Chevy Corvette, GM Firebird III, Buick Wildcat II,
GM Le Sabre, Cadillac Cyclone and many more

GM's Legendary Show and Concept Cars

# MOTORAMA

DAVID W. TEMPLE

# CarTech®

CarTech®, Inc.
838 Lake Street South
Forest Lake, MN 55025
Phone: 651-277-1200 or 800-551-4754
Fax: 651-277-1203
www.cartechbooks.com

© 2015 by David W. Temple

All rights reserved. No part of this publication may be reproduced or utilized in any form or by any means, electronic or mechanical, including photocopying, recording, or by any information storage and retrieval system, without prior permission from the Publisher. All text, photographs, and artwork are the property of the Author unless otherwise noted or credited.

The information in this work is true and complete to the best of our knowledge. However, all information is presented without any guarantee on the part of the Author or Publisher, who also disclaim any liability incurred in connection with the use of the information and any implied warranties of merchantability or fitness for a particular purpose. Readers are responsible for taking suitable and appropriate safety measures when performing any of the operations or activities described in this work.

All trademarks, trade names, model names and numbers, and other product designations referred to herein are the property of their respective owners and are used solely for identification purposes. This work is a publication of CarTech, Inc., and has not been licensed, approved, sponsored, or endorsed by any other person or entity. The Publisher is not associated with any product, service, or vendor mentioned in this book, and does not endorse the products or services of any vendor mentioned in this book.

Edit by Paul Johnson
Layout by Monica Seiberlich

ISBN 978-1-61325-534-6
Item No. CT533P

Library of Congress Cataloging-in-Publication Data

Temple, David W.
  Motorama / by David Temple.
     pages cm
  ISBN 978-1-61325-159-1
1. Motorama (New York, etc.) 2. General Motors Corporation–Exhibitions. 3. Experimental automobiles--United States--Exhibitions--History. I. Title.

TL7.U62N4895 2015
629.222074'73--dc23

2014016925

Written, edited, and designed in the U.S.A.
Printed in the U.S.A.
10 9 8 7 6 5 4 3 2

**Front Cover:**
The Le Sabre was sent to the 1951 Paris Salon aboard the *DeGrasse* inside a special aluminum container built by Alcoa Aluminum. This rarely seen overhead view at the event shows an amazed crowd gathered around the experimental car. (Photo Courtesy GM Media Archive)

**Endpapers:**
In 1954, the GM Motorama show visited Chicago for the first time. Here, a Corvette roadster is front and center, but two other Corvette concepts were added to the line-up. The Nomad was effectively a Corvette station wagon, and the Corvair was a fastback version of the Corvette. (Photo Courtesy General Motors)

**Frontispiece:**
The Corvette and Corvette-based show cars were photographed together in various poses on Pan American Drive in front of the Dinner Key Auditorium in Miami prior to the February 6 opening of the 1954 GM Motorama there. The yellow Corvette with the prototype detachable hardtop joined the GM Motorama at this time.

**Title Page:**
Harley J. Earl was the styling genius and his designs and the designs of his team populated the show floors at Motorama. This photo of Harley Earl shows him with the full-size clay model of the Le Sabre. (Photo Courtesy GM Media Archive)

**Back Cover Photo:**
The Firebird III was the only dream car on exhibit at the 1959 GM Motorama held only in New York City and Boston. This photo was taken at the show in New York City. (Photo Courtesy GM Media Archive)

*Author note: Some of the vintage photos in this book are of lower quality. They have been included because of their importance to telling the story.*

OVERSEAS DISTRIBUTION BY:

PGUK
63 Hatton Garden
London EC1N 8LE, England
Phone: 020 7061 1980 • Fax: 020 7242 3725
www.pguk.co.uk

Renniks Publications Ltd.
3/37-39 Green Street
Banksmeadow, NSW 2109, Australia
Phone: 2 9695 7055 • Fax: 2 9695 7355
www.renniks.com

# CONTENTS

Preface ..................................................................... 6
Acknowledgments ..................................................... 8
Foreword .................................................................. 9

## CHAPTER ONE: Origins of the Dream Car and the GM Motorama .................................. 10
The Beginning ........................................................................... 12
Harley J. Earl: Styling Engineer and Master Showman ............... 13
The Modern Concept Car is Born .............................................. 14
Projects XP-8 and XP-9 ............................................................ 16
The Grand Spectacle ................................................................ 23

## CHAPTER TWO: Transportation Unlimited and the Mid-Century Motorama .......................... 30
Transportation Unlimited ........................................................... 30
Mid-Century Motorama ............................................................. 35
GM Canada at the CNE, 1951–1952 ......................................... 38

## CHAPTER THREE: The 1953 GM Motorama .......... 40
Chevrolet Corvette: An American Sports Car ........................... 40
The Parisienne: A Formal Pontiac ............................................. 48
Oldsmobile Starfire: Excitement Abounds ................................. 51
Buick Wildcat: Trial Flight in Fiberglass ..................................... 53
Cadillac Orleans: Ultra-Luxurious Forerunner to
   the Eldorado Brougham ........................................................ 59
Cadillac Le Mans: A Sporty Luxury Car ..................................... 60
Other Special Displays of the 1953 GM Motorama .................... 70

## CHAPTER FOUR: The GM Motorama of 1954 ....... 72
Chevrolet Corvette: In the Spotlight .......................................... 72
The Nomad: A Two-Door Wagon .............................................. 74
Chevrolet Corvair: Sleek Styling ................................................ 80
Corvette with a Hardtop ............................................................ 82
Pontiac Bonneville Special and Strato-Streak:
   A Racy Sports Car and a Sport Sedan .................................. 83
Oldsmobile Cutlass and F-88: Sleek Sports Cars ...................... 90
Buick Landau and Wildcat II: Going Retro and Going Wild ...... 104
Cadillac Park Avenue, La Espada, and El Camino:
   Links in the Chain ............................................................... 110
GM Firebird I: Turbine Research ............................................. 115
Other Notable Show Cars of the 1954 GM Motorama ............. 116
Oldsmobile Skylark and Eldorado: Updated ........................... 119

## CHAPTER FIVE: The GM Motorama of 1955 ...... 120
Chevrolet Biscayne: From Show Car to Junk to Show Car ..... 122
Pontiac Strato-Star: A Radical Design .................................... 126
Oldsmobile 88 Delta: Daring Departure .................................. 129
Buick Wildcat III: A Man's Car ................................................ 131
Cadillac Eldorado Brougham: Steel-Bodied Prototype ........... 134
GMC L'Universelle: A Practical Cargo Vehicle ....................... 136
GM LaSalle II: Advanced V-6 and a Story of Recovery .......... 140
Other Notable Show Cars of the 1955 GM Motorama ............ 146

## CHAPTER SIX: The GM Motorama of 1956 ........ 150
Chevrolet Corvette Impala: Five-Passenger Luxury Sport ..... 150
Pontiac Club de Mer: Real Potential? .................................... 154
Oldsmobile Golden Rocket: Aptly Named .............................. 158
Buick Centurion: Innovative Predictor of the 21st Century .... 161
Cadillac Eldorado Brougham: Publicity Prototype and Town Car .. 164
Cadillac Castilian, Gala, Maharani, and Palomino:
   The "Mood Cars" ................................................................. 168
GM Firebird II: Next Generation .............................................. 170
Other Notable Exhibits of the 1956 GM Motorama ................. 176

## CHAPTER SEVEN: The Final GM Motoramas ..... 178
GM Canada Motorama ............................................................ 178
1959 Motorama ....................................................................... 178
1961 Motorama ....................................................................... 186
1958 GM Firebird III ................................................................ 189
1959 Cadillac Cyclone ............................................................ 193

## CHAPTER EIGHT: Modern Concept Cars ............ 196
2003 Cadillac Sixteen ............................................................. 197
2007 Chevrolet Volt ................................................................ 198
2008 Buick Riviera ................................................................. 199
2012 Cadillac Ciel .................................................................. 199
2013 Opel Monza ................................................................... 199
2013 Cadillac Elmiraj ............................................................. 200
2014 Chevrolet Corvette C7 .................................................. 200
2015 Chevrolet Corvette Z06 ................................................ 201
2015 Cadillac ATS Prototype ................................................ 201

Appendix A: Number Built and Status of the Motorama Show Cars .......... 202
Appendix B: Motorama Dates and Locations ................................................ 203
Index .................................................................................................................. 206

# PREFACE

For many years, the dream cars of GM's Motorama have been the source of fascination for automotive enthusiasts. They certainly have fascinated me for many years! Two events in particular sparked this interest. The first was discovering photographs in the mid-1970s that my dad took at the 1953 GM Motorama at the San Francisco Civic Center, two of which are shown in this book. The second event was reading an article in the August 1976 issue of *Motor Trend* titled, "The Case of the Lost Albanita: And Other Cars That Have Mysteriously Disappeared." It told the tales (some rumor, some factual) of numerous concept, exotic, and unusual cars that had been lost over the years. The article began with the author, John Pashdag, relating a dream in which he comes upon a junkyard aglow in moonlight while ". . . driving along a two-lane road through the semi-urban sprawl on the outskirts of—where? I'm never quite sure. Sometimes it looks like Detroit . . ." The sight of a giant tarp flapping in the gentle breeze captures his attention. Curious, he walks over to the edge of the tarp and, in his own words, ". . . with one quick motion, whip it into the air like a magician uncovering his rabbit-bearing hat, and fall back in awe as I see . . . a boat-tailed Duesenberg, a brace of 1939 Pierce Arrows, a 1904 Royce, a dozen Chrysler dream cars, two dozen Ferraris, an Italian Mustang, three Hudson Italias, a fiberglass Cadillac . . ." The story ended with, "For every historic automobile found, two more seem to vanish, and by the time they're found, the one that was found when they were lost has been lost again. It's a vicious circle, a losing battle for the collector and a winning battle for time." The images that Pashdag's dream produced in my mind were captivating. This may have been when I began thinking of such cars as art treasures.

These dream cars certainly qualify as art. They are also compelling in some cases because of rumors suggesting that some of the dream cars long thought to have been scrapped in the late 1950s might still exist in a garage or warehouse. Mysteries like that have a way of captivating people who love a good car story. John Pashdag's magazine article, written decades ago, reflects this idea very well even today.

In late 2002, the editor of *Car Collector* magazine, Dennis Adler, fortuitously approved a story proposal

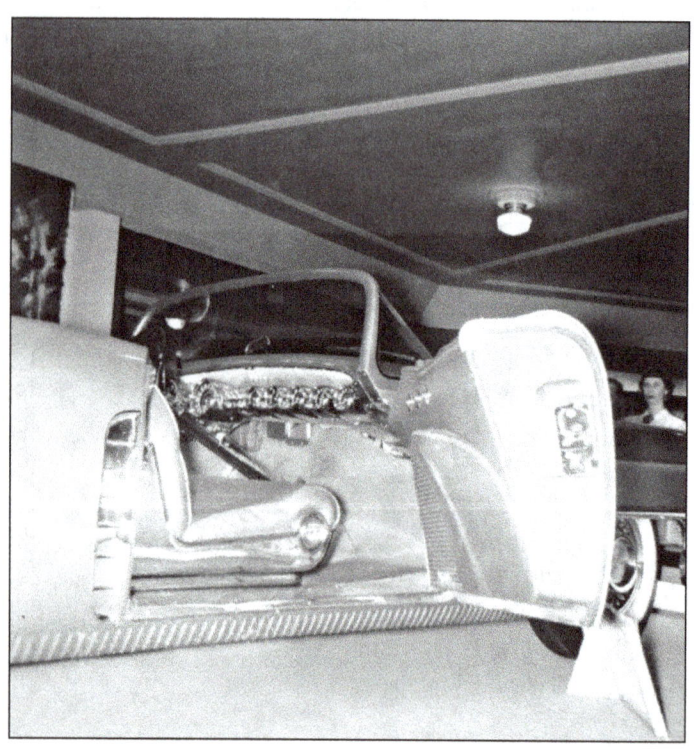 

*These were among the photographs taken by my father at the 1952 GM Motorama in San Francisco: 1953 Cadillac Le Mans interior (left) and 1951 GM Le Sabre with its styling updates (right). They sparked my life-long interst in the cars of the GM Motorama.*

from me about the lost dream cars of the GM Motorama. The three-part story titled, "Fate Unknown," published in the October, November, and December 2003 issues resulted in some interesting letters to the editor. One of them, from John Perkins, a retired GM engineer, included a photograph of the front seat removed from a 1953 Oldsmobile Starfire dream car. It was purchased by his father, a chassis engineer for Oldsmobile, at an Oldsmobile salvage auction and is now a part of the memorabilia in John's collection. Another letter was about a 1953 Cadillac Le Mans that had been on display in a Maryland Cadillac dealership in the 1980s.

Some months later I began my quest to compile every fact I could into book form. The effort became an automotive history "archeological exploration." Two years later, *GM's Motorama: The Glamorous Show Cars of a Cultural Phenomenon* was published and it went far beyond my original goals. Many people, including members of the Cadillac & LaSalle Club and former stylists, contributed important details and photographs to help chronicle virtually forgotten and seemingly lost history about GM's dream cars of the GM Motorama. Even the late Chuck Jordan, who designed two of the dream cars, wrote a wonderful foreword to the book.

Since then, much more has been learned about these cars and the GM Motorama itself. There are some surprises awaiting readers of this book, especially for those who read my first one on the subject.

Beyond the many updates, there is another purpose for this book. It is essentially one of the same purposes of the original and it is in regard to what little is said and written about the Motorama show cars tends to give the impression they were nothing more than flashy shells built to impress the crowds who saw them. These cars were much more substantive than that. In some ways each was a forecast or a possible forecast of the future of GM's cars despite the fact some of them did not actually run. Then there is the matter of claims that GM's dream cars lacked engines, had their hood gaps scribed in place, or were built of clay! None of these claims are true. Years of research have not resulted in discovering that any of these cars lacked an engine. Some, in fact, were made operable from the start and others made drivable some time after being built.

Furthermore, over the years much erroneous information has been perpetuated about these show cars. I am aware of having done so myself. My three-part series for *Car Collector* has errors picked up from various sources. As for the matter of mistakes, they are ultimately inescapable, especially with a subject as complex as this one. My first book on this topic was not error free either, but it was the best that could be done with the information available at the time. Newly discovered information has led to a much better account of this unique era of automotive history. This book, then, supersedes my original work. Even so, it is certainly not the complete history. Regrettably, some information is likely lost forever.

One other purpose of this new book is to, I hope, correct a misunderstanding about the dream cars of the GM Motorama era. Seemingly every dream car or show car General Motors built in the 1950s and early 1960s is called a "Motorama car" even if it never appeared at a General Motors Motorama. The phrase "Motorama car" has mistakenly become a synonym for dream car/concept car. "GM Motorama" is, in fact, the title of the traveling auto show produced by General Motors. While having this discussion with another car enthusiast, he got the impression that I meant if a concept car was not at the GM Motorama it is somehow less significant. There are many significant show cars that did not occupy a turntable at a GM Motorama. The dream cars of the Motorama simply became among the best known of all such cars.

This fresh look into GM's dream cars will be an adventure; the next best thing to actually stepping back in time to attend the GM Motorama.

# ACKNOWLEDGMENTS

A book such as this does not get written and published without the cooperation of many people. The following provided important information and/or photographs for this book: the late Charles D. Barnette (Cadillac & LaSalle Club), Matt Banchek (GM Media Bureau), Don Baron, Dick Baruk, Bruce Berghoff (H. B. Stubbs Company, retired), Joe Bortz (Bortz Auto Collection), Linda Cobon (Mgr., Records & Archives Exhibition Place, Toronto, Ontario), Lou Commisso (Cadillac LaSalle Club), Christo Danti (GM Media Archive Lead Archivist), Lea Lenz-Dunham, Richard Earl, Wayne Ellwood (former editor, *SHARK Quarterly*), Phillip Frances (GM engineer, retired), Mitch Frumkin (Chicago Automobile Trade Association photo archivist/historian), Hillary Hess, Jim Jordan (Cadillac & LaSalle Club), Warren Kostelny, Donald Keefe, John Kyros (GM Media Archive), Ed Lucas (FEL Enterprises), Marty Martino, Jim McDade, David McGee, Dick Page, Tim Pawl (Cadillac & LaSalle Club), John Perkins (GM Oldsmobile Division, retired), Steve Plunkett, Carter Ross, Bill Warner (Chairman, Amelia Island Concours d'Elegance), Ed Welburn (VP of GM Global Design), and Steve Wolken (GM Tech Center, retired).

To all of you, I extend my sincere thanks.

# FOREWORD

At a time when the primary mode of communication between the automotive industry and the American buying public was through black and white newspaper photography and weekly magazines, General Motors took on a massive initiative of connecting directly with the public on a much grander scale.

It was called "GM Motorama," an extravagant presentation of automotive design and technology like the world had never seen. On a broader level, it also presented an optimistic vision for the future of America.

General Motors Styling, under the leadership of Harley Earl, pioneered the dream car "concept" with the 1938 Buick Y-Job. It was followed by the 1951 Buick Le Sabre, and in 1953 the GM show car parade took off with feature vehicles for every brand, including the 1953 pre-production Corvette prototype. That design was so well received it went into production just six months later in June 1953.

Today, 60 years later, we're currently launching the seventh-generation Corvette Stingray, a car that continues to be a true American classic.

Although the last major GM Motorama season was in 1956, Motorama shows continued into the early 1960s, with the last date being February 5, 1961, in Los Angeles. More important, the development of GM show cars has continued on to this day, and it remains an important component of GM's design activities globally.

I am proud of GM's heritage. The Motorama was a significant chapter in our company's history and the many Motorama show cars have become the crown jewels of General Motors. The spirit of Motorama and the creative energy of the people who developed those show cars continue to drive our Global Design organization to this very day, and I must thank them for their efforts.

Ed Welburn
GM Vice President, Global Design

## Chapter One
# ORIGINS OF THE DREAM CAR AND THE GM MOTORAMA

Between 1949 and 1961, General Motors and GM Canada staged lavish auto shows, dubbed "The GM Motorama," in major cities for the purpose of telling the public about the company's products, which included not just its automobiles from Chevrolet, Pontiac, Oldsmobile, Buick, Cadillac, and GMC, but also its auto parts (such as the AC division) and non-automotive divisions (such as Electro-Motive Diesel and Frigidaire). Essentially, it served as a sales tool for selling the current crop of new GM automobiles and other products and it also informed people of GM's latest developments in scientific research and engineering. More notable, it featured a large variety of so-called dream cars (concept cars in today's vernacular) to test public reaction to innovative styling and mechanical features. These cars exposed the public to advanced concepts so as to acclimate them to characteristics to be found on automobiles in the near future as well as what might be seen in the distant future.

GM's head of styling, Harley Earl, knew that the public did not respond well to too much change too soon, but he also knew that people could and would view changes in most instances as desirable if given in the proper doses over time. This was accomplished through interactive exhibits, orchestras with troupes of dancers, lavish décor, and of course the dream cars, all done at GM's expense and free of charge to the public.

Although free of any monetary investment, the public paid for their experiences at the GM Motorama with an investment of time. The free show brought hundreds of thousands to each venue so lines were long. Even so,

*In the collection of the GM Heritage Center is this 1920 Cadillac, custom-designed by Harley Earl while at the Don Lee Coach and Body Works. In 1920, Earl sold his company, Earl Automobile Works, to Don Lee, a Cadillac distributor and owner of dozens of GM dealerships. Note the early version of a wraparound windshield.*

*The first production Cadillac Eldorado in Artisan Ochre (left of center), the Oldsmobile Fiesta (lower right), the Pontiac Parisienne (upper left), and the experimental 1951 GM Le Sabre (on stage) were just a few of the highlights of the 1953 GM Motorama. This setting is inside the Waldorf-Astoria where every GM Motorama made its debut. (Photo Courtesy GM Media Archive)*

# CHAPTER ONE: ORIGINS OF THE DREAM CAR AND THE GM MOTORAMA

*The "Kitchen of Tomorrow" was an exhibit highlighting GM's Frigidaire Division. Of course it displayed advanced concepts for the home of the future. This is the exhibit for 1954. (Photo Courtesy GM Media Archive)*

most attendees evidently felt the GM Motorama was exciting enough to warrant the wait. Once inside, they saw not only the new cars for the current model year, but also gazed in wonderment at the dream cars, such as the Cadillac Le Mans, Chevrolet Nomad, Buick Wildcat II, and a plethora of others. Many people wanted to buy these special cars, but were turned away in disappointment. Still, many were awed enough to place orders for a new Chevrolet, Pontiac, and so on. However, in a very few instances, VIPs managed to acquire some of the exotic dream cars and that makes for some interesting stories, which will be told later in this book.

The GM Motorama proved to be a great sales tool and helped propel General Motors to number one in the industry with as much as half the car market during this era. Let us now explore how this phenomenal success came to be.

## The Beginning

General Motors was incorporated on September 16, 1908, in Flint, Michigan, when William Durant filed incorporation papers for the new company. Durant, who was known as the "the king of carriage makers" as a result of his great success with the Dort-Durant Company, had an eye for seeing opportunity. Shortly after the filing, he added Buick and then Oldsmobile to his new company. In 1909, Oakland and Cadillac were added to the growing roster.

Car companies were not the only divisions acquired for the ever-expanding General Motors. Many others were brought in under the GM banner, such as A.C. Spark Plug, DELCO, Hyatt Roller Bearing, Harrison Radiator, and even Dayton Wright Airplane! General Motors also bought a 60-percent interest in Fisher Body. Furthermore, McLaughlin Motor Company was another acquisition. McLaughlin was a joint venture with Buick even before the formation of General Motors. The McLaughlin cars were built and sold in Canada and exported to other countries. In 1931 the German company, Opel, joined the GM family. General Motors was spreading across the globe!

Not all of these acquisitions happened under William Durant's presidency, however. Unfortunately, the expenditures made under his leadership put his company in financial jeopardy. Creditors' demands made matters even more difficult for Durant and he was soon forced out of General Motors. Alfred P. Sloan, Jr., who served as GM's president and CEO beginning in 1923, wrote that, "Mr. Durant was a great man with a great weakness; he could create but not administer . . ." Sloan, incidentally, was serving as president of Hyatt Roller Bearing at the time the company was bought by General Motors.

Durant was not yet through with the automotive business. He established Chevrolet in 1911 and returned to General Motors in 1915 as president after buying enough GM shares to regain control. By 1920, William Durant was again forced out of General Motors, this time permanently.

Over the years, General Motors continued to grow. It entered the Diesel train market with the Electro-Motive Division and the business of mass transportation

Harlow "Red" Curtice (left) and Alfred P. Sloan, Jr. (right) held various positions within General Motors including the presidency. Sloan, who was instrumental in bringing Harley Earl to General Motors, wondered why more attention was not given to the appearance of the automobile even before joining General Motors. (Photo Courtesy GM Media Archive)

through GM Coach and a relationship with Greyhound. Appliance-maker, Frigidaire, also became a division of General Motors.

The company became stronger in the 1920s and the Chevrolet division overtook Ford as the number-one automaker in the country. The latter part of this decade brought still another important acquisition; not a company this time, but rather a new employee of great talent.

## Harley J. Earl: Styling Engineer and Master Showman

In 1927, GM President Alfred P. Sloan hired Harley J. Earl, a man who greatly altered the way automobiles were designed. Earl brought art to the automobile as a means to entice people to buy GM brands. His design methods led to the rise of General Motors as the sales leader during the 1930s, 1940s, and especially the 1950s when it held half the market share of car sales. Earl, who spent his early years in the Hollywood, California, area, became involved with the Earl Carriage Works, the company founded by his father, Jacob W. Earl. Harley later took charge of this company and transformed it into the Earl Automobile Works, a custom-car business. It had a customer base ranging from wealthy businessmen to the stars and starlets of Hollywood.

In July 1920, Earl sold his company to one of his major customers, Don Lee, a Cadillac distributor who owned nearly four-dozen dealerships throughout California. Earl's work at Don Lee's shop put him in contact with Lawrence Fisher, the president of Cadillac, who visited the shop in late 1925. A friendship developed and the two discussed the subject of styling automobiles while playing golf together; in the past, Fisher had discussed styling with Sloan. They all agreed that styling should be a great sales tool, and Harley Earl clearly knew how to shape cars into desirable status symbols by designing and integrating every panel, line, and curve of a car.

Earl's success was due not only to his natural talent for design, but also because of his approach to customers: He provided a real-world look at his proposals through full-scale clay models. Clay models, as well as trips to the European auto shows, became valuable tools to Harley Earl, who reportedly said, "A picture is worth a thousand words, but a model is worth a thousand pictures."

Earl was asked to come to Detroit in early 1926 to do some design work for what became the 1927 LaSalle. His work on that project led to a job offer and the beginning of a remarkable career lasting more than three decades.

Harley Earl organized and became head of the "Art and Colour Section" of General Motors soon after being hired by Alfred Sloan. Earl's Art and Colour Section merged perfectly with Sloan's thinking regarding planned obsolescence. Model year changes were meant to entice the public to buy new cars through just enough changes to make the next new model seem better while avoiding making too radical a change too quickly. Earl's talents led to his appointment as a vice president in 1940; no automaker to that point had elevated styling to such a high management level. It was a fundamental change for General Motors.

During an early 1954 interview, Harley Earl explained how cars were designed in the days before the Art and Colour Section and how he changed the methodology. He said, "Fisher Body would draw up the body and the hood, and then they would model the body . . . then the divisions would take that drawing and they would put on their front end and their fenders and wheels, and they . . . would put them together. Well, when I worked on the

# CHAPTER ONE: ORIGINS OF THE DREAM CAR AND THE GM MOTORAMA

LaSalle, we didn't do it that way. We made it all one; we built it right together as one unit rather than separate it."

He also explained his managing style: "I often act as a prompter. If a particular group appears to be bogging down over a new fender or grille or interior trim, I sometimes wander into their quarter, make some irrelevant or even zany observation, and then leave. It is surprising what effect a bit of peculiar behavior will have. First-class minds will seize on anything out of the ordinary . . ."

Harley Earl left General Motors in December 1958, and Bill Mitchell became the head of GM Design. Two years earlier, the new Design Center was opened (and is still in use today) and with Mitchell at the helm, the company went in a new direction in terms of styling. Heavy applications of chrome trim and fins had gone about as far as they could go.

In 1945, Earl had established a consulting firm, Harley Earl & Associates. Earl's retirement contract with General Motors forbade him to perform any design work for their competition. Therefore, he created packaging for Nabisco and Ban Roll-On Deodorant, designed aircraft interiors, showrooms, etc. In 1964, Carl & Associates merged with Walter B. Ford Design Associates to become Ford and Earl. He also served as a consultant to General Motors.

Earl's seemingly limitless imagination was extinguished due to complications of a stroke; he passed away on April 10, 1969, at the age of 75.

Strangely, Harley Earl's achievements have been forgotten over time. In fact, some stories imply that he was not much more than a figurehead at General Motors. Only in recent years has Earl's impact on automobile design during his time with General Motors become known again.

## The Modern Concept Car is Born

In 1937, The Art and Colour Section became GM Styling and its first major assignment was a first in the automobile industry. Harley Earl was responsible for creating what is known today as the concept car. The first acknowledged modern concept car was dubbed the Buick Y-Job and it was Earl's personal "laboratory on wheels." For the 1933 "Century of Progress" World's Fair, a Cadillac V-16 show car (dubbed the Aerodynamic Coupe) was exhibited; it later went into a very limited production run. However, this Cadillac did not include multiple experimental mechanical *and* styling features, as did the Y-Job.

## THE NUMBERS

Throughout this book are references to each dream car's "EX", "XP," and/or "SO" number. According to retired Oldsmobile engineer, John Perkins, this system was employed simply to help accountants for GM log the expenses incurred by these projects. The late Chuck Jordan also confirmed the meaning of this abbreviation.

*Many of the custom-crafted cars of General Motors wore a metal tag with a shop order number. This one was attached to the 1954 Buick Landau.*

Chevrolet alone used the "EX" designations and therefore they were not assigned by General Motors. Most of the EX documentation from Chevrolet was evidently destroyed long ago.

Shop Order (SO) numbers were also assigned to "bucks" or functional mockups such as experimental convertible tops as well as experimental cars. Hence, while the 1954 Olds F-88s were all XP-20s, they each received their own unique shop order number. Not all SO cars were exotic dream cars, though. Some were simply production models with non-production paint and upholstery schemes, sometimes in combination with other non-production hardware, such as a vinyl-covered top. Most of these cars had a metal tag affixed to the body with their respective SO identification.

There were also instances in which SO meant Special Order, but this designation appears to have been used before World War II and for atypical customer orders at dealerships.

*Harley Earl created the modern concept car at General Motors. His Buick "Y-Job" was remarkably advanced in its styling and mechanical features for the late 1930s. This rare photo shows the car painted silver for its display at the 1940 National Auto Show at the Grand Central Palace in New York City. The car is owned by General Motors and is sometimes displayed at car shows and special events.*

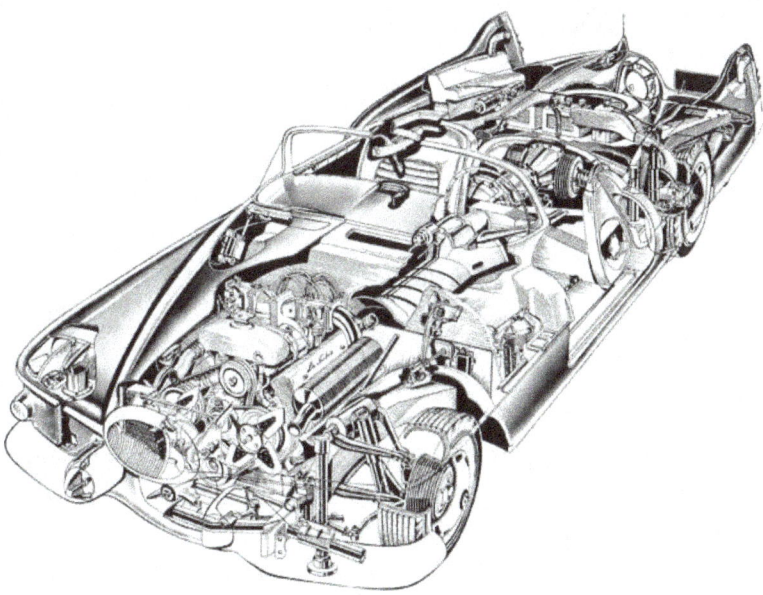

*This cutaway view of the Le Sabre reveals very little empty space underneath its skin. It was filled with complex mechanical systems including a supercharged aluminum V-8, transaxle, two independent fuel cells, hydraulic systems to operate jacks at all four wheels, trunk-mounted batteries, and more.*

The Y-Job "laboratory" had many advanced features, both in terms of styling and its mechanical systems. Advanced features of the Y-Job included hidden headlights, horizontal grille, wraparound bumpers, prototype "Dynaflow" torque-converter transmission, electric power windows and top, power steering, 13-inch wheels, and no running boards. It was very low for the time; from the ground to its peak, it measured only 58 inches. The length stretched to 208 inches and the width was 74 inches. Lower, longer, wider was part of the formula for styling the Y-Job. In summary, the car was radically different (but not overly radical) for the day.

Company president Alfred P. Sloan, Jr. and Buick Division head Harlow H. Curtice approved Earl's "semi-sports car," as he called it. The Y-Job was Earl's personal transportation for many years and served as the basis for the

*Harley J. Earl began his automotive career while he was in his 20s in California at his father's carriage shop. His work there later led him to a 31-year career at General Motors as the vice president of GM Styling. He believed art had a place in the products of industry. He once said, "To be successful, a stylist must always keep pace with progress. His ideas must not run ahead of, or lag behind, the amount of change that the public will accept when his designs go into the marketplace." This photo shows him with the full-size clay model of the Le Sabre. Earl pioneered the concept of modeling automobiles in clay. (Photo Courtesy GM Media Archive)*

MOTORAMA 15

styling of the 1942 Buick. The Y-Job generated a lot of free publicity for General Motors. It also provided a substantial number of styling features that eventually appeared on GM cars in the following years.

## Projects XP-8 and XP-9

By about 1946, the Y-Job was beginning to appear more like something from the past rather than a forecast of the future. A new concept car was needed. GM's vice president in charge of engineering, Charles Chayne, and Harley Earl got together with GM executive vice president and Buick general manager, Harlow Curtice, to discuss what they had accomplished with the Y-Job and what should be built to replace it.

Chayne authored an article about the XP-300 for the February 1952 issue of *Motor Trend* in which he explained the purpose and origin of the Le Sabre and XP-300: "We decided that it was time to build a successor to the Y-Job to see if we could better our mark of 'good after ten years' by doing one that would be still fresh and new after fifteen years. We weren't very far before it was clear to us that one car could not possibly contain the things we wanted to try, so we worked out a program for two cars."

General Motors made the decision to build two cars, designated XP-8 and XP-9, a few months later. These models were later formally named the Le Sabre and XP-300, respectively. Although Buick eventually claimed the model name Le Sabre, the XP-8 was not specifically associated with any GM division; it was simply the General Motors Le Sabre, even though the XP-300 would be identified as a Buick. In May 1951, the Le Sabre and XP-300 projects were formally approved. Ed Glowacke from the Chevrolet division was put in charge of a newly created studio, Special

*This photo from 1959 shows the cast-aluminum door skin removed, perhaps for the purpose of servicing the power-window system. (Photo Courtesy Steve Wolken collection)*

Automobile Design, and jumped into the styling of the Le Sabre. As a side note, photographs taken on August 1, 1949, show a mock rear license plate reading "Chevrolet" on the plaster model. As the design progressed, the Chevrolet designation was removed and the Buick nameplate appeared on the front of the car in late 1949. This is as close as the Le Sabre got to being associated with a specific division of General Motors.

Charles Chayne led the design, development, and creation of the XP-300, although Harley Earl provided input into the project. The designers of this car and the

*Harley Earl took the Le Sabre, his personal transport, to Watkins Glen in 1952. It drew crowds during the festivities leading up to the race. (Photo Courtesy GM Media Archive)*

16  MOTORAMA

Le Sabre were instructed to create a styling and engineering masterpiece. They raised the bar on what represented an advanced automobile in the early 1950s, but it was really the Le Sabre that raised the bar the most.

Aircraft design strongly influenced Harley Earl and he incorporated numerous elements into his automotive designs. In fact, GM's Allison division built the engines for the Lockheed P-38 Lightning and other World War II–era aircraft, and later built jet engines; it was easy for Earl to keep abreast of the latest trends in aviation. The P-38, as many enthusiasts are aware, inspired the tail-fin age beginning with the all-new 1948 Cadillac models. During the Korean War era, the U.S. military used many different jet fighters and these innovative and evolving aircraft provided a wealth of styling ideas for Earl.

Boats also provided influence in the design of his cars. Glowacke, a very talented stylist, raced cars and boats; he also piloted gliders and his personal airplane. He contributed a number of aviation-themed features to the Le Sabre: the oval grille (that is actually a hidden headlight system) inspired by the North American F-86 Sabre, the bumper bullets (later named "Dagmars" after Dagmar, a shapely actress of the era), its gull-wing bumpers, and the car's aircraft-style gauges.

In an article written for *Motor Trend,* Chayne explained that the design of both cars was dictated primarily by the "decision to build them just as low as possible. Doing this, pretty well forced the cars into being two-passenger convertibles, since with the necessary mechanical parts ahead of and behind the passenger space we would have been forced into an excessively long wheelbase had we attempted to use a second seat." Another important goal of the two projects was that the cars must be "complete in every sense of the word and still be capable of really terrific performance."

### Engine Innovation

The all-aluminum V-8 engine of the Le Sabre and XP-300, though, was the heart of these cars and a landmark innovation for that era. It displaced just 215.7 ci (3.25 x 3.25-inch bore and stroke), yet provided 335 hp, far surpassing what was then a magical ratio of one horsepower per cubic inch. Alcoa cast the aluminum block and heads of the engine, which weighed 550 pounds. The block was strengthened with cross-bolted main caps and its wet cylinder liners were centrifugally cast from Ni-Resist iron with a high coefficient of expansion very close to that of the aluminum heads and pistons. Designing the engine's intake manifold required an extra dose of creativity.

A mockup of the complete engine was crafted and sent to GM Styling for a fit check. Suddenly, Harley Earl demanded that the hood line of the Le Sabre be lowered 6 inches. Joseph Turlay, in charge of engineering the special V-8, instinctively thought the new specification was impossible to meet. However, he knew that saying, "no," or "it can't be done," to Earl was not typically good for continued employment with GM Styling. After some deep thought, Turlay dealt with the challenge by reducing the height of the oil pan, which then necessitated the addition of a windage tray to keep the crank throws from aerating the oil. Furthermore, replacing the iron flywheel with a bronze flywheel (which had a higher specific gravity) substantially decreased the size without sacrificing the required mass. This change netted 1½ inches of reduced height.

These changes reduced the overall height of the engine enough to comply with Harley Earl's "impossible" order. A Roots-type supercharger was placed just above the intake manifold, which also served as the valley cover.

Other features of the special V-8 included a chain-driven camshaft suspended below the intake and hemispherical combustion chambers (yes, it had a Hemi) in combination with domed pistons. This provided efficient burning of the air/fuel mixture compressed

*Like the Le Sabre, the XP-300 was very low in height, as demonstrated in this photograph. (Photo Courtesy Chayne family archives)*

## CHAPTER ONE: ORIGINS OF THE DREAM CAR AND THE GM MOTORAMA

*An advanced, supercharged aluminum V-8 displacing 215 ci powered the GM Le Sabre. The supercharger provided 18.2 psi of manifold pressure at 5,000 rpm. This photo was taken in July 2012 at the GM Heritage Center.*

to a high-for-the-day 10.0:1 ratio. Sodium-filled valves greatly dissipated heat and were positioned in the head at a 90-degree angle to each other. The positioning of the intake valves in combination with the cylinder banks at 45 degrees to horizontal led to a short, unobstructed flow of fuel. The rocker arms for the intake valves were mounted transversely, while those of the exhaust side were oriented in a fore/aft position. This unusual arrangement helped to make the engine more compact so it fit within the confined engine compartments of the Le Sabre and the XP-300. Double valvesprings were employed and valveseats were stainless steel inserts. The experimental engine's hydraulic lifters were designed to operate without clatter or bounce up to 6,500 rpm.

This high-tech engine could run on either gasoline or alcohol fuel, and this was long before any flex-fuel production vehicle was offered to the American public. Bendix-Eclipse 2-barrel carburetors were fitted to both the Le Sabre and XP-300. The carb streamed gasoline into the engine for typical street driving and the alcohol injectors delivered methanol for more horsepower under competition or aggressive driving. A pair of aircraft pressure-type (rather than conventional float-type) carburetors was fitted to the engines of both cars. Fuel flowed from two separate fuel cells and two electric fuel pumps. One carburetor ingested premium gasoline until nearly wide-open throttle, at which point the other carburetor (via progressive linkage and a valve) received a spray of methanol. Pressing the accelerator pedal to nearly full travel increased the flow of methanol to the rear carb and also engaged the supercharger.

On each side of the Le Sabre, the fuel fillers were clearly embossed: one filler door for "GASOLINE" and the other for "ALCOHOL." In addition, the filler caps were integrated into the filler doors. When filling the methanol fuel cell, a special funnel with a petcock and overflow tube was used to prevent the liquid from spilling onto the paint.

### Le Sabre Body Breakthroughs

Beyond the all-new aluminum engine, Harley Earl and his team integrated lightweight *cast magnesium* into the body of the car. The front fender valance, cowl, door-lock pillars, and deck lid (with ribs cast into it) were single large castings of magnesium. Casting components in magnesium was a challenging task at the time; multiple attempts were generally required to get the correct shape for these panels to obtain perfect alignment of each one. The remaining body panels were of aluminum sourced from and cast by Alcoa. The floors were aluminum honeycomb sandwiched between aluminum sheets.

Another of the car's breakthroughs was its tinted, wraparound (or, as General Motors called it, "Panoramic") windshield. The Le Sabre and the XP-300 were the first cars to have this feature. Harley Earl tried to have wraparound glass created in 1918, but the glassmaker simply could not discover a method of bending the glass into the desired shape without breakage. In 1949, GM's glass supplier, Libby-Owens-Ford, was finally able to solve the problem after four years of experimentation.

A wraparound windshield also offered the benefit of increased interior space. But Earl's priority was obtaining the largest field of vision possible and at the same time have a visually appealing automobile. The wraparound windshield, as well as tail fins, were adopted (actually copied) by the competition and were incorporated into the early 1960s. General Motors received the patent on the Panoramic windshield and likely made a handsome profit from royalties paid by the competition.

As originally built, the Le Sabre was upholstered in black leather. It was restyled for 1953 and this is likely when the upholstery was changed to blue. Note the two-toned steering wheel and the instrumentation on the console consisting of a chronograph, radio controls, and a rain sensor, which automatically raised the top if rain began to fall when the car was left parked in top-down mode. The interior design is credited to Henry Lauve.

Even though its interior had the look of a typical sports car, the XP-300 was certainly much more comfortable. Its finely pleated blue leather seats were adjustable in four directions and had bladders that were inflatable via a squeeze-bulb to change their contours. The steering column was telescopically adjustable as well. The console housed most of the gauges and controls.

### Le Sabre Suspension Features

A ladder-type boxed frame made of chrome-molybdenum steel supported the stylish and complex body. Underneath the bodywork was a parallel double-wishbone suspension that provided excellent handling characteristics; this same suspension is used on today's cars. The A-arms were made of cast-alloy; the upper A-arm pivot rod was imbedded in a solid piece of cylindrically shaped rubber encased in a steel casting. Hydraulic tubular shock absorbers were mounted between the steel casings and the lower A-arms. The setup acted as an effective springing medium for a time. Eventually, Chayne had to have the steel-encased rubber replaced because it had lost its elasticity; torsion bars were substituted.

A transaxle comprised of an altered Buick Dynaflow and a de Dion differential drove the car's rear wheels. (Some years later a 4-speed Hydra-Matic replaced the Dynaflow.) A de Dion differential is a type of semi-independent suspension with a drop-center beam axle connecting the two driving wheels aft of the open, double-jointed

*The 1951 Le Sabre generated a tremendous amount of free publicity for General Motors. It was a marvel in this country and abroad.* Motorsport *magazine featured the Le Sabre in its October 1951 issue. The November issue pictured the unique car on its front cover and detailed the XP-300 inside.*

# CHAPTER ONE: ORIGINS OF THE DREAM CAR AND THE GM MOTORAMA

driveshafts; it is separate from the final-drive unit attached to the frame. A transaxle combines the final-drive unit with the transmission located between the driving wheels and separates the transmission from the engine, thus moving a significant percentage of the weight toward the rear to help provide the desired weight distribution for a rear-wheel-drive car.

The rear-mounted torque converter was driven at engine speed, making possible the installation of a generator and hydraulic pump in the rear of the chassis. The input shaft of the transaxle drove the generator and the pump. The hydraulic pump operated four built-in jacks (one at each corner) to raise the car when required (i.e., changing a flat tire).

The double-jointed axle shafts were formed of magnesium and the rear suspension was a tapered, single-leaf spring mounted transversely. Thirteen-inch wheels helped make the car low, but to get adequate braking, 3½-inch-wide 9-inch-diameter finned brake drums with four brake shoes per drum were needed. The overall height with the top raised measured just 50 inches; the cowl height as measured from the ground peaked at a mere 36.25 inches. The Le Sabre's wheelbase spanned 115 inches.

### Le Sabre Styling and Design

The Le Sabre looked way ahead of its time and it was. The styling was inspired by jet aircraft of the era, but that was just one aspect of the car. It was far lower and wider than any contemporary car on the road. The interior and dash resembled a fighter plane cockpit as well.

A pair of side-by-side headlights appeared when the headlight switch was turned on. The hood-mounted center grille flipped 180 degrees, and the headlights moved into position to illuminate the road. Instrumentation comprised an altimeter, compass, clock, ammeter, digital speedometer, as well as gauges for oil pressure, oil temperature, and engine coolant temperature. A console sat between the black leather-covered bucket seats and housed a chronograph, radio controls, and a rain sensor to automatically raise the top in the event rain began to fall when the car was left parked in top-down mode.

Earl was said to prefer to leave the Le Sabre parked with the top down if the weather forecast predicted a strong possibility of rain. The car always drew crowds, so people witnessed first-hand the automatic top actuation. When a drop of rain struck the moisture sensor, the cowl vents closed while the convertible top and windows began to rise automatically. The convertible top retracted into a well with a pivoting, flush-fitting cover much like the Y-Job and the Corvette that followed a couple years later.

Additional advanced features of the Le Sabre were its rheostatically controlled, electrically heated seats and an ultraviolet light used to make the instruments glow at night. A 12-volt electrical system was installed to power all this gadgetry.

Magnesium castings, complex electrical and hydraulic systems, and extensive labor were responsible for the staggering price tag of this one-of-a-kind car, which totaled approximately $500,000 (or even as much as $1 million according to some reports) in circa-1950 dollars. However, the free publicity generated by the car made the expensive project more than worthwhile.

### XP-300 Suspension Features

The XP-300 shared many design and mechanical similarities with the Le Sabre, but one significant difference was that the XP-300 used a de Dion axle design based on

*This glamorous publicity photo is one of many taken by GM Photographic. Note the black sidewall tires of the XP-300, which reveals that the photograph was taken prior to 1953. Ned Nichols was assigned to head the styling of the unique car.*

*The Le Sabre was sent to the 1951 Paris Salon aboard the* DeGrasse *inside a special aluminum container built by Alcoa Aluminum. This rarely seen overhead view at the event shows an amazed crowd gathered around the experimental car. (Photo Courtesy GM Media Archive)*

a Daimler-Benz unit (used for the Grand Prix race cars) while the Le Sabre used torsion bars as previously mentioned. In addition, the XP-300 also had a 1-inch-longer wheelbase, coil springs at each corner, methanol and gasoline fuel tanks mounted behind the seat, a single fan in the engine compartment, as well as other suspension and steering component differences. Its hydraulic system was more complex than Le Sabre's; it operated the hood, windows, seats, locking devices for the doors, cowl vents, and jack system. This system, though, was prone to leaking and needed constant attention by the system project manager, Lee Furse. Moreover, there were notable differences between the two cars' braking systems.

### XP-300 Body Design

The XP-300's body was of heat-treated aluminum panels painted Venus White placed over a steel inner structure. Like the Le Sabre, the XP-300 had a gorgeous and ingenious body design incorporating a Panoramic windshield, simulated jet exhaust nozzle at the rear, and a low overall height. Each car also had bucket seats and a console. However, there were more differences than similarities. The hood and front fender tops were constructed as a single welded piece; the hydraulic system flipped the hood forward for access to the engine compartment. Functional chrome louvers extended down the side of the car; those on the front fenders and the forward one-third of the louvers on the doors served as engine compartment heat vents. The louvers at the rear of the door were fitted with adjustable dampeners so the driver or passenger could control the amount of air entering the interior compartment. An opening in the center of the massive bumper allowed air to reach the radiator.

Functional styling characteristics included a sealed-beam floodlight-type backup lamp mounted in the simulated rear jet exhaust. In addition, a chrome fin down the rear deck centerline concealed the hinges for the deck lids, which could be opened from either side.

The XP-300's interior consisted of finely pleated blue leather-covered seats with inflatable bladders. A squeeze-bulb adjusted the air level in the bladders and provided more or less support depending on the air pressure. A console housed most of the car's gauges and controls. A telescopically adjustable steering column allowed the driver to correctly position the steering wheel, and a combination tachometer/speedometer was mounted on the dash directly ahead of the driver's position. With the push of a button, the fuel gauge could be used to determine the fuel level in each tank.

Two tops were available for the XP-300: a hard top and a convertible top that could be folded and stowed in the compartment behind the seat; the latter was used almost exclusively. Originally, a retractable rear window (called a Riviera type) was also installed, but this was later removed from the car. It served as the rear window (or backlight) regardless of which top was in place. At the time the Riviera-type backlight was removed, the hardware to secure the hard top was also deleted. Although the hard top still exists (stored at the Alfred P. Sloan Museum's Buick Gallery), it is no longer possible to fasten it in place because of this change. A conventional convertible top with a fixed backlight replaced the original and remains in place today.

The XP-300 incorporated Earl's prevailing design philosophy of long and low. In fact, it only had 6½ inches

# CHAPTER ONE: ORIGINS OF THE DREAM CAR AND THE GM MOTORAMA

*The 1951 GM Le Sabre is a part of the GM Heritage Collection in Sterling Heights, Michigan. It can often be seen at special events across the country throughout the year.*

of ground clearance, which was extremely low for the time. The body and frame were welded together into an integral, solid unit. When the doors were closed, hydraulically operated steel bar locks slipped into place like the bolts of a vault door making the doors almost a structural part of the body. The XP-300's weight (only 3,125 pounds) and high-horsepower engine translated into excellent performance. Charles Chayne reportedly drove the XP-300 at 140 mph on at least one occasion!

## Public Debuts

Le Sabre was the first of the two experimental cars to be publicly revealed. In February 1951, the XP-300 was shown at the Chicago Auto Show although it was not quite finished. Several months later, both cars were shown together to members of the press at the GM Proving Grounds. Earl also drove the Le Sabre in the 1951 Watkins Glen race-day parade with a crowd of 100,000 fans and race-car drivers watching. The car then went on display for a few days at the 1951 Canadian National Exhibition (CNE) in Toronto and the Paris Salon where it drew large crowds. During its stay there, Leonard McLay, the chief mechanic for the Le Sabre, took General Dwight Eisenhower for a ride in the experimental car. Eisenhower was so impressed with the Le Sabre he wrote a complimentary letter to Harley Earl.

Both the Le Sabre and XP-300 were shown on the 1953 GM Motorama tour, although by then the Le Sabre had been updated with new wheels, deleted fender skirts, as well as additional air intakes and outlets to improve engine compartment and brake cooling.

The Le Sabre was a fully functional and drivable road car. In fact, Harley Earl drove the Le Sabre frequently and he eventually put about 45,000 miles on the car. During that time, it appeared on the cover of numerous publications, and by that fact alone, the Le Sabre probably more than paid for itself in terms of advertising for General Motors. The Buick XP-300 logged nearly 10,400 miles, and generated a fair share of publicity, too.

*The 1951 Buick XP-300 was donated to the Alfred P. Sloan Museum in Flint, Michigan, in 1966 and can be seen there when not being exhibited at a special event.*

*General Motors produced more than automobiles. Shown here is a cutaway exhibit of the company's Allison Division turbine aircraft engine on display at the 1949 Transportation Unlimited show. (Photo Courtesy GM Media Archive)*

The Le Sabre has been preserved by General Motors and is now a part of the collection of the GM Heritage Center. In 1966, the XP-300 was donated to the Alfred P. Sloan Museum in Flint, Michigan, after GM Styling refurbished it.

### Le Sabre and XP-300 Today

The legacies of the two experimental cars differ considerably. The Le Sabre greatly influenced car design for years to come while the XP-300 actually had little influence. The XP-300 was more of conventional design for that era, but even so, its frontal design and upper quarter panel shape were adopted for the 1953–1954 Buicks. As for the Le Sabre, its fin shape can be seen in the 1953–1954 Pontiacs as well as the 1957 Cadillac; its gull-wing bumper design showed up on other GM dream cars as well as production Cadillacs.

The Le Sabre's influence went beyond American automobiles; European designers were at least as awestruck by this car as their counterparts in the United States. The car even inspired a few semi-replicas during the 1950s including the Spohn-bodied Veritas. It was also copied by the Soviet Union automaker ZIS as the ZIS-112. Three versions of the 112 were built and used in competition for propaganda purposes. Thus, the Le Sabre played a small part in the Cold War!

The late GM stylist and vice president, Chuck Jordan, was in charge of two GM Motorama vehicles, the 1955 GMC L'Universelle and the 1956 Buick Centurion plus, much later, the 1985 Buick Wildcat concept car. He retired from General Motors at the end of 1992. Jor-

*The GM Motorama featured many interactive exhibits to demonstrate various qualities of the company's products. This scene from a 1953 venue illustrates the improved visibility afforded the driver of a new Buick. (Photo Courtesy H. B. Stubbs Co.)*

dan explained the impact of the Le Sabre: "The Le Sabre had dramatic proportions and shape. The Le Sabre really knocked us for a loop. It represented Harley Earl's design philosophy and it influenced all of us; it was a very exciting car. We knew we had to go all out." Jordan learned the value of having a place where a stylist "could design freely and take risks to develop new ideas." Such was the impact of Harley Earl on car design.

### The Grand Spectacle

The GM Motorama evolved from GM's Industrialist Luncheons of the 1930s held against a backdrop of special décor such as Persian rugs and landscape paintings at the Waldorf-Astoria on Park Avenue. This invitation-only event served as a platform to promote the products of the company. The Industrialist Luncheons continued until World War II interrupted automobile production. General Motors also set up sophisticated displays at the World's Fair for 1939–1940 under the banner of "Futurama" that included a special 1939 Pontiac with a plexiglass body as one of the exhibits. These experiences and many others gave General Motors the skills to produce even more attractive and entertaining displays to draw interest in their products.

Within a few years after the end of World War II, automakers (including General Motors) began introducing all-new cars. General Motors again produced its own

## CHAPTER ONE: ORIGINS OF THE DREAM CAR AND THE GM MOTORAMA

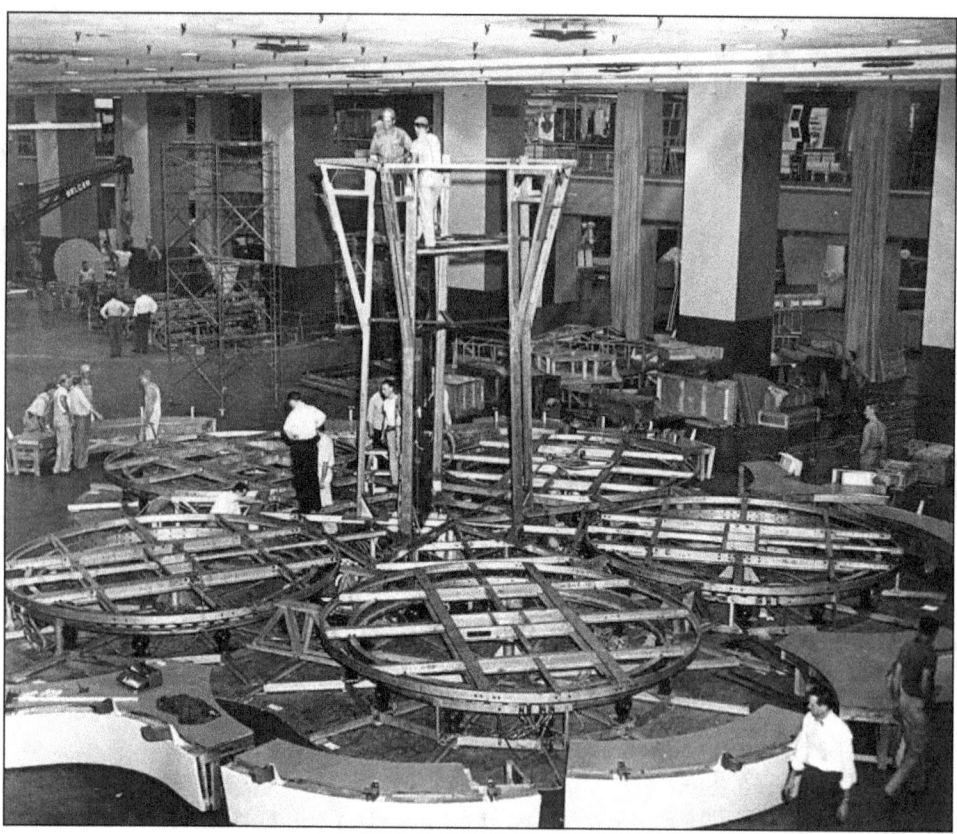

*The set up of the various exhibits and platforms such as this "cloverleaf" was contracted to H. B. Stubbs Company. This scene is from the Municipal Auditorium in Kansas City, Missouri, the final venue of the 1953 GM Motorama. (Photo Courtesy H. B. Stubbs Co.)*

auto show to promote its products. The first was 1949's Transpiration Unlimited followed the next year by the Mid-Century Motorama. This led to the more extravagant auto show known as the GM Motorama.

"Motorama" is often a misunderstood term because it has been loosely used to describe many things non-Motorama. People used "Motorama" as a more sophisticated word for "motor show," a label that had been in use for many years when GM's traveling auto show came into being. Furthermore, the title "Motorama" had been in use for other auto shows involving customs and sports cars for some time as well. The "ama" portion of the word means "spectacle" and GM's first "ama" was the 1939–1940 Futurama. But as part of the automotive lexicon it has often been misused. Often, people inaccurately refer to a "dream car" or "concept car" as a Motorama car, but to be accurate, only Motorama cars appeared at the Motorama show.

In 1947, General Motors initiated the use of the name Motorama for the company's spacious exhibit at the Chicago Museum of Science and Industry. The company also staged other "ama" shows in the mid-1950s including the Wonderama in Dayton, Ohio, and for a singular show in Chicago called Powerama. General Motors used "Motorama" well into the 1960s for foreign exhibitions of its Opel and Vauxhall automobiles. Chevrolet sponsored its "Featurama" in the 1960s.

For 1951 and 1952, General Motors did not produce similar shows because of the Korean War and the associated rationing of materials needed for war materiel. Extra promotion of automobiles simply was not needed as production was somewhat restricted, but the company still participated in such events as the Chicago Auto Show.

By the time the 1953 model year arrived something was needed to help boost sales back to pre–Korean War levels and beyond. Showing GM's products in an audience-drawing way to high-population centers was seen as a means to attain greater sales.

*Approximately 100 to 125 trucks were needed to move the GM Motorama cars and exhibits. This photograph was taken during setup at the Pan Pacific in Los Angeles in 1956. (Photo Courtesy H. B. Stubbs Co.)*

The first GM Motorama with dream cars was in 1953 and it began its six-city national tour in January; the first stop was at the Waldorf-Astoria. The display of new GM automobiles, mildly modified production vehicles, and dream cars along with Broadway-style stage shows brought 1.5 million visitors.

## Cost of Success

General Motors spent more than $5 million to produce a unique Motorama each year. An army of personnel was required to produce the show at each venue and a caravan of more than 100 tractor-trailers was necessary to transport it.

GM Motorama was said to be "GM's top salesman, its best prognosticator, and barometer of business." The GM Motoramas dramatically raised the profile of the company, and as a result, sales soared for 1953 and continued to climb during GM's Motorama years. More than 2.3 million people attended the 1956 GM Motorama making it the most visited of all. According to the May 1956 issue of *Auto Age*, General Motors received $1.3 million in orders for their cars at the New York City showing alone. Despite this, the GM Motorama was canceled for 1957, but did return for the 1959 and 1961 model years. However, the venues were minimal for each: New York City and Boston for 1959; New York City, San Francisco, and Los Angeles for 1961. Furthermore, the Firebird III was the only dream car exhibited at these two tours.

Within the short span of a few years, staging the GM Motorama had become cost prohibitive. With expenses skyrocketing, and the ever-increasing popularity of television, the fate of the Motorama show was sealed. Management found that with more and more people owning a TV set, advertising through that medium was more cost effective. Additionally, GM's ideas were essentially being given away to their competitors for free. Anyone, including stylists from Ford Motor Company and Chrysler Corporation, could and did attend the Motorama. In fact, Vince Kaptur, Sr., an engineer on Harley Earl's staff, was quoted in an article published in the January/March 1971 issue of *Special Interest Autos* as saying, "Ford engineers came to the New York show and literally fell all over the Corvette, Corvair, and Nomad, measuring every possible dimension. There's little doubt they did this to compare specs with their own Thunderbird, which was going into its final development phases at the time." Ford Motor Company went as far as producing a leather-bound book consisting of photos taken at one of the venues of the 1956 GM Motorama for distribution to their stylists.

Incidentally, GM's Futurliner buses are often associated with the GM Motorama, but it was a separate program known as the Parade of Progress. It, too, was a free, traveling educational exhibition involving a fleet of twelve special buses known as Futurliners.

Adding some spice to the Parade of Progress, on occasion, were various GM dream cars such as the Bonneville Special, Wildcat II, F-88, etc. Chapter Four gives a detailed account of this traveling show.

## GM Canada

Even though the 1957 GM Motorama tour was canceled, the show did go on in Canada. In fact, the 1955 to 1961 GM Motoramas were held in consecutive years (approximately coinciding with the time of new-model introduction) in Toronto at Exhibition Place on the CNE grounds. These were the full productions including stage shows, but the dream cars were one-year old when they were shown there. In other words, the 1955 dream cars were shown with the new 1956 model GM cars; the same held true for the 1957 show.

*Celebrities, dignitaries, dealers, and GM officials attended the preview night before the official opening of the GM Motorama. Here, actress-singer Shirley Jones is sitting on the hood of a 1954 Corvette possibly at the Pan Pacific Auditorium in Los Angeles. (Photo Courtesy GM Media Archive)*

CHAPTER ONE: ORIGINS OF THE DREAM CAR AND THE GM MOTORAMA

# THE PARADE OF PROGRESS AND THE FUTURLINER

*Charles Kettering, the head of research at General Motors from 1920 to 1947, is credited with the concept of the Parade of Progress. It began in 1936 and continued until World War II interrupted it. It then resumed in 1953 with the 12 Futurliner buses, such as these, built and used just prior to the U.S. entering World War II. (Photo Courtesy GM Media Archive)*

The concept of the General Motors Parade of Progress is credited to Charles Kettering, the man in charge of GM Research Laboratories from 1920 to 1947. Kettering, who went on to obtain more than 140 U.S. and international patents, saw an opportunity for General Motors to create a kind of nationwide road show so that the corporation could communicate scientific and engineering advancements at General Motors to the public. The idea for such a show came as a result of GM's displays at the "Century of Progress" 1933 World's Fair and similar exhibits at the GM Building. People were amazed and told family and friends of the wonders they had witnessed.

Alfred Sloan, Jr., GM's president, described the purpose of the traveling show: "The GM Parade of Progress is an undertaking to bring industry to people, and by showing the individual citizens in his home community what the contributions of industry mean to him and his family, to establish a basis of mutual understanding and friendliness and at the same time to increase confidence in the future progress of America."

The first Parade of Progress began on February 11, 1936, in Lakeland, Florida. Eight specially crafted Streamliner buses were filled with displays related to science and technology and were presented in an entertaining way.

The Parade stayed at each destination about five days. During that time visitors could view walk-through exhibits such as a nineteenth century home compared with a modern home, a blacksmith's shop compared with a modern service station, etc. A film, *Progress on Parade*, was shown inside a large silver tent; between showings up to 500 people watched scientific demonstrations such as music on a light beam, how a voice appears in sound waves, and other such marvels. Other displays included a running 4-cylinder engine with a quartz glass window to allow spectators to watch the entire process of combustion, studying sound with an oscillograph, photoelectric cells, automotive safety through engineering, etc.

In 1939, construction began on new buses called Futurliners; 12 were hand built. They were significantly larger than the old Streamliners with dimensions of 33 feet long, 8 feet wide, 11 feet 4 inches tall, and a weight of 12.5 tons. The red and silver vehicles reportedly cost $100,000 each. A bubble canopy was fitted over the driver's compartment and each was shaped over a wooden form in a vacuum chamber. One out of about every three or four was usable. Over the years, the buses underwent various cosmetic changes.

The show tour with the new buses continued to travel all over North America until it was interrupted by the start of World War II. Its success was not forgotten. Harley Earl certainly did not forget. The Parade was resumed again for 1953, but this time with input from Earl.

When the Parade of Progress came to town it attracted a lot of attention. Shown here is the scene in San Bernardino, California, in February of 1956. This proved to be the final year of this traveling exhibition. (Photo Courtesy GM Media Archive)

The cars of General Motors were also included among the many exhibits of the Parade of Progress. This photo is believed to have been taken at Aberdeen, Washington, and shows a 1956 Pontiac Star Chief convertible. The Futurliner in the background held the scale model of a modern city setup. (Photo Courtesy GM Media Archive)

General Motors ultimately sold its collection of Futurliner buses. Some were modified for various purposes by their new owners. Many years ago, dream car collector Joe Bortz bought five of them when no one else wanted the relics. He eventually sold four of them and donated another to the National Auto & Truck Museum before they became collectible. (Photo Courtesy Bortz Auto Collection)

In April 1953, the Parade again displayed products related to modern engineering, science, and ongoing research. However, for some of the tour various dream cars were on exhibit as well as examples of GM's newest line of cars. Exhibits and demonstrations included a two-cycle Diesel engine, how high-compression engines boost fuel economy and power, animations of how a car was built, a cutaway jet engine, plus science lectures. The most popular was "America at the Crossroads" carried by Futurliner Number Two. This 16-foot-long diorama showed the transformation of a rural crossroads community of a half-century earlier into a thriving, modern community and how the automobile played a part in it.

With the last show held at Spokane, Washington, in early July 1956, the Parade of Progress came to an end. Increasing costs helped put an end to the impressive spectacle just as had happened with the GM Motorama. Soon after, two of the Futurliners were donated to the Michigan State Police with the provision they never be brought back to General Motors for repair or reconditioning. One individual reportedly purchased several of the others for $300 each.

In the 1980s, when five of the unwanted relics were about to be scrapped, dream car collector Joe Bortz purchased them with the intention of converting them into car haulers. His plans changed and four of them were sold and one (unit Number Ten) was donated to the National Auto & Truck Museum and underwent a total restoration. In 2006, it was sold for $4.2 million at the Barrett-Jackson auction in Scottsdale, Arizona.

CHAPTER ONE: ORIGINS OF THE DREAM CAR AND THE GM MOTORAMA

*Every location of the GM Motorama was modeled in scale to get everything right. This particular model was of the 1955 show at the Waldorf-Astoria. GM president Harlow Curtice (left) and Harley Earl (right) appear to be pleased with the layout. (Photo Courtesy GM Media Archive)*

By 1958, however, there was no set of 1957 dream cars to exhibit so the 1958 GM Motorama in Toronto focused on the company's new cars. For the following year, the Firebird III was shown just as it was at the two venues of the 1959 GM Motorama, New York City and Boston. Interestingly, the Cadillac Cyclone, which was not shown at the GM Motorama in the United States, was placed on exhibit at the 1960 GM Motorama in Toronto.

Before this, GM Canada participated in annual auto shows held at the automotive building of Exhibition Place in Toronto even well before World War II. After the war ended and automobile production resumed, GM Canada resumed its participation in auto shows. In 1954, for instance, the company was represented in two major shows there: A kind of miniature version of the GM Motorama was held in conjunction with the National Motor Show in March. It was followed several months later by the GM Wonderama at the annual CNE beginning in late August.

For the most part, production vehicles were shown along with a few dream cars. Among the cars shown at the former event was the Buick Longhorn, a modified production station wagon described as "fully equipped for an African safari, complete with rifles and pistols in special holsters." Other small-scale exhibitions were conducted in Canada under the banner of "The GM Motorama," too. (See Appendix B on page 203.)

General Motors evidently held similar small-scale shows in the United States; at least they did in Oregon in 1959. A postcard commemorating the event is offered occasionally on the Internet auction site, eBay.com. Presumably, this was not a unique event.

*Even the exterior of the buildings were dressed up for the Motorama. This is the front of the Dinner Key Auditorium in Miami in February 1955.*

### Ford Stylerama

The success of GM's Motorama motivated Ford Motor Company to try to produce a road show with dream cars to be dubbed "Stylerama" and was scheduled to begin in 1957. In 1956, one of Ford's designers suggested to George Walker, the company's vice president and general manager of Ford's Styling Center, that the company should build several show cars to be hauled with special trucks and trailers for exhibition across the United States and Canada. (This was actually done with the one-off 1956 Mercury XM-Turnpike Cruiser, so it either served as the inspiration for a fleet of such cars shown in this manner or was the singular result of the proposal.) Company president Henry Ford II was very receptive to the idea.

However, the Stylerama was ultimately canceled after several clay model designs were completed. The Edsel fiasco that cost Ford Motor Company a few hundred million dollars and the high cost of everything associated with producing the show led to the termination of the project. Furthermore, some of the concepts coming from the design studio, such as the nuclear-powered Nucleon, were simply too revolutionary to appeal to the public. Harley Earl's philosophy of not going too far too fast evidently was not fully appreciated at the time in the Ford Advanced Design Studio. Or perhaps, in an attempt to outdo General Motors, they simply went overboard.

*GM dream cars were shown at dealerships across the country. Goad Cadillac in Corpus Christi, Texas, displayed the Apollo Gold La Espada in its showroom for one day prior to the car's appearance at the Parade of Progress held on the grounds of the local high school on February 25, 1955. (Photo Courtesy GM Media Archive)*

## Chapter Two
# Transportation Unlimited and the Mid-Century Motorama

GM's first major postwar show, Transportation Unlimited, took place in New York City in January 1949, and then again in Detroit in April; it featured the new lineup of 1949-model coupes, sedans, convertibles, etc.

For January 19 to January 27, 1950, General Motors sponsored its Mid-Century Motorama, also at the Waldorf-Astoria, the sole venue for this event. Five special cars were built for auto shows in Canada including the Mid-Century Motorama at the CNE in Toronto.

For 1951 and 1952, General Motors did not sponsor similar shows due to the rationing of materials (such as steel) needed for the Korean War. Extra promotion of automobiles simply was not needed, as production was somewhat restricted. However, General Motors still displayed show cars at various events: the Le Sabre and the XP-300, of course, along with the 1952 prototypes, the Cadillac Eldorado, Buick Skylark, and mildly customized production cars.

### Transportation Unlimited

At the Waldorf-Astoria, the public got its first chance to view a prototype Buick Riviera two-door hardtop months before its official release, which was not until June. Other vehicles included were prototype two-door hardtops consisting of the Chevrolet Bel Air, Pontiac Catalina, Oldsmobile Holiday, and Cadillac Coupe de Ville, plus three modified production Cadillacs: a Series 62 convertible (named El Rancho) and two altered Fleetwood Sixty Specials (dubbed the Caribbean and Embassy).

*General Motors' advertising agency, Campbell-Ewald very likely designed this colorful cardboard poster. It was used to promote GM's first major postwar auto show, dubbed "Transportation Unlimited," held at New York City's famous Waldorf-Astoria hotel in January 1949. The exhibition went on to one more venue: Detroit, in April.*

*Centered in the grand ballroom of the Waldorf-Astoria was the "Pillar of Progress" covering 1,500 square feet of floor space with five electrically synchronized turntables upon which sat a car from each of the passenger car divisions. (Photo Courtesy GM Media Archive)*

30   MOTORAMA

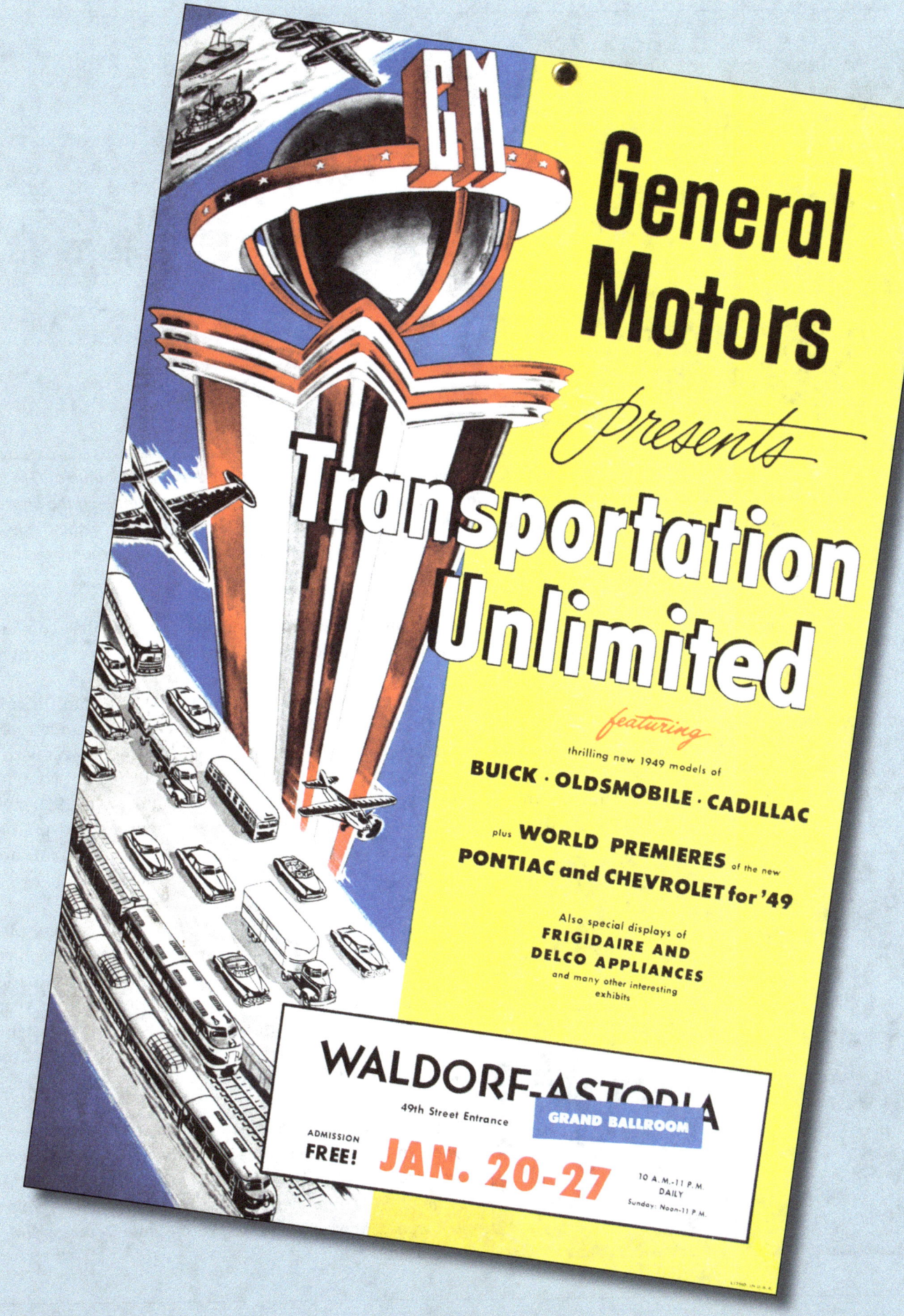

# CHAPTER TWO: TRANSPORTATION UNLIMITED AND THE MID-CENTURY MOTORAMA

*An array of Oldsmobile models can be seen here inside Convention Hall, the site of the second and final venue of GM's Transportation Unlimited. Note the Eighty-Eight convertible in the foreground, left. The Eighty-Eight combined the standard Olds V-8 of the Ninety-Eight with the shorter, lightweight chassis of the 6-cylinder Seventy-Six series. Behind it is a station wagon with wood-panel inserts. An all-steel version replaced it later in the model year. In the foreground, center, is an Olds with a see-through hood. (Photo Courtesy GM Media Archive)*

The February 1949 issue of *General Motors World* provided a rather prosaic description of these Cadillacs as being "sleek sybaritic specimens of automotive splendor."

### Cadillac Coupe de Ville

The show at the Waldorf-Astoria was the first public unveiling of the prototype two-tone Coupe de Ville (SO 9717). It was enthusiastically received, so much so that it was rushed into production, with some changes though.

The prototype was based on the 1948 Cadillac convertible. Its cowl braces were attached to the floor, a telltale sign that it was a convertible.

The prototype was distinctly different than the production version that appeared later in the model year. The car was much longer than the production car with a 133-inch wheelbase. It also had a simulated air scoop for the rear fenders, one-piece curved windshield, 1950-style Series 75 backlight, short-wave telephone, and pullout desk. Side glass and vent windows were hydraulically operated. The prototype's seat covers and headliner were gunmetal-colored leather.

Rather than being built to the specifications of a nearly production-ready car, this car appears to have been built per the specifications of GM president Charles E. Wilson, who became Secretary of Defense four years later. After the car had made its rounds on the Motorama circuit for two years, Wilson used it for daily transportation until 1952.

*This is the interior of the 1949 Chevrolet Bel Air prototype exhibited at Transportation Unlimited. (At least two prototypes were built.) Revealed in this photograph are some of the differences between it and the actual version that went into production for 1950. (Photo Courtesy GM Media Archive)*

## Cadillac El Rancho

A western-themed interior was the principal lure of the El Rancho convertible (SO 9770). The car's upholstery was of waxed saddle leather, trimmed with dark suede kip hides, and saddle-stitched in white cord. In addition to the special upholstery, antiqued hand-engraved silver hardware further dressed up this show car. The El Rancho's exterior was finished in a special color named Mexican Dawn, a brown hue.

*The grand ballroom of the Waldorf-Astoria was used for the debut of GM's prototype hardtop models, the Chevrolet Bel Air, Oldsmobile Holiday, and the Buick Riviera. (Note the side trim on the Riviera show car was not used on the production version of the car.) Two others, the Pontiac Catalina and Cadillac Coupe de Ville prototype, were shown in adjoining rooms. All of them later went into production. The silver Buick (to right of the Riviera), identified in GM Media Archive records as a Super Series 50 Sedan Model 51, is also a show car with special paint and a bright silver interior. (Photo Courtesy GM Media Archive)*

*The Pontiac Catalina two-door hardtop prototype was two-toned as were the other two-door hardtop prototypes General Motors displayed during Transportation Unlimited. Two-toning emphasized the hardtop design, which mimicked the appearance of a convertible with the top in the up position. (Photo Courtesy GM Media Archive)*

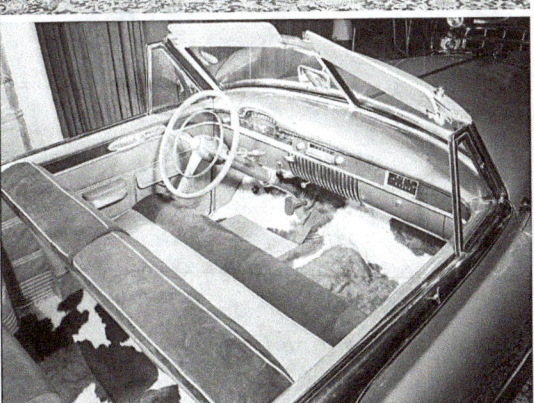

*Four special Cadillacs were exhibited for GM's Transportation Unlimited (from top left, clockwise): the Cadillac Coupe de Ville prototype, Caribbean, Embassy, and El Rancho. The Caribbean and Embassy were built from Fleetwood Sixty-Specials. (Photo Courtesy GM Media Archive)*

### Cadillac Caribbean and Embassy

Special features of the Caribbean Daybreak metallic green Caribbean sedan included antiqued silver hardware, door saddles, and fold-down trays concealing smoking and vanity sets mounted in the back of the front seat. Upholstery was French broadcloth and iridescent green leather and the headliner was green broadcloth. The instrument panel was painted to match the exterior.

The black Embassy had a number of luxurious appointments. The roof was leather-covered and it had simulated rear fender air scoops. The front passenger-side door had a recess for a tool kit of chrome-plated tools and the driver-side front door contained a storage compartment for maps.

The interior had silver hardware, pearl-gray clipped sheepskin carpet, a hydraulically operated divider between the front and rear compartments, a tubular umbrella storage pocket in the right side of the front seat, a vanity case housed in the passenger-side rear door, and a shortwave telephone mounted within the driver-side rear door. Upholstery in the front compartment was black leather while the rear compartment was custom-woven broadcloth with black leather for the door panels.

### Buick Riviera

In addition to the show cars, a specially prepared two-toned Riviera with a pleated silver leather interior was also exhibited.

### A Major Success

According to an article published in the January 21, 1949, edition of *The New York Times*, "New York's unabated craving for new cars and insatiable curiosity as to what makes the automotive wheels go around were emphasized yesterday by the 65,000 visitors attending the opening session of the General Motors exposition 'Transportation Unlimited' at the Waldorf-Astoria Hotel.

"Show officials estimated that one out of every three who inspected the automobiles on display wished to purchase at once and take delivery at the same time. On receiving the sad tidings that they could place orders with dealers, and hope for the best, at least 80 percent of those who applied turned away with long faces."

Of all the special show cars that appeared at Transportation Unlimited, only the Coupe de Ville prototype is known to have survived. However, it was virtually hidden away for decades before being purchased in early 2011 by collector Steve Plunkett.

The unique car belonged to Charles Wilson for nearly a decade. (The other three 1949 Cadillac show cars were given to Alfred Sloan and other GM executives.) After President Eisenhower appointed Wilson as Secretary of Defense, he gave the car to his secretary, who then moved to California and took the unique car with her. According to Plunkett, in the late-1970s the car was located in the San Diego area. It later made its way to Connecticut where it was in storage for many years. The beautifully restored car was shown for the

*This Buick Roadmaster Riviera show car was equipped with pleated leather upholstery. The pattern and the color, silver, were unlike the production version. This car's side trim was also unlike that of the production Riviera, which had a "sweepspear" molding. (Photo Courtesy GM Media Archive)*

*Another Buick show car at GM's Transportation Unlimited was a silver Super Series 50 Sedan Model 51 with a silver interior nearly identical to the one specially made for the Riviera show car. It differed in having a fold-down center armrest in the back seat. (Photo Courtesy GM Media Archive)*

*Of the four special Cadillac show cars exhibited for Transportation Unlimited, only this Coupe de Ville prototype is known to have survived. It was recently restored and is currently owned by Canadian collector Steve Plunkett.*

first time since its recent restoration at the 2013 Amelia Concours d'Elegance.

### Mid-Century Motorama

The Mid-Century Motorama featured specially trimmed cars in addition to the regular line of automobiles, which, without a doubt, impressed the 320,000 visitors who attended.

### *Cadillac Debutante*

One of the Waldorf-Astoria Mid-Century Motorama show cars, the Cadillac Debutante, was a sensation with the crowds. Leopard skins covered the upper portion of the front and rear seat backs, the upper side panels, and the complete floor in the front and rear compartments while the armrests were covered with iridescent gray leather. Every unpainted metal surface within the interior was gold-plated.

Obtaining perfect, matching leopard skins was the greatest challenge in creating the Debutante according to Don E. Ahrens, Cadillac General Sales Manager.

*The 1950 Cadillac Debutante featured Tawny Yellow Buff paint, leopard-skin upholstery, and gold-plated interior trim. It was quite the sensation at the Mid-Century Motorama. (Photo Courtesy GM Media Archive)*

MOTORAMA 35

## CHAPTER TWO: TRANSPORTATION UNLIMITED AND THE MID-CENTURY MOTORAMA

Planning ahead was critical; many months before the car was built, a Detroit furrier was commissioned to obtain the necessary skins. Ultimately, he brought 187 of the finest Somaliland leopard skins in the country to his business establishment and after a careful examination, 14 of them were judged as the best that could possibly be obtained. Further work was needed to match each piece for the best layout.

The exterior was every bit as striking. A pearlescent paint, Tawny Yellow Buff, was developed to "complement the Rufous Buff color in the leopard skins." To get the pearl luster effect, miniature moon-shaped fish scales were sprayed over the base paint. These fine scales were obtained through a special process of dissolving large fish scales, leaving only the tiny pearl essence. The car is often reported to have inspired the 1956 comedy film, *The Solid Gold Cadillac*, although the movie must have been inspired by the Broadway play of the same name that premiered in 1953.

### Buick Riviera

One particular Buick Riviera two-door hardtop exhibited at the Mid-Century Motorama must have caught the eyes of the ladies. This show car was painted salmon pink and its interior was upholstered in pink broadtail and fabric.

### Oldsmobile Palm Beach

Another car that made quite an impression on show attendees was the two-door hardtop Oldsmobile Palm Beach Holiday Ninety-Eight. Painted Cabana Sand over Surf Green, the Palm Beach was upholstered in green alligator leather with a contrasting fine cane-mesh fabric.

*The two-door hardtop Oldsmobile "Palm Beach Holiday" Ninety-Eight show car's interior was upholstered in green alligator leather with a contrasting fine cane-mesh fabric.*

### Pillar of Progress Display

Other highlights of the Mid-Century Motorama included displays of the newly redesigned 1950 Cadillac Series 61, Series 62, and Series 75 models; restyled models of the Buick Division; a new series of "Futuramic" Oldsmobile Ninety-Eights in five models; Chevrolet and GMC trucks; plus a special display of the 5,500-hp T-40 turbo-prop engine built for the U.S. Navy by GM's Allison Division.

Centered in the grand ballroom of the Waldorf-Astoria was the "Pillar of Progress" covering 1,500 square feet of floor space with five electrically synchronized turntables upon which sat a car from each of the passenger car divisions. A 30-foot-high pylon was mounted at the center of the platform; its apex featured plaster relief models of the autos going back to 1900. These plaster relief models were in keeping with the theme of emphasizing progress during the first half of the twentieth century.

*Chassis had long been common sights at auto shows when this one for a Buick was shown at GM's Mid-Century Motorama. I suspect the hood of the car visible in the foreground is that of the Buick specially painted in salmon and upholstered in pink. (Photo Courtesy GM Media Archive)*

![Stars of an All-Star Cast presented by General Motors at the Canadian National Exhibition promotional brochure]

*Five cars were built for auto shows in Canada including the Mid-Century Motorama at the Canadian National Exhibition in Toronto: two Oldsmobiles dubbed Golden Jubilee and Westward-Ho, a pair of Pontiacs named Magnificent and Fleur de Lis, plus the Chevrolet Royal Canadian. This promotional brochure for the GM exhibits at the CNE illustrated each of these cars along with the Buick Riviera and Cadillac Series 62 convertible also in attendance.*

*The 1950 Pontiac Fleur de Lis (within the "corral") appeared at that year's Canadian National Exhibition. It was among five specially built, GM Canada show cars shown at this as well as other events. (Photo Courtesy CNE Archives, Alexandra Studio Collection, MG5-5903-4)*

The five cars built for the Canada Mid-Century Motorama were two Oldsmobiles dubbed Golden Jubilee and Westward-Ho, a pair of Pontiacs named Magnificent and Fleur de Lis, plus the Chevrolet Royal Canadian. However, this show was also open for all makes.

Features of these cars included an interior finished in silky black broadtail and salmon nylon waffle weave with details in black leather for the Oldsmobile Golden Jubilee; Cudahy Yellow and Cadillac Black leather interior with Cudahy Yellow exterior for the Oldsmobile Westward-Ho; metallic green lower body and a special crinkle champagne finish, the Pontiac Magnificent; gray-white paint with French Blue tapestry and leather upholstery for the Pontiac Fleur de Lis.

The Chevrolet Royal Canadian featured a rich Carteret Red and Oyster White paint scheme that provided a striking color combination. It was further enhanced by gold plating for the bumpers, grille, and other trim along

MOTORAMA 37

# CHAPTER TWO: TRANSPORTATION UNLIMITED AND THE MID-CENTURY MOTORAMA

with a spectacular interior. Upholstery for the show car consisted of white leather at the seat ends and white tartan and plain scarlet for the seating surfaces.

### Survivors

The special show cars of the Mid-Century Motorama are not known to exist today. However, Cadillac & LaSalle Club member Tim Pawl believes he may have seen the 1950 Debutante, but was not familiar with this show car at that time (around 1979), and assumed that he was viewing a customized 1950 Cadillac convertible in deteriorated condition. After nearly 30 years, the Debutante had become a forgotten show car. A former GM employee offered it for sale.

## GM Canada at the CNE, 1951–1952

*This postcard commemorated the appearance of the Le Sabre at the General Motors Vision-Era exhibit at the 1951 Canadian National Exhibition in Toronto, Ontario. It was there for the first three days of the event before departing to its next scheduled venue. The car was a sensation wherever it appeared.*

After the 1950 Mid-Century Motorama at the CNE, the Motorama banner was not used again until 1953. However, for 1951, General Motors made a good impression on the attendees of the CNE in Toronto. Along with the new models was the Buick Le Sabre (three days only) and a set of modified production cars that comprised the Chevrolet Royal Canadian, Pontiac Plainsman, Oldsmobile Rancher, as well as the upscale hardtop Chevy Bel Air, Pontiac Catalina, Buick Riviera, and a Cadillac Series 62 convertible.

How the 1951 production-based show cars differed from standard factory specs is unknown, but of course each had special paint colors and interiors. Most likely the Chevrolet Royal Canadian featured gold-plated exterior components, as did its 1950 predecessor. Presumably, the Pontiac Plainsman and Olds Rancher had western-themed appointments judging by their names.

The Le Sabre returned to the CNE for 1952. Shown with it was another version of the Chevrolet Royal Canadian along with the Pontiac Catalina Supreme, Oldsmobile Caribbean, Buick Ranger, Cadillac Coronation Coupe, and Chevrolet Special Delivery trucks. Unlike the show cars of the prior year, some information is available on the 1952 show cars of GM Canada. The Chevrolet Royal Canadian was painted brilliant Parade Scarlet and deep Guards Blue. As in the past, the bumpers, grille, and other exterior trim were gold-plated. Georgian White with contrasting shades of red made the Pontiac Catalina Supreme a standout at the show. Little information is available on the Catalina Supreme; the same is true for the Oldsmobile Caribbean, other than it was "finished in glowing Carib Green."

The Buick Ranger featured a western theme. It was built from a Roadmaster convertible and was said to be painted El

38  MOTORAMA

Pawl does not recall seeing gold trim on the car he inspected, but the 24-carat gold used on it (although spectacular) was not durable and neither was the leopard skin upholstery. I suspect that an owner who was also unfamiliar with the car's history and made the same assumption as Pawl may have restored the car to a stock configuration, or that it was ultimately sent to a junkyard. Even if found today, restoring this car's interior to its show car configuration would be a costly and ultimately impossible project. The only choice available to restore the interior would be the manufacture of faux leopard skin to match the original as closely as possible. Restoring all the 24-carat gold-plated hardware would certainly be pricey, as would be duplicating the special paint finish.

*A modified Buick Roadmaster convertible featured a western theme. Fitted on at least the driver-side door (possibly both doors) were a rifle (type unknown) and a holster! (Photo Courtesy CNE Archives, Alexandra Studio Collection, MG5-5914-6)*

Rancho Beige and Canyon Brown. However, a black and white photo of this car shows it to have had a monotone scheme. The wheels were clearly darker so perhaps the brown paint was applied to them. Brown may also have been the color of the convertible top's fabric. A rifle (type unknown) and a holster were fitted on at least the driver-side door (possibly both doors)!

An advertisement for GM Canada's show cars at the CNE said, "The dignified styling of the Cadillac Coupe de Ville is given a new distinction by the exquisite use of Sequoia Beige and Royal Maroon." Chevrolet Special Delivery trucks were displayed in Parchment Cream and coral with a matching interior. Carpet covered the cab and body floors.

Other special exhibits included the "Preview of Progress," a science show conducted by GM technicians, an Oldsmobile Rocket V-8, and cutaway displays of the Hydra-Matic and truck transmissions.

*The theme for GM Canada's presentation at the 1952 Canadian National Exhibition was "Travelera." Special show cars at the event included the Chevrolet Royal Canadian, Pontiac Catalina Supreme, Oldsmobile Caribbean, Buick Ranger, Cadillac Coronation Coupe, and Chevrolet Special Delivery trucks. The Le Sabre made a repeat appearance, too.*

MOTORAMA 39

## Chapter Three

# THE 1953 GM MOTORAMA

General Motors resumed its own large-scale show beginning in January 1953. This year the exhibition went to New York City, Miami, Los Angeles, San Francisco, Dallas, and Kansas City. The theme for the elaborate stage show presentation at this year's Motorama was "Motorythms and Fashion Firsts" choreographed by Richard and Edith Barstow of the Barnum & Bailey Circus. It was the first such auto show produced by General Motors to include the so-called dream cars. Among them was a prototype of the Corvette, planned for release for the 1954 model year. (Public reaction to the stylish sports car changed GM's planning considerably.) Others included the Pontiac Parisienne, Oldsmobile Starfire, Buick Wildcat, Cadillac Le Mans, and Cadillac Orleans. Also shown were the 1951 experimental cars, the Buick XP-300 and an updated GM Le Sabre.

### Chevrolet Corvette: An American Sports Car

The chain of events leading to the creation of the Corvette included the refinement of the relatively new material, glass reinforced plastic (GRP), and the increasing popularity of European sports cars in the United States. Another important link in the chain of events leading to the Corvette took place in September 1951 when Harley Earl attended the sports car races at Watkins Glen and watched the European and special-build sports cars in competition.

*This publicity photo of the original 1953 Corvette was taken at the Key Biscayne Hotel, a popular lodge in the 1950s and 1960s.*

*The 1951 Buick XP-300 (in background) was shown on the 1953 GM Motorama show tour. A Buick show chassis (left, center) and a pair of Roadmasters (foreground) are also seen in this view inside the Waldorf-Astoria.*

# CHAPTER THREE: THE 1953 GM MOTORAMA

*An elegant silver-blue gown worn by the model matches the color of the 1953 Cadillac Sixty Special appearing during the stage show at a GM Motorama. (Photo Courtesy Jim Jordan)*

*Bill Mitchell of the GM Design staff sat in the driver's seat of the restyled 1951 GM Le Sabre for this photograph taken at the Waldorf-Astoria before the official opening of the 1953 GM Motorama. Mitchell was Harley Earl's successor as the head of GM Design. (Photo Courtesy Steve Wolken)*

Briggs Cunningham is reported to have innocently poked fun at Harley's Le Sabre, which he drove to the event, by suggesting that Earl should have brought a car he could race. During an interview, Earl said the idea for the Corvette was born while driving the Le Sabre as the pace car for this race. Earl decided that General Motors should build an *American* sports car.

Earl assembled a team of bright and talented engineers to tackle the project. Robert McLean, who had engineering and industrial design degrees from Cal Tech, and Maurice Olley, director of Chevrolet Research & Development, were part of the team. Others involved in the styling of the car were Bill Bloch, Tony Balthasar, Vince Kaptur, Sr., Clare McKichan, and Joe Schemansky.

### Original Show Car EX-52

After a fast eight months of development, Harley Earl's version of an American sports car debuted at the Waldorf-Astoria, the first venue of the 1953 GM Motorama. The fiberglass-bodied prototype was displayed on a turntable as the Polo White roadster, EX-52/SO 1737. It was officially named "Corvette," and generated much excitement wherever it was shown. GM personnel were positioned around the dream cars to eavesdrop on the comments made by spectators; much of what they overheard indicated interest in the sports car.

The original show car featured functional cowl scoops, which were painted red inside. Interestingly, General Motors fitted similar scoops to the 1956 Corvette. Hydraulically operated hood and trunk lids were installed on EX-52 for display purposes; these panels opened and closed as the show car revolved on its turntable. The recessed headlights were covered with a

*This rare original poster was likely produced by GM's ad agency, Campbell-Ewald. It was used to promote the 1953 GM Motorama held at the Civic Auditorium in San Francisco.*

*Various minor alterations were made to the original prototype of the Corvette before its first public appearance at the Waldorf-Astoria in January 1953. In its original form, prototype EX-52/SO 1737 was equipped with Bel Air–type hub caps and trim rings and lacked the anodized gold model name script later installed in the front and rear of the car. It was not displayed publicly as seen here. Script on fender says Cougar, a name that was only briefly considered. (Photo Courtesy GM Design Center)*

"fencing mask" grille, which could be lifted to simplify cleaning the headlight lenses; on the production version, this feature was replaced by larger bezels minus the hinged grilles. Controls on either side of the AM-radio allowed these scoops to open independently.

An element of the prototype's design maintained for production was the flush-fitting folding lid for the car's black convertible top. This was evidently one of Harley Earl's favorite features as it was used many times beginning with the Buick Y-Job.

The prototype's other features included two-piece bumper bullets and anodized-gold Corvette script under the crossed-flags emblem and on the deck lid. The bumper bullets were changed to a one-piece unit for production and the script on the front and rear was deleted.

Incidentally, the original hood emblem had to be altered on the first prototype before its debut. Chevrolet interior designer Robert Bartholomew first designed crossed staffs with the checkered flag on the driver's side and the American flag on the passenger's side. The identical design also appeared on the steering wheel hub. Just days before the Corvette was to go on display at the Waldorf, Chevrolet management learned the proposed emblem was actually illegal because it featured the American flag, which cannot be used on a commercial product. The illegal emblem from the front of EX-52 still exists and is displayed at the National Corvette Museum in Bowling Green, Kentucky.

Newly redesigned emblems were quickly crafted and installed. A red flag emblazoned with the Chevrolet bow-tie symbol and a fleur-de-lis replaced the American flag.

Another last-moment substitution on EX-52 was the replacement of the Bel Air wheel covers (actually used on about the first 25 production Corvettes) with a set featuring a simulated knock-off hub with a two-bar spinner. The prototypes' wheel covers differed from the production units in a couple of minor ways: longer bars for the spinner or "flipper" and the Chevy bowtie emblem's long axis being perpendicular to the bars of the flipper.

The bottom of the folding-top storage well for the original show car was covered in fabric held in place with a pair of metal bands. Hinge design for the lid over this compartment allowed the trunk lid to be opened at the same time, something not included on the production cars. The convertible top frame had inward-folding, long side rails, but this arrangement proved to be somewhat troublesome. A redesign did not totally solve the problems that prevented the top's smooth operation. However, the folding side rails were further developed and adopted for full-size Chevys some years later.

Even before the Corvette was unveiled at the Waldorf-Astoria, it had already been approved for production. However, production was pushed months ahead of the planned 1954 release because of the public's response to the prototype. The first Corvettes rolled off

# CHAPTER THREE: THE 1953 GM MOTORAMA

*The rear-end styling of the 1953 Corvette remained virtually unaltered from that of the original prototype (shown) at the GM Motorama in Miami.*

the Flint assembly line on June 30, 1953, just a few weeks after the end of that year's GM Motorama.

GM management determined that the Corvette belonged with Chevrolet. Therefore, certain mechanical aspects of the car became set in stone. For one, Chevrolet's inline 6-cylinder engine was coupled to the 2-speed Powerglide; it was the only choice offered to power the sports car. Chevrolet was designing a modern V-8, but it was two model years away and a 4-speed manual transmission truly befitting a sports car would not be available until 1957. These facts and the lack of conveniences such as roll-up windows (instead of plexiglass snap-in panels) that most Americans expected in their automobiles diminished enthusiasm for the car. The Corvette had other issues that left the car's future in doubt at General Motors, which have been well documented in other books and magazines over the decades.

### Prototypes 852, 853, 856

Three Corvette prototypes were built. The original prototype Corvette (or "Waldorf Corvette" as it was often referenced inside GM Styling) was assigned the Chevrolet Engineering internal tracking number of "852." Four more prototypes were ordered, but only "853" and "856" were actually built; the two canceled orders were for a complete chassis ("854") and another complete car ("855") to be used for assessing new components and systems as well as to serve as a Proving Grounds test car. The "855" chassis, however, was assembled and used for V-8 installation trials.

GM Styling and Chevrolet Engineering assembled car 852 (aka EX-52). The other two bodies were supplied by Fisher Body and assembled by the Chevrolet Experimental Department.

Car 856 ("EX" number unknown) was the test car; it received heavy-duty test-driving on GM's Proving Grounds to investigate how well the fiberglass body could withstand the stresses imposed by driving as well as how it responded to temperature extremes. Car 856 was completed on January 15, 1953. Because it was a test mule, it was not built to show car standards.

Car 853 (EX-53) was the second show car, but actually the third prototype to be completed (on February 1,

# EX-52 Differences

The first prototype's red interior differed only in minor details from the 300 production cars. These differences included:

- Chrome-plated inside door release knob (white for production cars)
- White vinyl-covered door panel trim (painted for production cars)
- Different control knob layout on dash
- Smaller inside rearview mirror
- Red knob on gear selector lever (white for production cars)

Not surprisingly, EX-52 had distinctive features under the hood not used in production including:

- Radiator header tank mounted on driver's side of the engine
- Chrome-plated, "pancake" truck-type air cleaners
- Chrome-plated rocker arm cover
- No shield for the ignition system
- Shrouded fan

In addition to the above, the inline-6 installed in the prototypes had a published horsepower rating of 160, rather than the 150-hp rating for the mass-produced Corvettes.

**Among the minor differences between the interior of the original prototype of the Corvette (shown) and that of the production model included the size of the dash-mounted rearview mirror, control knob layout, and color of the gear shift lever knob. (Photo Courtesy GM Design Center)**

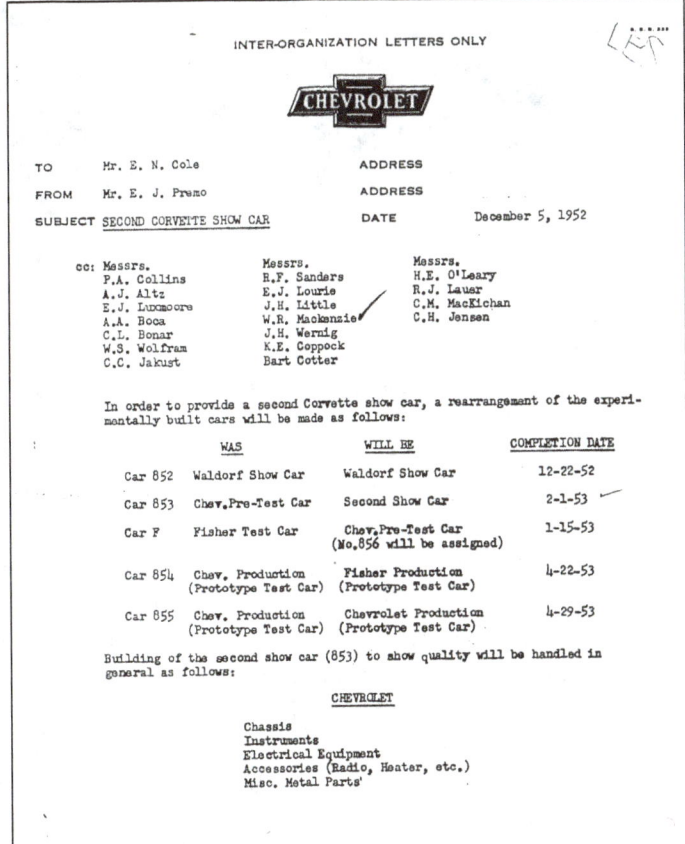

**This letter described the shuffling of the internal reference numbers for the Corvette prototypes once a second show car, built by Chevrolet, had been authorized. Car 852 was the first prototype that was used for the GM Motorama, car 853 was displayed at various auto shows, and "Car F" was the test car that was later designated car 856. The other two, 854 and 855, were later canceled, although the latter's chassis was used for V-8 fit tests.**

CHAPTER THREE: THE 1953 GM MOTORAMA

# THE FATE OF EX-52

Corvette EX-122 is the car often said to be the original GM Motorama display car. GM documents indicate EX-122 began as the second production Corvette off the assembly line, however. This is the way the car appeared after its final rebuild at General Motors. (Photo Courtesy Don Keefe)

What happened to Corvette EX-52 (aka Car 852) and the other 1953 Corvette prototypes? In 1993 John Amgwert, one of the founders of the National Corvette Restorers Society (NCRS), wrote an article, "The Earliest Corvettes," for the club's official publication, *The Corvette Restorer Magazine*. He detailed the history of the first several Corvettes using original GM work orders, which were illustrated in the article. At that time the work orders were in the possession of the NCRS, but they have since been donated to the Antique Automobile Club of America Library (AACA). Automotive historian Don Keefe also reported the same conclusions as Amgwert regarding the fate of EX-52 in an article he wrote for *Corvette Fever* not long afterward.

According to these memorandums, the body of EX-52 was burned at the Milford Proving Grounds for a flammability test and its frame was salvaged and modified for use on the 1954 "Waldorf" Nomad. One of the GM work orders, dated November 6, 1953, provided a detailed description of the results of a fire-resistance test; the final notation described the body as collapsing from the flames at 11 a.m.

This test was performed to determine whether a flame retardant should be mixed into the fiberglass. Adding the retardant would have added to the cost of building each car. The tests revealed that a "reinforced plastic body is superior in resistance to fire than a conventional steel body."

Despite these facts, most references state that EX-122 is the original Corvette prototype even though it is known to have a production body atop its chassis. (About a dozen or so years ago its current owner rebuilt EX-122 to the appearance of the original prototype.) Amgwert and Keefe, however, both concluded from GM's work orders that EX-122 actually began as the second production Corvette, E53F001002. General Motors retained this car for testing of the experimental Chevrolet small-block V-8 and other components beginning in 1954 and continuing into 1955.

According to official GM documents examined by Amgwert and Keefe, the frame was replaced during the time it was being modified for an experimental V-8 installation. It was later rebuilt for ride development and in about May 1955 a new body was installed but by then the original frame and body had been replaced. After a 25,000-mile durability test the car was torn down and inspected. Finally, it was totally rebuilt in late 1955 and assigned a VIN of EX-122 since it could not be given a standard serial number.

The rebuilt car served as a courtesy car for a short time before being sold on April 11, 1956, to Russell Sanders, who was assigned to Chevrolet's Engineering Department. Sanders later served as Director of Engineering & Sales at GM's Rochester Products Division in New York. He sold EX-122 on October 10, 1959, for $1,000 to John Ingle, a resident of New York. Ingle kept the car for approximately 40 years. Sanders wrote a letter to Ingle describing in detail the history of EX-122. (The letter was included with the sale of EX-122 to its current owner.) In this letter Sanders explained the history of the car from the time it was "built up originally in the Experimental Department of Chevrolet Engineering" and that it was constructed with the "best possible" workmanship because it was to be used for display at the GM Motorama at the Waldorf-Astoria.

Furthermore, Sanders stated in his letter that EX-122 was not the first Corvette built, but rather it was the "first one built for show. There were other test cars... that were far from good looking..." The evidence available does not support his recollections, as two prototype show cars were built along with one test car that was not the "best possible" workmanship, as Sanders expressed it.

Currently, the available information indicates that the second production Corvette, serial number E53F1001002, was replaced piece by piece over time to become EX-122.

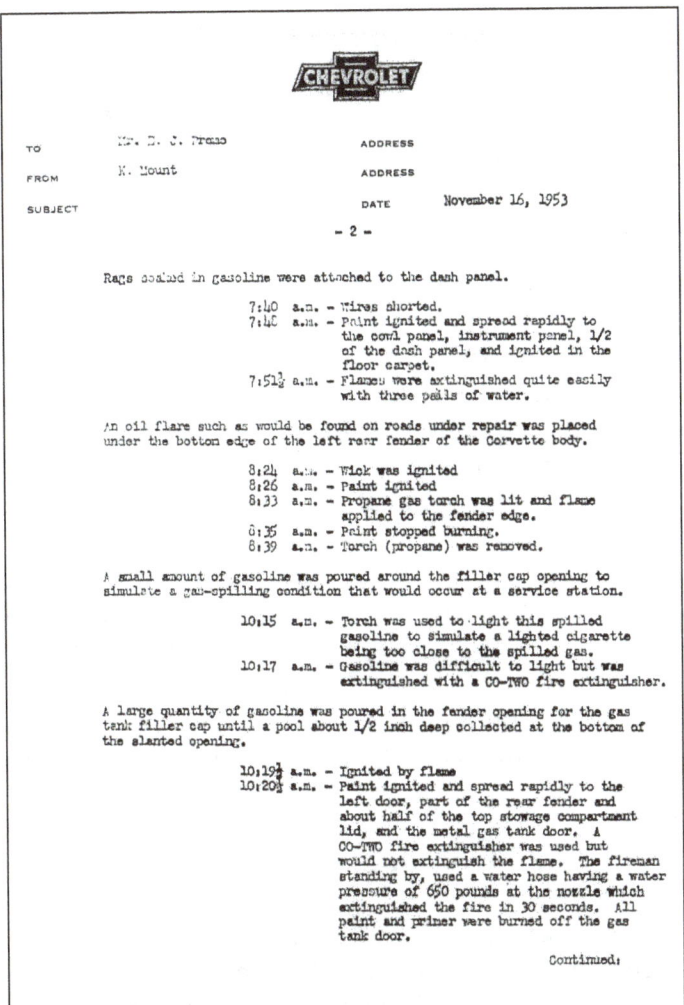

*This inter-organization letter confirmed the scrapping of EX-52, but its folding top was kept for use at GM Styling. The letter states the "chassis was retained by the Research and Development Group." Note that the car had accumulated 111 miles.*

*A detailed report was made regarding the fire resistance test of fiberglass conducted on EX-52. Shown here is page two of that report. The results of the tests showed that no fire retardant needed to be incorporated into the fiberglass body of the Corvette.*

# CHAPTER THREE: THE 1953 GM MOTORAMA

*The Fisher test car was not finished to show car standards. Note the grille, black sidewall tires, and hubcaps. Its body was eventually replaced with that of the second show car. (Photo Courtesy GM Media Archives)*

> ## EX-53 Differences
>
> Differences between the first show car and the second included:
>
> - No cowl scoops on show car Number Two
> - Push-button door releases deleted on car Number Two
> - White piping around the door panel storage compartment lid
> - White piping around the convertible top's well lining
> - Different trunk lid hinges and mounting locations
> - Varying brackets, fittings, hoses, etc. within the engine compartment

1953). It was displayed in Canada on two tours and at various auto shows in the United States including the Denver Auto Show (April 6–11), the Custom Car Show in Indianapolis (May 25–31), and the Michigan Motor Show in Detroit (June 2–7). It was also seen in a GM promotional film, *Hall of Wonders*, narrated by Dave Garroway of NBC's *Today* television program.

### The Parisienne: A Formal Pontiac

The Parisienne (SO 1759) or La Parisienne (as it was sometimes referenced, especially when shown in Canada) featured nostalgic, classic-era styling as a chauffeured town car. Similar to other cars of the GM Motorama, the Parisienne was long and low. It was a full 7 inches lower than a production Pontiac and 56 inches overall in height. However, the car did not simply have a lower roofline but numerous body modifications.

Although based on a very early production 1953 Chieftain (probably a convertible) and still appearing much the same as the production car from which it was built, its modifications created the aura of something much more upscale than a Pontiac. The changes made to the body were generally subtle yet wide-ranging. (A special metal tag on the upper right firewall bearing "SPEC. BODY-X70–E0235" attests to these changes.) Paul Gillan rendered these alterations with the assistance of Homer LaGassey from the Pontiac studio. They resulted in a lower and more sophisticated-looking car, as well as one that was much heavier due to extensive use of lead filler.

Other than its lowered roofline, other body modifications included a sectioned hood, lowered cowl shaped to accommodate a wraparound windshield, as well as cut-down front fenders and doors, rear deck, and quarters. A fixed landau-styled top made of fiberglass covered the passenger compartment and of course there was the open chauffeur's compartment.

Press releases stated that a "plexiglass dome" could be installed over the chauffeur's compartment although the car was most likely never shown with it installed. However, according to Homer LaGassey, the plexiglass cover was actually fabricated. No quarter windows were provided, but the rear backlight did wrap around to aid in visibility to the rear.

The Parisienne's front bucket seats were upholstered in pink cowhide and the rear bench seat was beige and black button-tufted nylon. As an aid to entry into the rear seat, the passenger-side bucket seat moved forward automatically via a hydraulic system when the passenger door was opened.

General Motors often added a little extra pizzazz to the engine compartment of its show cars in terms

*This photo of the 1953 Parisienne was taken inside GM's Argonaut Building. The car's fixed landau-style top, lowered height, and sectioned body made it a very distinctive show car. Adding to the formal and luxurious look of the Parisienne was its meticulously hand-lacquered exterior finish described by General Motors as "black-black."*

of a higher-than-stock horsepower power rating and chrome-plated parts. However, the Parisienne was one of the exceptions. It was powered with a stock straight-8 (without any chrome dress-up items) and a Hydra-Matic.

For the 1954 season, General Motors freshened up the Parisienne; the most notable features were a new 1954 grille and color scheme. The formal-looking black was changed to blue-tinted silver and the pink leather was replaced by white. The updated car made appearances at various auto shows including the International Motor Show in Toronto as well as the Canadian National Exhibition (also in Toronto) several months later, but not the 1954 GM Motorama. It was also placed on exhibit at car shows in the United States, such as the 1954 Milwaukee Auto Show.

No production version of the Parisienne was ever intended; it was strictly a design exercise meant to impress potential Pontiac buyers. The show car's name was used for Canadian Pontiacs some years later.

For many years car enthusiasts assumed the Parisienne was crushed. Instead it left General Motors intact, although exactly how is a bit fuzzy. It may have been sent to a Pontiac dealer where it was reportedly used as a courtesy car. In 1959 the Parisienne was sold to a Michigan resident who eventually had some restoration work performed on it. This owner then sold the car to a New Jersey antique dealer in 1981. Some time later, the Parisienne, which by then had already been restored to its 1953 configuration, was the subject of a story in *Old Cars Weekly*.

Noted dream car collector Joe Bortz learned of the car's existence thanks to the article and later negotiated with the owner to buy the one-of-a-kind automobile. It still remains part of the Bortz Auto Collection and has been displayed at many auto shows over the years including the 2008 Pebble Beach Concours d'Elegance.

*This 1953 Pontiac Parisienne, with its chauffeur-driven town car design, sits inside the Waldorf-Astoria, the first venue of the new GM Motorama. Those "silver streaks" across the hood were recessed into the panel rather than bolted over it as on standard Pontiacs.*

*The rear bench seat of the Parisienne was covered in beige and black button-tufted nylon. The headliner was pleated. (Photo Courtesy GM Media Archive)*

CHAPTER THREE: THE 1953 GM MOTORAMA

Here is the interior of the Parisienne as it appears today. General Motors altered the show car for the 1954 show circuit, but a private owner later restored it to its 1953 scheme. (Photo Courtesy Bortz Auto Collection)

Yes, that is a French poodle dyed blue sitting in the Parisienne! The car's front seats were upholstered in "high-luster Roulette Pink" cowhide. Tinted poodles were included in the stage show presentations but canceled afterward because of protests from the American Society for the Prevention of Cruelty to Animals.

The 1953 Parisienne received a new color scheme and was updated with 1954 components. This scene is at the Canadian National Exhibition Automobile Building in Toronto.

Dream car collector Joe Bortz bought the 1953 Pontiac Parisienne from a New Jersey collector after it had been restored to its 1953 configuration. (Photo Courtesy Bortz Auto Collection)

### Other Pontiac Showpieces

Another Pontiac showpiece for the 1953 GM Motorama was a modified four-door sedan dubbed Avalon, which, according to a GM press release, featured "Catalina styling." (The Catalina itself was Pontiac's top-of-the-line two-door hardtop model.) It was painted in a non-production color scheme of chartreuse with a black top. The interior was hand-buffed top-grain chartreuse cowhide and black waffle-patterned nylon. Chromed window moldings and ribbed-steel plates on the door panels brightened the luxurious customized interior.

### Oldsmobile Starfire: Excitement Abounds

This low-slung fiberglass-bodied Oldsmobile Starfire convertible was named after Lockheed's F-94A Starfire Interceptor powered by the J-33 turbojet manufactured by GM's Allison Division and resembled, to some degree, a stretched Corvette. Although this particular model never went into production, many of the styling cues, including the oval grille, were used on future Oldsmobile models and its name was applied to a specially trimmed Olds convertible produced the following model year.

The six-passenger Starfire X-P Rocket (its official full name, SO 1621) was painted a stock color, Regal Turquoise. It reportedly had a matching turquoise Orlon convertible top, but it may not have actually been installed. The chief of the Oldsmobile Studio, Art Ross, headed the design of this dream car.

*The 1953 Pontiac Avalon, a modified four-door sedan, was painted in a non-production color combination of chartreuse with a black top. Chartreuse leather and black waffle-patterned nylon upholstery matched the car's exterior colors.*

*An impressive display made for the 1953 GM Motorama was this Pontiac cutaway car. The red four-door sedan was bisected in such a manner "as to retain all of the lines and style which have made the 1953 Pontiac so popular," according to a Pontiac news release. (Photo Courtesy GM Media Archive)*

*The Regal Turquoise 1953 Starfire "X-P Rocket" featured a wide, oval bumper/grille combination, panoramic windshield, and 200-hp Olds V-8.*

## CHAPTER THREE: THE 1953 GM MOTORAMA

Underneath the hood, General Motors installed the 303-ci "Rocket V-8," said to produce up to 200 hp, which was 35 hp more than the 1953 Olds Ninety-Eight engine. The compression ratio was raised from 8.3:1 to 9.0:1 to achieve the increase; it presumably received other modifications that were left unspecified. Oldsmobile introduced a 12-volt electrical system in 1953. The Starfire's upgraded equipment included the new electrical system, power steering, power brakes, and power twin aerials.

Turquoise and white ribbed-leather seating styled to give the appearance of four individual seats added sports car flair to the Starfire. Chrome moldings decorated the front seat. The rear seat wrapped around to smoothly blend into the rear side panels. Interestingly, Ford had not conceived of the second-gen Thunderbird in 1953, and yet the wraparound rear seat was featured on the four-seater 1958 Thunderbird. This may be one instance in which General Motors gave away an idea to a competitor. The Starfire's two-toned interior was another concept pioneered with this experimental car and a styling feature that was used extensively in the following years.

The Starfire's wide, oval bumper/grille combination, side trim, and beltline dip was similar to that of Oldsmobiles for the 1955–1957 model years. However, not every idea shown on the Starfire made its way into production. One of those was the Starfire's door opening shape (wider at the bottom than at the top), made to ease backseat entry and exit for passengers. Another feature not used in production was the sleek, clear bubble over the headlights, but the idea was carried forward to the next GM Motorama on the 1954 Oldsmobile F-88.

An Oldsmobile Engineering logbook originally belonging to the father of Michigan resident, John Perkins, lists three Starfires being built. Evidently they were identical to one another; no photographs have surfaced to indicate otherwise.

A 1953 Starfire may have survived to this day but others certainly did not. According to Perkins, two were scrapped in 1954 or 1955. He and his brother each own a complete set of seats from what must be the two scrapped cars. John recalls that his father, Ralph Perkins, who worked as a chassis engineer for Oldsmobile, purchased the two identical sets of turquoise and white seats in 1954 or 1955 through the Oldsmobile Factory Salvage Department for a total price of around $40. A wood base and casters were added to make the seats easier to move.

In the mid-1970s, John (now retired from Oldsmobile) attempted to locate the only 1953 Starfire known to him at the time for the purpose of restoring it. Also at that time, he simply assumed that the second set of seats had been a spare set. His search finally led him to a man at General Motors who surprised John when he said he was given the task of cutting up *two* Starfires. John remembered having his father's Oldsmobile Engineering logbook and soon discovered the entries regarding the Starfires and other special Oldsmobiles; the entry listed three Starfires. Of course, it's possible that the entry is incorrect and only two cars were actually constructed.

At least one of the Starfires was fully operable. According to Art Ross' son John, his father got to drive one of the Starfires briefly. There was even a plan to let Art's wife drive it for an extended time, but according to John, the car suffered from several mechanical issues and as a result the plan was abandoned.

However, one Starfire appeared in September 1953 at Grosse Point, Michigan, a stop on that year's Glidden Tour. The same car, or another one, was evidently successfully driven in a motorcade on the newly completed Turner Turnpike in Oklahoma City on October 15, 1953, as part of the Oklahoma Oil Progress celebration.

A couple of other interesting anecdotes about the 1953 Starfires include a *Milwaukee Journal* newspaper account of the car shown at the 1954 Milwaukee Auto Show, which opened on February 6. It says that the dream car was reported to have cost $127,000 to build. Interestingly, from January 30 to February 7, a 1953 Starfire was on display at the St. Louis Auto Show; the dates for these shows overlap by a couple of days, which provides additional evidence for the construction of more than one 1953 Starfire.

*From this angle, the Starfire's bucket-style front bench seat, as well as details of the virtually symmetrical dash, is clearly seen. The recessed license plate mount was covered with a clear-plastic shield and the exhaust ports were underneath the back-up lamps. (Photo Courtesy GM Media Archive)*

## Buick Wildcat: Trial Flight in Fiberglass

The 1953 Wildcat (retroactively renamed Wildcat I with the creation of the 1954 Wildcat II) began simply as SO 1714 and was Buick's Motorama dream car for 1953, which was the 50th anniversary of Buick. This dream car was created under the guidance of Buick's chief engineer, Ned Nickles, who some years earlier, oversaw the design of Buick's first hardtop, the 1949 Riviera.

An eight-page booklet titled *Buick Wildcat: Trial Flight in Fiberglas and Steel* was available to those who were interested in learning more details about this experimental car. The three-passenger car was described in this booklet as a "revolutionary sports convertible" and it certainly was that as it was unlike any other Buick since the Y-Job and XP-300.

### Innovation Through and Through

The Wildcat exhibited a plethora of novel styling and mechanical elements, such as the concave vertical grille bars and "buffer bombs" integrated with a massive wraparound front bumper/oval grille frame, twin hood scoops for improved airflow into the carburetor, a trio of fender-top "ventiports," push-button-actuated doors, a slim sweepspear line traversing from bumper to bumper, and cooling vents for the rear tires and brakes. It also had Roto-Static front hubs that consisted of a stationary hub with a scoop on the forward-facing side designed to improve cooling of the brake drum. The 15 x 6.5-inch wheel revolved around the scooped hub.

A power convertible top folded into a well covered by a flush-fitting lid, an idea carried over from the old Y-Job. Styling for the rear of the Wildcat included very modest tail fins with integrated taillights similar in shape to those of Buicks produced for the 1954 model year. This dream car's deck lid was given parallel fin-like projections spanning from the passenger compartment to the rear center bumperettes surrounding the license plate housing. In between was a lengthwise recess; at the forward end of this recess was an air vent with "Roadmaster" spelled out in chrome block lettering. The small vent provided flow-through ventilation when driving with the top up. A set of grooves (each one aligned with each of the chrome-plated letters) ran the length of the deck. An ornament similar to the car's hood ornament sat at the end of the deck lid, which was held shut by a set of twist locks. The Wildcat's dual exhausts with chromed tips exited through openings in the split roll panel.

Fine leather was used throughout the interior including the steering wheel rim and padded dash panel pads. Gauges, radio dial, and clock, all surrounded by a chromed panel, were recessed between these pads. The heater, defroster, and air vent were controlled with chrome-plated levers positioned to the right of the steering column within easy reach of the driver. The inside rearview mirror was mounted on the top of the double-roll dash. Finely grooved chrome-plated inserts adorned the pleated door panels.

The new Roadmaster version of the 322-ci V-8 supplied power and was coupled to an improved Twin-Turbine Dynaflow automatic transmission. The 188-hp engine was finished in light green enamel paint and fitted with chrome-plated valve covers and power

*A 200-hp version of Oldsmobile's 303 Rocket V-8 was said to power the Starfire dream car.*

*The instrument panel of the Starfire was equipped with a 130-mph speedometer, tachometer, coolant temperature gauge, radio, combination oil pressure/ammeter gauge, clock, and radio speaker. (Photo Courtesy GM Media Archive)*

# CHAPTER THREE: THE 1953 GM MOTORAMA

steering pump housing. Buick's 90-degree valve-in-head V-8 was oversquare with a bore and stroke of 4.00 x 3.20 inches. Maximum torque peaked at 300 ft-lbs at 2,400 rpm. Dual turbines in the torque converter were used in the Dynaflow to ensure quick shifting and crisp acceleration. The previous version of the transmission was said to convert the Wildcat's "magnificent power into whip-quick getaway with perfect smoothness at every pace."

Other equipment included on the Wildcat was power steering with a 22:1 ratio, power brakes,

This card produced by General Motors (front and back shown) provided the pertinent specifications of the 1953 Oldsmobile Starfire.

This page from an Oldsmobile Engineering logbook, originally belonging to the father of Michigan resident John Perkins, reveals that three of the 1953 Starfires were built. (Photo Courtesy John Perkins collection)

This front bench seat was originally installed on one of the three Starfire dream cars. Ralph Perkins, a chassis engineer for Oldsmobile, purchased it along with its companion rear seat (as well as a duplicate set) at an Oldsmobile Factory Salvage Department sale. His two sons now own the seats. (Photo Courtesy Photo by John Perkins)

One of the 1953 Starfires (at the rear of the caravan) along with one of the 1953 Buick Wildcats and the second 1953 Cadillac Le Mans were driven in the Oil Progress motorcade in October 1953 as part of a celebration of the oil industry in Oklahoma. Also present was a new Corvette as well as other makes. (Photo Courtesy GM Media Archive)

hydraulically adjusted seat and windows, a "Selectronic" radio with foot-control switch, and twin rear-mounted automatic antennas.

A modified Roadmaster frame shortened to a 114-inch wheelbase was underneath the Wildcat's fiberglass body. Coil springs and direct-action shock absorbers were used front and rear.

Dimensions of the Wildcat were an overall height (top up) of 54.0 inches, overall length of 192.0 inches, overall width of 79.4 inches, front overhang of 35.1 inches, rear overhang of 42.9 inches, ground to seat height of 19.7 inches, and a ground clearance of 6.0 inches.

Buick employed a 12-volt electrical system beginning in 1953, thus it was also included on the Wildcat.

The Wildcat I was the precursor of Buick styling for the next several model years. Its combination bumper/grille and buffer bombs were similar to those that appeared on the 1954–1957 models (though without the concave grille) and the sweepspear not only showed up on mid-1950s Buicks but beyond. Furthermore, its modest fin design was used on production Buicks the following year, as was the double-roll dashboard.

### Black, White, Pale Green, Two-Tone?

When the Wildcat made its debut at the Waldorf-Astoria it was black with a green interior; afterward, a different car painted white was used for the remainder of the GM Motorama tour. Pleated green leather upholstery with white piping was used for the

*Bright green leather upholstery with pleats and white piping covered the bench seat of the 1953 Wildcat. The rolled dash of the show car forecast that of the 1954 Buicks.*

interior of all the 1953 Wildcats. However, the black car was reported to have had pale green leather while the white car shown at the GM Motorama was said to have brilliant green upholstery. Thus, there may have been a difference in the shade of green for each. These cars were equipped with a two-toned steering wheel taken from 1953 production stock; the one difference was that it had a special center medallion.

At least one of the 1953 Wildcats eventually left General Motors, and in the 1980s it became part of the collection of dream cars owned by Joe Bortz. He found the car stored in a Michigan warehouse in fair condition after

*The Wildcat's 188-hp engine was finished in light green enamel paint and fitted with chrome-plated valve covers and power steering pump housing. Buick's 90-degree valve-in-head V-8 was oversquare with a bore and stroke of 4.00 x 3.20 inches. Maximum torque peaked at 300 ft-lbs at 2,400 rpm. (Photo Courtesy Bortz Auto Collection)*

*This photograph, taken at the GM Motorama at the Dinner Key Auditorium, shows the white Wildcat. The car began to be shown at that venue as well as the remaining sites of the 1953 tour. Like the black car shown previously at the Waldorf-Astoria, it had a green interior. Note the louvers along the quarter panel.*

# CHAPTER THREE: THE 1953 GM MOTORAMA

*A black 1953 Buick Wildcat was shown at the Waldorf-Astoria, the opening venue for that year's GM Motorama. An internal report for GM personnel noted the black car was a challenge to keep free of dust, as the fiberglass body seemed to develop a static charge. A black version was never shown again, at least not at the GM Motorama. (Photo Courtesy GM Media Archive)*

many years of neglect. Today, it is maintained in pristine condition after receiving a full restoration, which was completed in 1988. This only known surviving 1953 Wildcat is sometimes shown at special events, such as Eyes on Design, the 2008 Pebble Beach Concours d'Elegance, and recently at the Geneva Concours d'Elegance in Geneva, IL. I believe this is the car shown on the GM Motorama tour beginning with the Miami show.

In addition to the two Wildcats shown on the Motorama circuit, another white example with radiused wheel wells (similar to the 1953 Skylark) and a detachable hardtop was also built. Most likely, this Wildcat was a modified version of a pre-existing car rather than a separate build; four were constructed. This total construction number remained unknown until recently when I was able to examine the Shop Order book at the GM Heritage Center.

The book, which was found several years ago, offers a comprehensive listing of many (but not all) of the special cars and other projects of GM Styling/GM Design. The other SO numbers for the other three Wildcats were 1867, 1868, and 1877. Another number, 2056, is also listed in the Shop Order book as a "1953 Wildcat hardtop" for Harlow Curtice and is the car described above.

It is likely that the SO number was issued for a series of changes, such as the addition of the detachable hardtop, to one of the four cars. Perhaps, Curtice specifically ordered these changes instead of ordering a fifth car. Exactly which car was altered (assuming there was not a fifth car) is unknown.

After appearing at the Waldorf-Astoria, the black Wildcat seemingly vanished. Could it have become the white car with the Skylark-type rear wheel openings? No definitive answer for this question exists. According to the February 8, 1953, edition of the *Miami Herald* the black car, which appeared in New York, was repainted light green. Strangely, the light green car was said to be appearing at the GM Motorama there, but the car shown was actually white.

This was not the only instance of an erroneous report regarding a green Wildcat being shown at an event. A Chicago newspaper incorrectly reported that the Wildcat appearing at the 1953 Chicago Auto Show was pale green when in fact, it was also white. A pale green car, though, must have existed. It appeared at the 1953 Denver Auto Shows (April 6 to 11) if the newspaper account of its color was correct.

What is probably the pale green car was pictured in black and white inside GM's 1953 Quarterly Report to shareholders for the second quarter of the year. In this photo, the exterior and interior seem to be the same shade, suggesting it is the solid-green version.

Other than these references there is one more report concerning this elusive green Wildcat. Jim Jordan, a member of the Cadillac & LaSalle Club, recounted to me the story of a friend's father who saw this car being used as a courtesy car by a U.S. Air Force general at Bergstrom Air Force Base in Austin, Texas, in 1954 or 1955. The occasion was a Sports Car Club of America (SCCA) race. No photographs of the green Wildcat were available from GM Media Archives or through the GM Design Center.

*Sitting in this Wildcat is Jimmie Lewallen (left) and Buck Baker (right), both of whom were successful race car drivers in NASCAR competition. The venue is believed to be near the West Palm Beach Speedway, circa February 1, 1953. (Photo Courtesy Gary Lewallen)*

*Here is a photograph from the files of the Vancouver Public Library. Not likely seen in nearly 60 years, this photo shows one of the 1953 Wildcats in a two-tone scheme (probably white over green) as it was seen in Canada during 1955. This photo was taken at the Kerrisdale Arena in Vancouver, British Columbia, in early April 1955. The event was a small GM Motorama in which five 1954 dream cars were also shown: Corvair, Nomad, Cutlass, El Camino, and Firebird I. (Photo Courtesy Vancouver Public Library, Special Collections, VPL 82756A)*

Also adding a bit of intrigue to the story is the Wildcat painted in a two-tone scheme shown across Canada during 1955. This car was displayed in Vancouver, British Columbia, and Regina, Saskatchewan, and probably other Canadian cities.

Where do all these facts lead? Based on all of the information available, the Wildcat owned by Joe Bortz and probably the green example can be eliminated as the cars from which the open rear wheel wells and detachable hardtop were made. That leads to the black Wildcat shown at the Waldorf as a candidate.

Clouding the matter a bit of what's what with these Wildcats, though, is a report from Ed Lucas, the owner of FEL Enterprises, a restoration shop in Troy, Michigan, and a former owner of the 1954 Olds F-88 originally owned by E. L. Cord. Lucas says that he saw a *black* 1953 Wildcat in the garage of a GM employee in the late-1960s! Perhaps two of the Wildcats were initially painted black, but we may never really know for certain.

The cars have some interesting differences, which can be found by studying photographs of their interiors. The door panels of the black car and those of the white car seem to show minor variations in the door panels. Moreover, the banjo-style steering wheel for the black car was largely wrapped in mostly green leather (but off-white or pale gray at the 9- and 3-o'clock positions) while the white car had a reverse scheme. The photo in the aforementioned GM quarterly report shows a primarily dark-colored steering wheel on what is suspected to be the pale green Wildcat, which seems to add some

*This 1953 Wildcat is the only one known fitted with a detachable hardtop. It was probably modified from an existing Wildcat; it was used by GM president, Harlow Curtice.*

# CHAPTER THREE: THE 1953 GM MOTORAMA

*Fin-like projections on the Wildcat's deck lid bordered the grooved central surface of the Wildcat's deck lid. They were also integrated into the unusual bumper, which surrounded the license plate mount. Note the trunk ornament and twist locks.*

*Only one of the 1953 Wildcats had fully radiused rear wheel openings similar to those of the limited-production 1953 Skylark. This Wildcat was also fully operable and is believed to have been a modification of one of the four Wildcats built, rather than a fifth example.*

credibility to the report that it was the original black car repainted. Meanwhile, the open wheelwell version of the Wildcat did not have the banjo-type steering wheel, but rather a 1954-style steering wheel.

*This illustration of the 1953 Wildcat appeared in GM's second quarter 1953 Quarterly Report to Shareholders. I believe it is the elusive light green 1953 Wildcat. No photos of this car were available from GM Media Archive.*

### Production Predictions

The Wildcat I was evidently considered for production, although newspaper reports indicated otherwise. In the July 1953 issue of *Motor Trend* a note about the car was in the column titled, *Spotlight on Detroit*: "Another one of the sports cars shown by General Motors this year is rumored to be ready for production on a limited scale. Chevrolet's Corvette will be first, but Buick's Wildcat is likely to be the next. A Michigan supplier was contracted to perform body engineering for a slightly modified version. Planned for 1954 introduction, the car will be powered by a 220-bhp Buick V-8. Steel will replace fiberglass in the production version of the new two-seater."

According to the late Homer LaGassey, a GM stylist, upper management was a little "scared" of the Wildcat because it was so different from production Buicks. (Indeed, the *Trial Flight in Fiberglass and Steel* booklet made note of the car's atypical design in the opening paragraph: "Buick bypasses time and tradition to bring your 'dream car' closer . . .") Product identity was very important and the Wildcat was certainly a departure from the cars coming off the assembly line.

The "slightly modified version" as described in the *Motor Trend* report may have been represented by the car used by Harlow Curtice. Another departure from the show cars would likely have been deleting the Roto-Static wheels and replacing them with traditional wheel covers and steel wheels, or perhaps even with the wire wheels that were standard equipment on the Skylark and optional for other Buick models. The detachable hardtop might have been offered as an option had the car been put into production.

*The 2008 Pebble Beach Concours d'Elegance featured many of the surviving GM dream cars. Among them was the 1953 Buick Wildcat owned by Joe Bortz (in passenger seat). (Photo Courtesy Bortz Auto Collection)*

### Cadillac Orleans: Ultra-Luxurious Forerunner to the Eldorado Brougham

Cadillac's 1953 Orleans (SO 1619) was a pillarless four-door hardtop that allowed unobstructed access to the interior. This high-luxury sedan featured reverse-opening rear doors, or "suicide doors." Although the Orleans never became a production model, some of its innovative features appeared in the 1957 Eldorado Brougham. The Orleans was painted Damascus Steel Gray and its roof was covered with champagne-colored RW grain Naugahyde. A GM press release issued in 1956, which included an index of experimental cars from the company, referred to the Orleans as a "Cadillac Custom four-door hardtop Coupe de Ville for C. E. Wilson." The SO number stated in the press release was the one assigned to the Orleans: 1619. It was evidently built for Wilson, but was first used as a show car.

Unlike other models of GM show cars, the Orleans required a little more than a quick glance to see that it differed from those coming off Cadillac's assembly lines. It was built from a leftover 1952 Coupe de Ville body shell and was assigned the engine number 5362 00001. The car was sent to GM Styling for major structural changes that included reshaping the cowl for the installation of a "Panoramic" windshield and the installation of rear doors. Stiffness lost by not including the center (or B-) pillar, was restored to the body by making the rear of the front seat serve as a structural brace. Locks for the rear doors were designed to release only when the Hydra-Matic shift lever was in neutral.

The usual accessories, such as power windows, signal-seeking radio with pre-selector, rear speaker, and power antenna, were included. However, other equipment added was a Cadillac Series 75 heater with registers under the seat, air conditioning with airplane-style swivel controls in the center of the dash, an electric shaver and vanity case in a compartment in the back of the front seat, and finally, a standard household electrical outlet. The latter could supply electrical power to radios and other appliances through a converter, which changed the generator's direct current into alternating current.

Other luxurious appointments of the Orleans included seat cushions and backrests of gray leather with champagne-colored nylon inserts. The car's headliner was champagne-colored, perforated Naugahyde adorned with chrome-plated roof bows and scalloped moldings. The roof-rail moldings were painted gunmetal gray. Gray

*The Damascus Steel Gray 1953 Cadillac Orleans made its debut at the Waldorf-Astoria, the first venue of that year's GM Motorama. Built from a leftover 1952 Coupe de Ville body shell, the Orleans featured a wraparound windshield and a four-door hardtop body without center pillars. Surprisingly few photographs of this car exist. (Photo Courtesy GM Media Archive)*

leather covered the upper door panels while the lower portion was gunmetal gray. Carpeting was gray and champagne Craftex fiber with a gray leather binding.

A stock 331 V-8 evidently powered the Orleans. A copy of the original build sheet in the files of GM's Heritage Center does not specify any changes to the car's engine.

The Orleans had great appeal to those who bought Cadillacs and preferred hardtops, but wanted four doors for convenience. Reportedly, Harley Earl got the idea for this car during a visit to Italy where he saw a Lancia sedan built as a four-door pillarless hardtop. This concept had actually been used on some European cars in the mid-1930s, but those cars were much smaller than the Orleans.

Cadillac placed a four-door hardtop in production for 1956 called the Sedan de Ville; it had a short B-pillar but without the suicide doors. The Eldorado Brougham with suicide doors and no B-pillar went into limited production the following year.

Chevrolet, Pontiac, and Cadillac brought out four-door hardtop models for 1956 while Buick and Oldsmobile released theirs one-year earlier. All of them, however, employed a short B-pillar upon which to suspend the rear doors, which opened conventionally. Not until the Eldorado Brougham went into production for 1957 did General Motors use the pillarless four-door hardtop design seen in the Orleans.

*The interior of the four-door pillarless hardtop Orleans was equipped with cushions and backrests of gray leather with champagne-colored nylon inserts. The car's headliner was champagne-colored, perforated Naugahyde adorned with chrome-plated roof bows and inner roof-rail moldings. (Photos Courtesy GM Media Archive)*

The fate of the 1953 Orleans is unknown, although General Motors did not scrap it. Records at the GM Heritage Center show the car's ownership was transferred to Charles Wilson on March 31, 1953. Many years ago, Matt Larson, a Cadillac & LaSalle Club member, spoke with a former employee of the GM Styling facilities who had the chance to purchase the car in Louisville, Kentucky, in 1961 or 1962. He also heard through a credible source that the car was in the San Diego area in the late 1970s.

Today, that rumor appears to be a case of mistaken identity. In fact, the 1949 Cadillac Coupe de Ville prototype was in San Diego at that time and is very likely the cause of the rumor regarding the Orleans. Assuming that to be true, what became of the Orleans after the early 1960s is a mystery.

### Cadillac Le Mans: A Sporty Luxury Car

Cadillac took a bold departure with its three-passenger sports car at the 1953 GM Motorama show. Adorned in Metallic Blue (silver-blue), this Cadillac was dubbed "Le Mans" (SO 1709). Its namesake was the 24-hour race held near Paris, France, in which the two Cadillac entries finished 10th and 11th in 1950. Emphasizing the connection between the dream car and the Le Mans race was a large painting placed behind the show car depicting a scene from the *Vingt-Quatre Heures du Mans* road race.

Although the dream car represented a major departure from the typical Cadillac of the day, styling of the Le Mans was generally predictive of the look of the upcoming 1954 Cadillacs. This included the dream car's frontal design and wraparound windshield, which was a standard feature of the limited-production 1953 Eldorado and became standard on all Cadillac models for 1954. The fiberglass body of the Le Mans sat on a Cadillac frame with a wheelbase shortened to 115 inches. The overall length measured 198.1 inches, overall width spanned 80.6 inches, and overall height was said to be just 51 inches with the top raised; this was 7.9 inches lower than a standard Cadillac convertible.

According to press releases from General Motors, the 331-ci V-8 installed in the dream car produced 40 more hp than in stock form, cranking out 250 hp at 4,500 rpm. It is unlikely that any of the original three Le Mans prototype cars were fully operable cars in the beginning. The engine upgrades specified in these press releases comprised the installation of dual 4-barrel carburetors, 9.0:1 compression ratio, redesigned exhaust manifolds, high-lift valves, and special mufflers. The Hydra-Matic was also said to have been "adapted to the higher engine performance."

## Luxury with Pizzazz

As the Le Mans proved, it was not a pure sports car; rather it was a luxury car with sports car features. Indeed, one of GM's press releases about the car stated, ". . . the Le Mans represents an ideal of motor car enthusiasts—combining elegance with power."

General Motors let the motoring press put the Le Mans through its paces and confirmed the attributes of the car. Most likely the second Le Mans built was the one test driven at the GM Proving Grounds by Detroit area newsmen, according to the October 1953 issue of *Motor Trend* ("Spotlight on Detroit," page 11). According to this article, the road testers reported, "Floorboarding the engine with the reworked Hydra-Matic unit immediately sends the tach past 4,000, the car gets 0-to-60 in slightly under 9 seconds, and drops into fourth at about 87 mph. This performance is all the more surprising since the car weighs only 400 pounds less than a standard Cadillac convertible."

The test car was said to be "definitely too heavy and spongy for competition" and that the experimental car would not go into production although the 1954 Eldorado "looked much like the Le Mans but with a rear seat."

This brief report noted that three examples had been built up to that point at a cost of $1 million and that each was a little different from the other, even though the specifics were not provided. A newspaper writer for a Detroit newspaper reported driving the Le Mans past 100 mph on the Milford, Michigan, test track and that its "rated top speed is 135 mph."

## An Idea Takes Root

Inspiration for the Le Mans may have originated with a one-off, 1952 Cadillac Custom Convertible that Harley Earl had built for friend and co-worker Harold R. Boyer. Boyer was the plant manager of Cadillac Motor Car Division's Cleveland tank plant. His car, very similar in concept to the Le Mans, was born during a conversation with Earl.

Boyer mentioned that his dream car would be part Cadillac and part sports car (the same combination expressed in the aforementioned press release about the Le Mans). Evidently, Harley Earl took the idea of such a car seriously; he began designing one with Boyer's input. A Coupe de Ville (style 6237DX) was sent to GM

*The bench seat of the Le Mans, designed for up to three passengers, had a "V" Cadillac crest embossed on the center of the backrest. Note the open convertible top's well lid; it opened similarly to that of the Eldorado. (Photo Courtesy GM Media Archive)*

*These photographs (taken by an unknown visitor to a Canadian dealership and processed on July 27, 1953) show a Le Mans on display. The venue is suspected to be the Beattie Cadillac-Chevrolet-Oldsmobile, Ltd. in Toronto. Also suspected is that the car shown is the third Le Mans since it is known to have been present at the Canadian National Exhibition the following August/September.*

CHAPTER THREE: THE 1953 GM MOTORAMA

*This silver-blue 1953 Cadillac Le Mans, one of four built, represented a sporty luxury car and forecast the frontal design of the 1954 model Cadillacs. Its namesake was the 24-hour race held near Paris, France, in which the two Cadillac entries finished 10th and 11th in 1950. Emphasizing the connection between the dream car and the Le Mans race was a large painting placed behind the show car depicting a scene from the Vingt-Quatre Heures du Mans road race.*

Styling for conversion into a three-passenger Cadillac convertible. Its overall length was reduced 10 inches and the overall height was dropped 6 inches to achieve the sports car look. Like many of the dream cars, this one's power top retracted into a well where a flush-fitting lid covered it. Manifold and oil temperature gauges as well as a tachometer and an aircraft-type clock were added to the custom-built car's instrument panel.

A newspaper article about the custom convertible, which appeared in the *Cleveland Plain Dealer*, stated the car was equipped with a 230-hp engine with dual carburetors and that it had a top speed of 130 mph. According to the story, General Motors was "so impressed by the vehicle" that it was being considered for production. The March 1953 issue of *Motor Trend* featured a story on the 1953 GM Motorama cars. It reported that dealers were surveyed on the sales potential of the Le Mans; the sampling revealed a market existed for about 5,000 units.

Ultimately, only four were built. The first three were, of course, show cars and were followed by one more in late 1953 (almost complete in October). It was built for the president of Fisher Body, James E. Goodman. The Le Mans grabbed the attention of many during the GM Motorama tour, especially actor John Wayne. According to author Tim Howley in a story he wrote for the January/February 1999 issue of *Special Interest Autos*, designer Dave Holls (who designed the car's instrument panel) told him that when Harley Earl returned to Styling after the Waldorf-Astoria show he was telling everyone about the positive reaction to the car. According to Holls, Wayne told Earl that he wanted one. Earl explained that the car was just a show car and was made of fiberglass to which Wayne replied, "I don't care if it's made of pudding. I want one." (Incidentally, John Wayne never did get a Le Mans built for him; he did receive a 1953 Corvette, a car that still exists.)

Despite the excitement generated by the Le Mans, Harley Earl observed that those who would actually "back up their approval with a check" showed a stronger preference for the Orleans. Furthermore, the Corvette was controversial enough; only Harley Earl could have pushed it through. That car, along with the Oldsmobile Fiesta, Buick Skylark, and Cadillac Eldorado (all limited-production cars) probably seemed like enough specialty models for the time.

*This early photograph of the 1953 Cadillac Le Mans (taken in GM's Argonaut Building) reveals a clear view of the silver-blue dream car's rear styling with its trunk moldings and exhaust outlets through the bumperettes.*

*Inspiration for the 1953 Le Mans dream car may have originated with this one-off 1952 Cadillac custom convertible that Harley Earl had built for friend and co-worker Harold R. Boyer.*

### Le Mans Number One

What happened to the Le Mans dream cars? According to documentation at the GM Heritage Center, the original car, serial number 5300 00002 (the GM Motorama show car), was shipped to Clarence Dixon Cadillac in Hollywood, California, on July 7, 1954. The car was at the dealership for only a few months when shoe store mogul Harry Karl bought it.

Karl hired famed customizer George Barris to perform a makeover on the car using some motifs popular with custom-car builders at that time. Once it was completed, Karl gave it to his ex-wife and wife-to-be again, actress Marie McDonald, sometime in late 1954 or early 1955.

Barris customized the entire car, including the engine compartment. The 331 V-8 was originally painted the silver-blue color of the Le Mans, but Barris repainted it metallic green and dressed it up with chrome-plated components. Reportedly, the engine produced 300 hp, 50 more than the figure quoted by General Motors and 30 more than the official rating of a stock 1955 Eldorado engine. What modifications, if any, were made to obtain the extra 50 hp, or even if the engine was tested on a dynamometer, is not known.

The engine compartment was just the beginning.

*Special instrumentation was added to Boyer's 1952 Cadillac custom convertible. This feature was similar to that which appeared on the 1953 Cadillac Le Mans dream car.*

Barris' unique alterations included custom-formed, blue-white chrome-plated steel panels added to the lower fenders behind the front wheels and a Continental kit integrated into the deck lid. In addition, a 24-karat gold molding made with 1/2-inch steel bar was made to cover the seam where the steel panels joined the front fenders. The upper quarter panels were reshaped with polished stainless steel fins.

Furthermore, a multi-piece top of plexiglass with a chrome-plated steel frame was constructed that could be lifted off entirely or the forward portion only could be removed and the rear section (the rear window with a chrome tiara) left in place. Thirty coats of "platinum dust" sprayed over a polychromatic base sealer were applied to the body. The 30-spoke wheel covers were gold-plated; the spokes themselves were chrome-plated.

The interior was completely redone and fitted with many luxury appointments. These included a television, tape recorder, radio-telephone, and cocktail bar in the rear window sill, which had a red leather cover to keep it out of sight. An electrical current inverter connected the 12-volt electrical system for proper voltage to operate the television and other devices. The seats were either reupholstered in red leather or dyed red, and a number of gadgets were installed. Interestingly, some of the custom features of the restyled Le Mans were very similar to another Barris-built car, the 1954 *Golden Sahara*.

As a customized car, the Le Mans received national publicity again. It was pictured on the cover of the December 1955 issue of *Motor Trend* as well as the cover of the June 1956 issue of *Rod & Custom*. It was shown at the Sixth International Motor Revue (formerly known as the Petersen Motorama) and the Pacific International Auto Show in Oakland, California, in 1955.

Harry Karl's second marriage to Marie lasted only half as long as the first; the two divorced again in 1958. Perhaps Marie and the Le Mans also parted company at about that time.

According to a well-known classic car dealer from Ohio, Leo Gephart, another car dealer in Dayton, Ohio, purchased the customized Le Mans from someone in California. While being driven to Ohio by its new owner, the hood of the Le Mans was damaged when large rolls of carpet fell from a truck. It was immediately sold to another dealer who had the hood repaired and primed. It was then sold to a car dealer in Fairborn, Ohio, who later closed his business.

According to Gephart, this dealer, who was "quite wealthy and did not need to work," put his personal cars, including the Le Mans, into storage. This information fits well with the stories told to me by Cadillac & LaSalle Club member Bernie De Winter, IV, who saw the car on the streets of nearby Dayton from time-to-time during 1964 and 1965. This story was also confirmed by Ohio resident Fred Miller, who eventually acted as an agent for the sale of the car.

Beginning in 1966, the car was in storage, partially dismantled, after having been driven a total of 7,945 miles. Fred Miller, who was interviewed by phone in 2006, acted as an agent for the owner of the Le Mans. Miller still recalled many details about the car. He confirmed that a classic car dealer bought the Le Mans in California and took it to Ohio; it was later purchased by a son of a wealthy family.

Another Ohio resident and Cadillac & LaSalle Club member, Wayne Turner, saw the ad placed in *Hemmings Motor News* in late 1984 and responded to it, as did several others. Turner made an appointment with Miller to view the car in Centerville, Ohio, but it had already been sold (still partially dismantled) to California resident John Crowell on December 1.

Sadly, a fire destroyed Crowell's Le Mans (along with five other exotic and historic cars he owned) during the early morning hours of May 14, 1985, when green hay stacked against the building in which the cars were stored spontaneously ignited. Only the engine, wheel covers, and other miscellaneous parts, which had been removed and stored elsewhere prior to the fire, still exist.

A settlement was reached with Crowell's insurance company and they took possession of the remains.

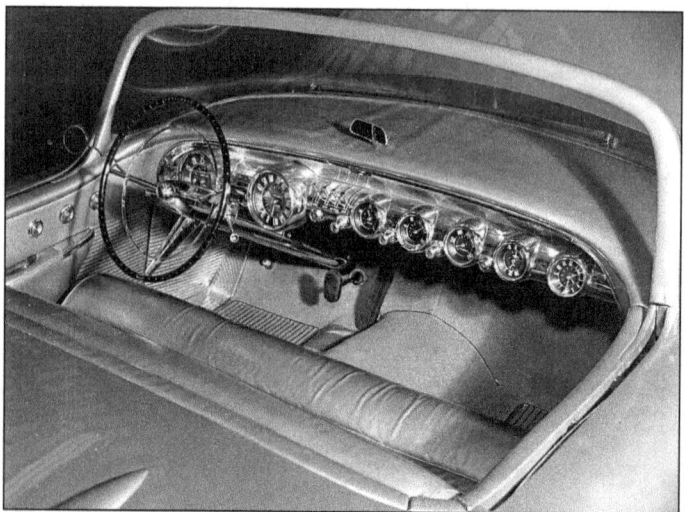

*Round dials and gauges were spread across the instrument panel of the 1953 Cadillac Le Mans. They included a 130-mph speedometer, Selectronic radio, tachometer, and clock. Levers were used to control the heater, defroster, and fresh air vents.*

Surprisingly, Crowell still had the bill of sale listing its serial number, 5300 00002, proving it was the first Le Mans. (Both Miller and Crowell had believed the serial number meant the car was the second of the four Le Mans until their respective telephone interviews for this project.)

Bill Pozzi, who was a California resident at the time, bought the surviving parts of the Le Mans in 1991. According to him, the metallic green engine block is stamped "5300 00002X." At last report he still owned them.

### Le Mans Number Two

The second Le Mans (SO 1865), serial number 5300 00003, also has an interesting history. Luckily, the build sheet for this car still exists and is in the files at the GM Heritage Center. On it is the note, "Cars in Company use, for use of Harley J. Earl." The car's ownership was transferred to Earl on August 21, 1953. Old interoffice correspondence at the Heritage Center makes reference to a Le Mans, titled to Earl, sitting in a warehouse. This correspondence authorized transfer of the car back to the company and gave its net asset value as $1. The serial number was not noted on the correspondence, but unless Earl owned two of the cars (a somewhat improbable scenario), Le Mans Number Two was the subject of the memorandum.

Other information in this file revealed that Earl's car was repainted black sometime in 1953. Although not mentioned in this memo, but rather in a GM press release, was the fact the upholstery was changed from silver-blue to yellow. Le Mans Number Two was already repainted black by the time it appeared in Cleveland, Ohio, for that year's Glidden Tour in September, as shown in photographs taken at the event. In October, the car was sent to Oklahoma at the request of the state's governor, Johnston Murray, to participate in the Oil Progress Exposition held mid-month. (The above-mentioned press release was about this event.)

*Le Mans Number Two was transported to Greenlease-Moore Cadillac-Chevrolet in Oklahoma City for display in their showroom in early November 1953. Greenlease-Moore was one of the largest distributors of Cadillacs at that time. Vice president and general manager of the dealership, Robert T. Moore, is shown standing with the Le Mans; the Oklahoma state capitol building is in the background. The car had been repainted just a few months earlier and titled to Harley Earl. (Photo Courtesy GM Media Archive)*

*This newspaper advertisement promoted the appearance of a Le Mans (show car Number Two) at Greenlease-Moore Cadillac-Chevrolet in Oklahoma City, Oklahoma, in early November 1953.*

CHAPTER THREE: THE 1953 GM MOTORAMA

The original 1953 Le Mans (serial number 5300 00002) was transferred to Clarence Dixon Cadillac in Hollywood, California, during July 1954. Some months later, shoe store magnate Harry Karl bought it and had famed customizer George Barris modify it. The restyled Le Mans was on the show circuit for a while during 1955. (Photo Courtesy Ina Mae Overman collection)

Le Mans Number Two, along with another pair of 1953 GM dream cars (the Starfire and Wildcat I) as well as a new Corvette were on display at the Oklahoma City Municipal Auditorium for two days before being driven in the Oil Progress Motorcade along the newly completed Turner Turnpike and into downtown Oklahoma City. The Le Mans and the other cars went on to make appearances in Chandler, Stroud, Bristow, and Sapulpa before proceeding to Tulsa where it was driven in a Saturday-afternoon football parade. It was then on display for the National Oil Progress Week show at the Pavilion of Tulsa Fairgrounds that same Saturday and Sunday.

From there, Le Mans Number Two returned to Oklahoma City for display in the showroom of Greenlease-Moore Cadillac-Chevrolet during the first week of November. The car's history after that showing remained totally unknown until mid-2011 when I found a posting left on the message board of the website Jalopy Journal by a man claiming to be a retired GM employee. His only posting to the site was regarding questions and remarks made about the 1953 Le Mans. He said that he drove a black Le Mans as a company car during 1956. My attempts to communicate with him to learn more failed.

Then in early 2013, Ed Lucas (a former owner of the 1954 Olds F-88 now in the Gateway Automobile Museum) told me that this Le Mans was sent to Warhoops Used Auto & Truck Salvage where it was supposed to be destroyed. Shortly thereafter, as the story goes, Warhoops owner,

*Several components of the original Le Mans still survive and those pictured here are now in the collection of Cadillac & LaSalle Club member Jim Jordan. These were not on the car when it was sold to John Crowell of Pleasanton, California, in late 1984. The engine from this car also still exists. Shown here are: convertible top switch knob (top left), warning lamp lens (top right), ignition switch components (bottom left), contol lever for either the heater, defroster, or circulation vents (bottom right). (Photo Courtesy Jim Jordan collection)*

Harry Warholak, Sr., was seen driving the car on Mound Road by a GM official who promptly reported the occurrence. Representatives were soon dispatched to Warhoops to oversee the destruction of Le Mans Number Two.

## Le Mans Number Three

Records in the archives of the GM Heritage Center about the Le Mans dream cars offer little information on the third Le Mans (SO 1866). There is a document showing it to have been a "Car in Company use" and that it was shipped by flatbed truck to Pemberton Cadillac Company in Toledo, Ohio, for display in the dealership's showroom May 14–16, 1953. Most likely, it was the same one that went on to Cleveland, Ohio, to be shown at Central Cadillac Company from May 19 to 22.

This Le Mans was shown in Canada on more than one occasion including the 1954 CNE in Toronto. By then it had been repainted Apollo Yellow and its interior color changed to black. This makeover may have been done at about the same time Le Mans Number Two was altered to its black and yellow color combination.

Le Mans Number Three was sold to Floyd Akers, owner of a Cadillac distributorship. The only documentation that seems to exist in GM's records about the sale is simply that one was sold; the document does not provide the car's serial number. Fortunately, a photocopy of the certificate of title issued by Washington, D.C., to Akers in 1955 does exist. The serial number printed on that document (5300 00004) confirms the car's identity as the third Le Mans built.

Buddy Abell (now deceased), a mechanic who worked at Capitol Cadillac when the Le Mans was delivered there in June 1955, told me that the dealership's mechanics had to make the car roadworthy. According to Abell, no wiring harness was present, thus it was delivered in non-running condition. To get the Le Mans running, a modified 1955 wiring harness was installed, functional instruments were made for it, and the suspension had to be modified with taller springs and spindles. The laws of Washington, D.C., specified a minimum road clearance, which the Le Mans, as built, did not meet.

*Sometime after being shown at the 1953 Canadian National Exhibition in Toronto, Le Mans Number Three was repainted Apollo Yellow (according to the sign) and its interior color changed to black. It appeared in this color scheme at the 1954 GM Wonderama at the CNE along with the red Corvette with the prototype hardtop, Buick Wildcat II, etc. (Photo Courtesy CNE Archives, Alexandra Studio, MG5-5891-1)*

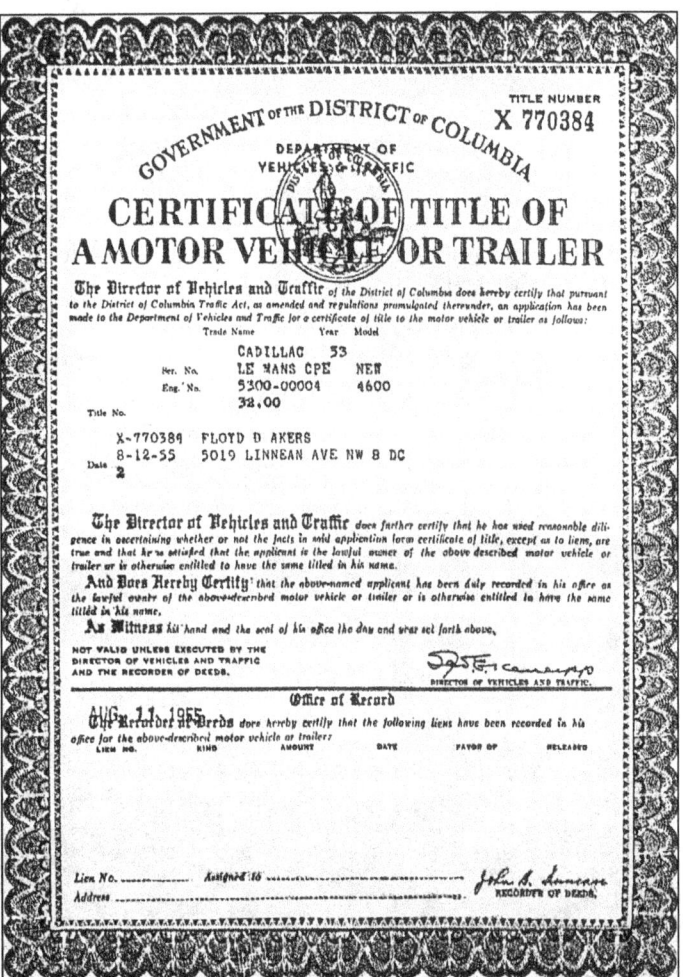

*This is a photocopy of the original title issued by Washington, D.C., to Floyd Akers for Le Mans Number Three sold to him by General Motors in 1955. The serial number typed on it proves the car to be the third Le Mans of the four built.*

## CHAPTER THREE: THE 1953 GM MOTORAMA

*Le Mans Number Three is now owned by collector Scott Milestone. He displayed the car in the showroom of Capitol Cadillac in Greenbelt, Maryland, during the meeting of the Potomac Region of the Cadillac & LaSalle Club in October 2008.*

Unspecified work was performed by Derham in Rosemont, Pennsylvania. (Derham's records, which are stored at the Gilmore Museum in Hickory Corners, Michigan, are almost non-existent from the 1950s.) The Le Mans script mounted on the deck lid was most likely made by this company; no period photo of the rear of a Le Mans shows such a script. In addition, this script differs somewhat from that mounted on the grille of all four cars.

One omission in the design of the car was addressed. A weather seal was made to stop rainwater from leaking into the interior through the base of its convertible top; however, it was not very effective.

During the early 1960s, after the car had been driven about 6,100 miles, it was placed in storage at Floyd Akers' other dealership, Suburban Cadillac. In 1977, the car was inadvertently sold with the dealership, which was subsequently renamed Coleman Cadillac. It was a mistake; no one thought to exclude the car from Suburban's inventory when the contract was written. Eventually, the car was repainted; the color was changed from Apollo Yellow (as delivered to Akers) to a shade of white (probably a contemporary Cadillac color). In the 1980s, the car was on display in the showroom of Coleman Cadillac in Bethesda, Maryland.

Around 1989, this Le Mans was purchased by Maryland resident Scott Milestone. He has shown the car at the AACA Museum and the 2013 Amelia Island Concours d'Elegance.

### Le Mans Number Four

The fully functional Le Mans Number Four (SO 2001/SO 90245/SO 90530) was built specifically for J. E. "Bud" Goodman, the CEO of Fisher Body. It was assembled very late in the model year judging by its engine number (5300 91300); a photo of the car dated October 9 shows it fully assembled. It was, however, unfinished. At a glance, this one appeared to be an exact copy of the original three show cars, but it was not.

The cornering lamp and corrugations (or "scuff plates") on the rocker panels included on the other three Le Mans were deleted from Le Mans Number Four. Goodman's Le Mans also was not equipped with the rain sensor supposedly present on the other three examples and is by all appearances the only one of the four to have a detachable hardtop. Furthermore, this car and Number Two are the only ones known to have been made operable by General Motors (even though the second car was made operable for Harley Earl, likely months after being built). Le Mans Number Four, therefore, is almost certainly the car used in the Rose Bowl Parade on January 1, 1954, since

*Some of the styling differences between Le Mans Number Three and Le Mans Number Four are evident in this photo taken inside the showroom of Capitol Cadillac in October 2008. This may have been the first time these two cars sat together.*

*Le Mans Number Four, built for Fisher Body president Jack Goodman, was nearing completion when this photo was taken in October 1953.*

*Le Mans Number Four is evidently the only one of the four to have a detachable hardtop. This car was later restyled and updated with a 1959 engine and transmission.*

it was silver-blue and Harley Earl's black car was the only other one known to be functional at that time.

According to the previously mentioned *Special Interest Autos* story written by Tim Howley, the car was later repainted Metallic Sea Mist Green. This may have taken place in 1957 as something was done to the car to result in the issuance of SO 90245 at that time. Next, it was heavily restyled and updated to 1959 specs (resulting in the new SO 90530) for Goodman shortly before Harley Earl left General Motors.

Changes in the styling included quad headlamps, flatter hood, lowered cowl, different windshield, a pair of simulated air scoops on the quarters, a major revision to the design of the tail fins and tail lamps, plus removal of the simulated trunk straps. The car was repainted silver-gray and reupholstered in leather of the same color.

A 1959 Eldorado 390 V-8 and Hydra-Matic as well as a low-profile Harrison radiator replaced the original units. What became of the accessory hardtop is not known, but it was either lost or discarded.

In 1963, Goodman gave the car to his son, who had become the owner of Clarence Dixon Cadillac in Hollywood, California. The car sat in the showroom and years later it was loaned to the Petersen Automotive Museum. Le Mans Number Four also made it to the big screen when it appeared briefly in the 1978 movie *The Buddy Holly Story*. Shortly after being shown at the 1999 North American International Auto Show in Detroit, the Cadillac Historical Collection purchased the car from Goodman. It became part of the collection of the GM Heritage Center when the center was organized in 2004. The car is still shown at various events.

*Le Mans Number Four is now a part of the GM Heritage Collection and is still shown at various events across the country.*

MOTORAMA 69

# Other Special Displays of the 1953 GM Motorama

During the 1953 model year, General Motors released for sale three semi-custom models: Oldsmobile Fiesta, Buick Skylark, and Cadillac Eldorado. All were essentially hand-built cars with price tags virtually guaranteeing limited production as well as unrestricted publicity for each division. That is what such cars did: They generated publicity that translated into showroom traffic. Then, most people bought a lower-priced mass-produced car with the higher profit margin that looked similar to the showboat that attracted them in the first place. Each was introduced to the public at that year's GM Motorama.

Pontiac had a powerful display: the four-door sedan cutaway car. It was bisected so it would "retain all of the lines and style that have made the 1953 Pontiac so popular," according to a Pontiac news release. The car's entire rear deck and Panoramic rear window, the full one-piece windshield, and the complete front end were retained in full. The engine and transmission were completely exposed. According to the official press release, all exposed parts and edges were finished in "brilliant duco [lacquer] and chrome so as to make the car a show model as well as an engineering display."

A rather dramatic demonstration of the newly optional (for Olds upper series, Buick, and Cadillac) Frigidaire air conditioning system was offered via an Oldsmobile cut in half lengthwise with a sheet of plexiglass over the open side. Visitors could put their hands through an aperture in the plexiglass to the feel the cold air inside.

*A two-toned blue Oldsmobile Fiesta, like this one, was on exhibit at the 1953 GM Motorama. This particular car is a part of the collection housed at the GM Heritage Center.*

*A 1953 Buick Skylark was made available for close-up inspection during that year's GM Motorama. The limited-production car featured special bodywork resulting in a hefty price tag of $5,000. Only 1,690 were built. (Photo Courtesy GM Media Archive)*

*This Azure Blue 1953 Eldorado is nearly identical to one shown on the 1953 GM Motorama circuit. Only 532 Eldorados were built for this model year.*

Additional displays included several 1953 Oldsmobiles in exclusive show colors, a cutaway "Power-Ride" chassis finished in chrome plating, and the division's one-millionth Golden Rocket engine (produced since its introduction in 1949) mounted on a pedestal.

Many production cars were shown in non-standard schemes throughout the years of the GM Motorama. The cars in special show colors in Miami in 1953 were:

- Fiesta in Surf Blue with darker teal blue deck and upper rear fenders
- Ninety-Eight convertible finished in copper metallic with solid ivory leather upholstery
- Holiday Ninety-Eight with a Philippine Green top and Hawaiian Pearl body
- Ninety-Eight four-door sedan with a Platinum Gray top and Shadow Gray body
- Holiday Eighty-Eight coupe with a Raven Black top and Inca Gold body
- Super Eighty-Eight four-door sedan painted Cosmic Blue over Planet Blue
- Deluxe Eighty-Eight in Shell Gray and Gulf Blue

The cars in special show colors shown at the Kansas City venue were:

- Fiesta in Raven Black and Ivory with a red leather interior
- Holiday Ninety-Eight with a Philippine Green top and Hawaiian Pearl body
- Holiday Eighty-Eight coupe with a Raven Black top and Inca Gold body
- Super Eighty-Eight four-door sedan painted Cosmic Blue over Planet Blue

Most or all of these cars were perhaps shown at other venues of that year's GM Motorama as well. It is likely several Buicks were shown in special schemes this year, but none were mentioned in the news accounts of the GM Motorama I found.

At least three specially painted and trimmed Cadillacs were displayed during the 1953 Motorama tour. One of them was shown at the Waldorf-Astoria if not elsewhere on the tour. It was a Coupe de Ville painted orange and equipped with a white Naugahyde-covered top. Another Coupe de Ville of an unknown color combination also received a Naugahyde-covered top. (A vinyl top was not a factory option for Cadillacs until the 1963 model year, but it was standard equipment for the 1956–1960 Eldorado Sevilles and the 1960 Fleetwood.) A Fleetwood Sixty Special wearing an unspecified shade of dark blue and a matching Naugahyde top was also exhibited during the 1953 tour.

## Chapter Four
# The GM Motorama of 1954

The 1954 GM Motorama toured five cities this year; Dallas and Kansas City were dropped from the schedule due to less-than-expected attendance and Chicago was added. This exhibition offered visitors a chance to see the largest array of dream cars General Motors ever assembled for the touring show. Among them was a car akin to an earth-bound jet plane powered by a turbine engine: the GM Firebird I. A set of Corvette-based concepts presented some interesting possibilities for the future, although at the time no one realized Chevrolet's fiberglass sports car was about to become dangerously close to being dropped from production.

The theme for this year's stage presentation was "Going Places" and was again choreographed by Richard and Edith Barstow of the Barnum & Bailey Circus. During the show, a car from each of GM's passenger car divisions appeared on stage.

### Chevrolet Corvette: In the Spotlight

Two Corvette-based concepts appeared at the Waldorf-Astoria in January 1954: the Nomad station wagon (SO 1954) and a Corvair fastback (EX number uncertain, SO 2071) painted a striking, deep red. The following month three vehicles were on exhibit at the Dinner Key Auditorium in Miami: the Nomad; a modified Corvette (SO 2000) with unique upholstery, roll-up windows, and a prototype detachable hardtop; and a different Corvair (EX number uncertain) painted a custom-blended color labeled Seafoam Green.

*The Corvette and Corvette-based show cars were posed together on Pan American Drive in front of the Dinner Key Auditorium in Miami prior to the opening of the GM Motorama in February 1954. The "hardtop" car joined the GM Motorama at this time. Note that the Corvair is painted Seafoam Green. A deep red Corvair was exhibited at the preceding Motorama in New York City.*

*This advertisement promoting the appearance of the Corvette-based show cars at the GM Motorama at the Pan Pacific Auditorium appeared in the March 7, 1954, copy of the* Los Angeles Examiner.

72   MOTORAMA

# CHAPTER FOUR: THE GM MOTORAMA OF 1954

Another Corvair (EX number uncertain) painted Seafoam Green was also built, but whether it appeared at any of the GM Motorama venues is not known. (The EX numbers for three Corvairs may have been EX-200-53, EX-210-53, and EX-215-53, though this has not been verified.)

The Corvette-based Nomad did not go into production, nor was it considered for production for more than a brief time. Its roofline, though, was adapted to the Bel Air, resulting in a sporty, two-door station wagon for 1955 through 1957. The positive reactions of visitors who attended the Waldorf-Astoria show to the 1954 dream car version resulted in the decision to proceed with production of the Bel Air–based car.

The Corvair may have gone into production had Corvette sales been high enough to justify it. As many as five Corvairs may have been constructed, with each being a little different from the other. An unverified source claims one was painted Pennant Blue and another Harvest Gold (but were not shown publicly) and that two others were painted Seafoam Green, a custom-mixed color. The latter certainly seems plausible, especially the name for the color. There appear to be no records on these other cars at GM Media Archive.

The features of the Corvette with the prototype hardtop were adopted almost exactly as they appeared on the show car versions for the restyled 1956 model. As with the Corvair, more than two of the hardtop cars were built, although how many is currently unclear.

## The Nomad: A Two-Door Wagon

For 1955, Chevrolet had a virtually all-new lineup of cars planned, but some designers were pushing for two more models to be added: the Executive, a three-window coupe with inward-facing jump seats in back, and a sport wagon. Only the sport wagon concept survived and ultimately became the Nomad, a two-door wagon based on the Bel Air. The first Nomad, however, was based upon the Corvette.

Carl Renner was a cartoon animator at Walt Disney Studios, but his true passion was cars. After establishing himself at General Motors, he was assigned to the "Project Opel" team, which was tasked with developing the Corvette. Ultimately, he was responsible for styling possibly the most famous dream car of the 1950s, the Corvette-based Nomad.

### Prototype Design

The frame from the EX-52 (aka, car 852) prototype Corvette, according to a GM work order, was to be

*The exact purpose of this illustration is not known, but it appears to be something produced as a brochure cover (probably by Campbell-Ewald, GM's ad agency) for a 1955 Corvette-based Nomad had it gone into production as such. This illustration seemingly suggests the Corvette-based Nomad may have been given more serious consideration for production than previously thought. (Photo Courtesy GM Media Archive)*

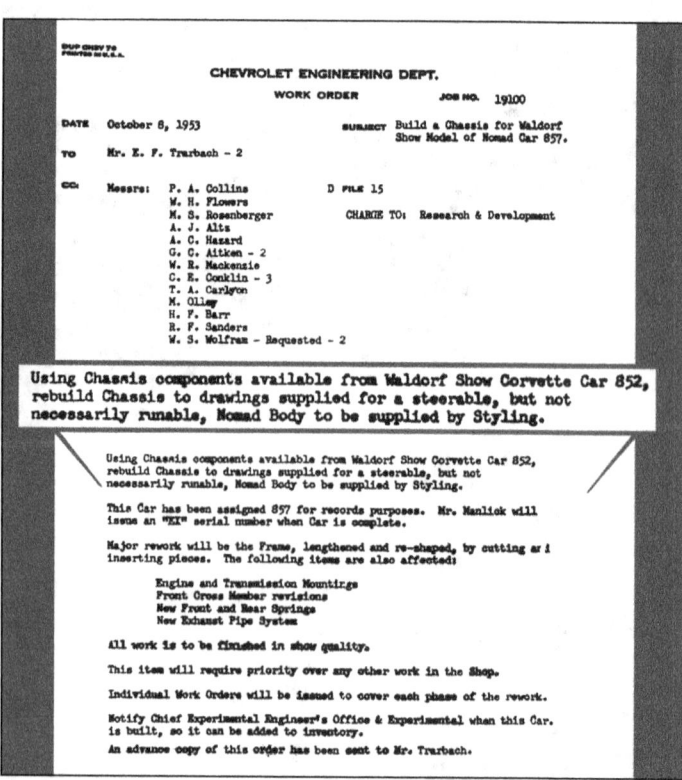

*This photocopy of a Chevrolet Engineering Department memo instructed that the chassis from the original Corvette prototype be modified as needed for use on the 1954 Nomad.*

*Compared to the Corvette, the Nomad was 8 inches longer from the firewall to the centerline of the front wheels and 1 inch shorter from the centerline of the wheels to the front-most part of the car. Thus, although the show car resembled a modified Corvette it was actually so different that it had to be fabricated from new molds. (Photo Courtesy David McGee)*

modified as needed for use on the Nomad. Work Order 19100 dated October 8, 1953, specified, "Using Chassis components available from the Waldorf Show Corvette Car 852, rebuild Chassis to drawings supplied for a steerable, but not necessarily runnable, Nomad Body to be supplied by Styling." The work order specified extensive changes for the dream car, which included lengthening, reshaping, and adding pieces to the EX-52 frame as required. Lengthening the frame meant stretching its wheelbase 13 inches to a span of 115 inches.

Work order 19100 also specified the chassis was to be "finished in show quality." Currently, no information is available as to whether or not the chassis from the original Corvette prototype was indeed adapted as ordered. According to the article "Nomads & Nomadmen" published in the January/March 1972 issue of *Special Interest Autos* and written by the late Pierre Ollier, a designer with General Motors, the Nomad was built on a production 1953 station wagon chassis (although, if correct, the station wagon frame had to have its rear wheel arches reshaped). Therefore, the possibility remains that Work Order 19100 was countermanded and a totally different chassis was used for the "Waldorf Nomad" which, incidentally, was also known at Styling as "Car 857."

*A small-scale GM Motorama was held at the Kerrisdale Arena in Vancouver, British Columbia, in early April 1955. Among the cars shown was this 1954 Nomad. (Photo Courtesy Vancouver Public Library, Special Collections, VPL 82756H)*

Although based on the Corvette, the Nomad was distinctly different. It was 8 inches longer from the firewall to the centerline of the front wheels and 1 inch shorter from the centerline of the wheels to the front-most part of the car. Because of such differences, it had to be fabricated from new molds. Other than some mechanical items, only the grille, bumperettes, headlight assemblies, wheel covers, taillight assemblies, and dashboard components were acquired from the Corvette parts bin.

# CHAPTER FOUR: THE GM MOTORAMA OF 1954

*These rarely seen photographs reveal various features of the 1954 Nomad including the bows on the headliner and the electrically operated tailgate window. The latter feature was adopted for the 1959 Chevy wagon. (Photo Courtesy David McGee)*

Reportedly, the Nomad was finished in white, but before its debut it was changed to a two-tone scheme (according to *The Hot One: Chevrolet 1955–1957* by Pat Chappell). The colors chosen may have been 1953 Oldsmobile Fiesta colors: Alpine White and Turquoise (a metallic color that looked more blue than green). Without an actual 1954 Nomad to inspect or GM records with the actual paint formula available, the true shades used are open to speculation.

Because of the low overall height of the Nomad (just 54 inches) the surface of its roof panel was much more prominent than typical station wagons of the day. Because of this, Harley Earl ordered that the roof panel be given some special feature or features to make it more visually appealing. One option strongly favored by Earl was to have retracting stainless steel panels over the rear half, but the concept proved to be impractical. A compromise (credited to Renner) emerged from the idea, however, consisting of a series of grooves running side-to-side aft of the B-pillars.

Styling of the concept car's interior was no less stunning than its exterior. Except for the dashboard and steering wheel, the Nomad's interior shared nothing with the Corvette. The upholstery was white leather with silver-blue fabric inserts. The front bench seat's backrest was split into a one-third (driver's side)/two-thirds (passenger's side) arrangement. The rear seat could be folded forward to lay flush with the cargo floor; when done, it provided a 75-inch-deep cargo compartment. Chrome-plated bows added some decoration to the car's white headliner; a feature carried over to the production Bel Air–based Nomad.

*The Corvette-based 1954 Nomad provided the basis for the 1955 Bel Air–based Nomad. Its roof and tailgate styling were carried over to the production station wagon. This photo was taken at the Waldorf-Astoria.*

### Production Features

The public was clearly impressed after its first look at the 1954 Nomad at the Waldorf-Astoria; so much so that Harley Earl is reported to have made a phone call from the hotel instructing Carl Renner to proceed with adapting the dream car's roof to the Bel Air body. (Not long afterward, Pontiac was also authorized to build its own version, dubbed the Safari.)

The production version kept the forward-sweeping B-pillars, sliding side glass, grooved roof panel, tailgate trim, and open rear wheel housings of the show car.

*This photograph taken prior to the opening of the 1955 CNE in August of that year reveals that a 1954 Nomad was on display six to seven weeks after one was reported to have been dismantled at General Motors. Note the presence of the 1955 Lincoln Futura show car spinning on its turntable to the right in the foreground. (Photo Courtesy CNE Archives, Alexandra Studios, MG5-5892-14)*

Later, the functional exhaust port surrounds on the lower quarter panels of the 1954 Nomad were adapted as a non-functional accessory; these were first offered for the 1958 model year. The Corvette Nomad's electrically operated tailgate window was not adopted until the 1959 models were designed.

The production version generated some decent sales and publicity for Chevrolet. However, the concept was dropped with the end of the 1957 model year as sales of two-door wagons were decreasing. The Nomad name continued for a few more model years, though.

Because the 1954 Nomad is one of the most popular, if not *the* most popular of GM's dream cars of the 1950s, a number of semi-replica Nomad street rods have been crafted over the past decade or so. A company, Superior 54, produced a limited run of 1954 Nomad-type bodies with a modern chassis.

*Another photograph from the CNE Archives shows the 1954 Nomad up close and sitting next to a 1955 Bel Air at the CNE auto show held in August/September of 1955. (Photo Courtesy CNE Archives, Alexandra Studios, MG5-5892-24)*

# CHAPTER FOUR: THE GM MOTORAMA OF 1954

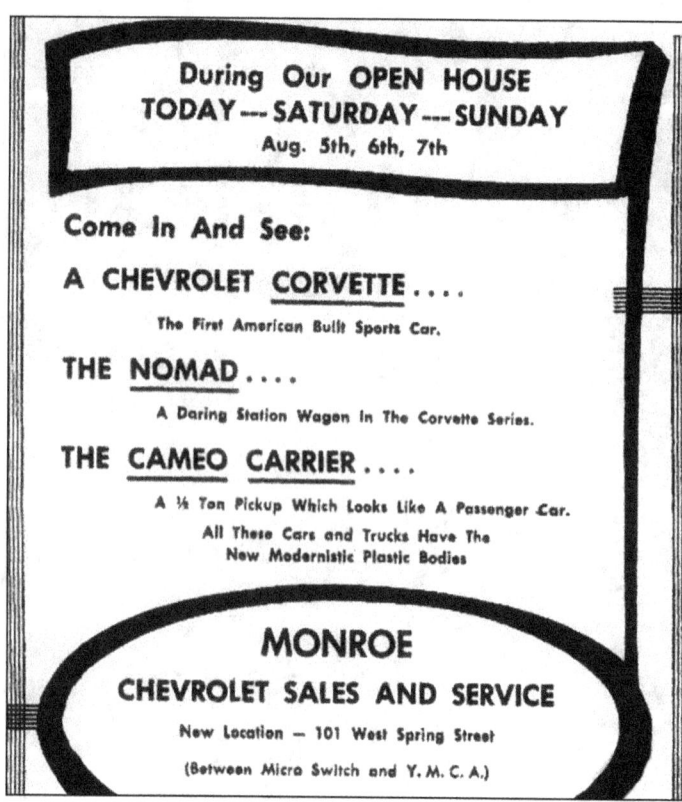

*This ad appearing in the August 5, 1955, Freeport Journal Standard promoted the appearance of the Corvette, Nomad, and Cameo pickup at Monroe Chevrolet Sales and Service in Freeport, Illinois, and noted that all had fiberglass bodies. The Nomad was even described as a member of the Corvette series. Therefore, this appears to be further evidence that a Corvette-based Nomad was in existence weeks after one was reportedly scrapped. Incidentally, only the pickup bed of the Cameo was of fiberglass.*

### One Nomad or Two?

Whether or not a 1954 Nomad still exists is a controversial matter. It was rumored, decades ago, that the Nomad was locked away in a warehouse in Newport Beach, California, but there is also a totally different version of its fate. Chapter 11 of Noland Adam's book, *Corvette: American Legend Vol. 2*, recites an interview conducted with Norm Brown, a retired GM employee who began working for the company in 1955. On his first day at work he assisted in scrapping some show cars, one of which was a 1954 Nomad. This took place on Friday, July 8.

Brown described the car that he helped strip as, "a miniature production Nomad; a 1955 Chevrolet vehicle I had seen . . . but this had a Corvette front end on it." According to Brown, his job was to assist in removing all the hardware that could be readily removed, damage it (i.e., bend it), and throw it into a trash barrel. When that was done, the rolling shell of the Nomad was pushed aside, presumably to be hauled to a crusher on the following Monday. Brown never saw the Nomad again. Reportedly, a work order calling for the Nomad's destruction was seen in GM's files, but without a completion order attached.

Contradicting this story is a 1987 article in *Nomad News* in which the author, Bob Jones, interviewed a Washington state Chevrolet dealer, Tom Dorsey, who said he saw the 1954 Nomad (along with other cars) in November or December *1959* in a Detroit warehouse basement used by General Motors. His description of what he saw painted a picture of a pristine 1954 Nomad. The car's existence in 1959 gives credibility to Chevrolet Studio head "Mac" McKichan's assertion that the Nomad was scrapped in the 1960s, at least in terms of the time line. Maybe another Nomad was scrapped in the 1960s, or maybe not.

According to, Pat Chappell's book, *The Hot One: Chevrolet 1955-1957*, Carl Renner, who headed the car's design, insisted that only one Nomad was built. McKichan was quoted as saying, "To the best of our knowledge, the original Corvette Nomad was scrapped sometime in the 1960s . . . Persistent stories crop up from time to time that we have it squirreled away in a warehouse somewhere in Detroit, but unfortunately this seems to be a myth." Most assuredly, the designers who said only one Nomad was built and scrapped believed just that.

Past research on these cars has led me to conclude the designers simply did not always know how many of a particular show car were built. The fact that the late Mac McKichan believed only one 1954 Nomad was built is not at all surprising. Clearly, the number of cars to be built was not a decision made by the stylists.

Supporting evidence for my belief that at least two 1954 Nomads were built is a set of photographs of one on display inside the Automobile Building of Exhibition Place during the CNE in Toronto, Ontario, in late August 1955. The photos seem to prove at least two of these dream cars were built.

In other words, if Norm Brown helped dismantle one in early July 1955 and one was on display about six to seven weeks later, there had to have been at least two of them. Among the cars around the Nomad in one photo are 1955 Chevrolets including a Bel Air two-door hardtop parked beside it. Clearly visible in two of the photos from the archives of Exhibition Place is the 1955 Lincoln Futura (the car which, incidentally, was reworked into the Batmobile used in the 1960s television program *Batman*). Therefore, the most plausible explanation for the conflicting information is that at least two 1954

Nomads were built (evidently identical); one of them was scrapped in July 1955 and another was scrapped in the 1960s as stated by Mac McKichan.

Nomad enthusiast and researcher, David McGee, contacted Brown in January 2012 by telephone. He reaffirmed to McGee that he did indeed help dismantle a 1954 Nomad on his first day of employment with General Motors; Brown, then 18 years old, specifically recalled removing the door panels and various chrome components from the show car at the Chevrolet Engineering Building on Van Dyke in Warren, Michigan. These vivid details seem to indicate Norm Brown's memory of this event is entirely correct.

### Three Nomads?

So, does that settle the issue of the number of Nomads built and their respective fates? Perhaps it does not.

David McGee stumbled upon some startling information while looking through the July 2011 issue of *Super Chevy* magazine. In response to an article about the GM Motorama in an earlier issue, a reader submitted a letter to the editor stating that he saw what had to be *two* 1954 Nomads at GM's Arizona Proving Grounds. Jim McDade wrote the letter, and both McGee and I later interviewed him.

According to McDade, he was employed at the Proving Grounds in late 1969 or early 1970. Early one morning, as he was driving on one of the many lanes of the test track, he noticed an early Corvette (a 1953–1955 type) approaching from the opposite direction. He was quite surprised to see such an old Corvette on the test track and even more surprised as it passed; it was a station wagon! Intrigued, he turned around as quickly as the track allowed and headed in the direction of the mysterious car.

After approximately five to seven minutes he spotted the Corvette station wagon behind a fence and sitting nose high as though the engine had been removed from it. The engine could not have been removed so quickly from the car he had just seen on the track, so this must have been another one. McDade found someone to ask about these unusual cars and was told they were trying to "get them roadworthy for the owner" who was a high-ranking GM executive with a home nearby. This executive was said to have other GM show cars.

Because Norm Brown scrapped a Nomad show car and Jim McDade believes he saw two of them, the only apparent explanation to reconcile all of these stories is that three identical 1954 Nomads must have been built! My conclusion is that Mac McKichan must have known about the Nomad scrapped by Norm Brown and others, but did not correctly recall when it happened and the two others survived at least until 1970. If two still exist, it helps explain the constant rumors of the Nomad being hidden away.

Some may find this hard to accept, but I have long believed that building just one 1954 Nomad made no sense. Two and three copies of other such cars were built for 1953 and 1954 and the Nomad was one of the most popular show cars of 1954, so why not build at least two for the show circuit?

One other matter settled by Norm Brown is the question of whether or not the Nomad had an engine. Many enthusiasts believe it had no engine and the hood was

The only known venue where the red 1954 Corvair was shown was at the Waldorf-Astoria in January 1954. This car was reported to have been present at Warhoops Used Auto & Truck Parts until about 1978. The trunk lid reportedly was only a scribed outline. (Photo Courtesy GM Media Archive)

A Seafoam Green Corvair appeared at the GM Motorama in Miami and for the remaining locations of the 1954 GM Motorama. This publicity photo showing the car's sleek design was taken in Miami near the Dinner Key Auditorium before the opening of the show. Note the engine heat vents on the front fender and the push-button door release. (Photo Courtesy GM Media Archive)

*The Corvair featured a panoramic windshield slanted back at a 55-degree angle, a trio of small rectangular vents on the fenders for interior ventilation, and twin bulges with chromed slotted vents on the hood. (Photo Courtesy GM Media Archive)*

simply scribed into the fiberglass. According to Brown, an engine was present. In fact, some frontal views of the car show the driver-side rear corner of the hood (which opened forward like a Corvette's) sitting a bit high. This slight misalignment (typical of fiberglass panels at the time) serves as proof of an opening hood.

## Chevrolet Corvair: Sleek Styling

The 1954 Chevrolet Corvair model name was created from a combination of Corvette and Bel Air. This new model was essentially a modified Corvette with a fastback roof sweeping back into a jet exhaust-type opening. Its Panoramic windshield was angled back at 55 degrees. The ventilation system included a set of three small rectangular intake vents mounted (one over the other) on the fenders and exhaust vents located on the C-pillars, which could be opened and closed with a manual control. Engine compartment heat was vented through chromed, slotted vents integrated into twin bulges on the hood. The so-called jet exhaust opening was fitted with the license plate mounting, a license plate lamp, and a pair of back-up lights. It was also filled with a bright-metal plate with a myriad of Chevrolet bowtie emblems cut into it.

The Corvair's rear styling was considered an update for the 1955 Corvette, but no money was released to fund the necessary tooling changes because of the poor sales of the sports car. Therefore, the Corvair was evidently intended to forecast the styling for the 1955 Corvettes, but in the end it did not.

*The Corvair's upholstery and door panels were completely different than those of a stock Corvette or other Corvette-based show cars of the 1954 GM Motorama.*

The interior was largely upholstered in light beige leather, but the pattern on the seats and door panels differed from that of the production Corvette. A bulkhead (as on the Corvette) sat directly behind the bucket seats while a filler panel covered the section from the bulkhead to the bottom of the backlight. A convenient storage compartment and an armrest were built into the door panels.

Interestingly, GM literature stated that the Corvair was equipped with a 150-hp engine joined to a Powerglide transmission, the stock arrangement for a *1953* Corvette from which at least one Corvair was likely built. The 1954 Corvette's engine, according to General Motors, gained 5 extra horsepower raising it to 155.

Roger Roberts, an Indiana resident, constructed a beautiful replica of the Seafoam Green Corvair using documents and photos he said he purchased from the estate of a former GM engineer who reportedly performed design work on the car. According to Roberts, the red version did not have an opening trunk; it was simulated with a scribed outline and an opening trunk was incorporated for subsequent versions.

*This very rarely seen photo of a Corvette with the prototype hardtop, shown during the 1954 GM Motorama show tour, was taken inside the shop at GM Styling. The show car's color appears to be the same or similar to Harvest Gold, a color offered for 1955. (Photo Courtesy GM Design Center)*

Other details differed between these prototypes and the red version, such as functional versus non-functional vents, according to Roberts.

According to Roberts, there were some issues with the hinge geometry, which the engineers later solved. One solution was to have the trunk pivot on hinges mounted at the rear (which is how Roberts built his replica). However, an old home movie taken by car enthusiast Don Baron (who transferred the movie film to DVD many years ago) has a brief scene showing the trunk of a Seafoam Green Corvair opening conventionally. This seems to indicate that two Seafoam Green cars were indeed built, but with vastly different trunk hinge mechanisms.

### Where Are They Now?

It seems that the red car was not shown again after its appearance at the Waldorf-Astoria, but there is no conclusive proof of this. There is, however, evidence that it was not scrapped as apparently intended. According to *two* eyewitnesses interviewed for a 2003 story about the GM Motorama cars in *Car Collector* magazine, a car described as a red 1953–1955-style Corvette fastback was seen at Warhoops sitting atop one or two other cars.

One of the witnesses, Mark Auran, now an East Texas resident, lived in Michigan in the 1960s and 1970s. As a teenager, he frequented the famed Warhoops wrecking yard in Sterling Heights to search for GTO parts and distinctly recalled seeing the Corvair as well as the Biscayne.

The other witness was Larry Muckey, an Eldorado Brougham enthusiast who also made repeated trips to Warhoops. Muckey said the car disappeared from Warhoops around 1978; Auran concurred with the approximate year of the Corvair's disappearance. Furthermore, according to Roger Roberts, a friend of his also saw the red Corvair at Warhoops, but it was upside down and badly damaged, but not beyond repair. Apparently, it had somehow fallen from its perch atop another car.

The red Corvair was rumored to exist some years ago according to author Don Keefe. He was told that the owner of it had also purchased a 1954 Nomad. Keefe cannot verify the story, but simply repeated to me what he was told by a friend of a friend involved in the Corvette hobby.

According to Roberts, Richard York salvaged roughly 50 components from a Seafoam Green Corvair that had been crushed; Roberts then obtained these from York's estate. The parts included the push-button door releases, script, trunk hinges, trunk mat, etc. Many of these parts are now on the Corvair replica built by Roberts.

*The interior details of the Corvette with the prototype hardtop differed significantly from the production version. In fact, it forecast the interior design of the 1956–1957 Corvettes. Some or all of the hardtop-equipped show cars were built from 1953 models. (Photo Courtesy GM Design Center)*

# CHAPTER FOUR: THE GM MOTORAMA OF 1954

*Shown here is a Corvette with the prototype hardtop on display at the 1954 Chicago Auto Show held March 13–21. The dates overlap those of the GM Motorama in Los Angeles (March 6–14), which indicates two cars were being shown in the U.S. simultaneously with a third shown in Canada. (Photo Courtesy GM Media Archive)*

Furthermore, Roberts believes that five Corvairs were built; each was a little different because General Motors was serious about a production version. Based on available information, the red Corvair disappeared from the Warhoops wrecking yard about 35 years ago, one green car was crushed, and three others have an unknown fate.

## Corvette with a Hardtop

The other special Corvette, displayed during this year's GM Motorama tour (starting with the Miami show), had a prototype fiberglass detachable top in addition to roll-up windows. (Production Corvettes made do with snap-in panels.) A windshield that was reportedly about 3 inches higher than the stock unit as well as a cast bronze frame were installed and the body was repainted to match or closely match Harvest Gold, which was a color offered for 1955.

The interior was outfitted with non-production upholstery and door panels with round-dimpled waffle-pattern inserts, as well as a small glove box on the passenger-side kick panel. A similarly patterned upholstery and door panel design (with square dimples rather than round ones), along with the hardtop, appeared for the 1956 Corvette, although the latter item was, of course, offered as an extra-cost option.

Without question, at least three Corvettes with the prototype hardtop were built. While one was being shown at the Pan Pacific Auditorium in Los Angeles (March 6–14), another was on exhibit at the Chicago Auto Show

*A Corvette with a prototype hardtop again appeared at the International Amphitheatre in Chicago; this was for the GM Motorama held there some weeks after the Chicago Auto Show. (Photo Courtesy GM Media Archive)*

82 MOTORAMA

(March 13–21). The dates of these shows overlap a couple of days so the cars must have been two separate vehicles.

The two cars appear to have been in the same color scheme, but this is based on comparing a black-and-white photograph of the "hardtop" car at the Chicago Auto Show to a black-and-white photo of the car known to have been yellow; the gray shading representing the color of the paint for each car appears to match. Obviously, this is not a reliable method to determine the color of the car at the Chicago Auto Show. (Even if they were both yellow, they may not have been the same shade of yellow.) At least one of these two cars was built from an early 1953 Corvette, although most likely both were 1953 models.

Another Corvette "hardtop" show car was built from a 1953 Corvette with serial number E53F001260. This car was displayed at various Canadian auto shows throughout 1954 including the 1954 CNE in Toronto, Ontario, and the 1955 GM Motorama at Calgary, Alberta. It existed simultaneously with the other two show cars. It was given nearly the same modifications as the pale yellow car. Other than its color scheme (gold-tinted red exterior with a white interior) the only apparent difference between it and the yellow car appearing on the GM Motorama circuit was that its wheel covers were stock Corvette units without the crossed-flags centerpiece seen on the yellow hardtop, the Corvair, and the Nomad.

According to an article written by Wayne Ellwood and Noland Adams for the Summer 1999 issue of *SHARK Quarterly* magazine, Corvette E53F001260 was sold by General Motors on August 17, 1957, to an employee in the Truck Sales Department in Oshawa, Ontario. This car still exists and has had numerous owners since 1957. However, since 1973, it has had one Canadian owner who has performed a partial restoration. It is missing its original cast bronze windshield frame, which was replaced when the original custom-made windshield had to be replaced with a production unit in the 1960s.

## Pontiac Bonneville Special and Strato-Streak: A Racy Sports Car and a Sport Sedan

For 1954, GM Styling broke new ground for Pontiac with its first two-seat sports car, called the Bonneville Special (SO 2026). The other Pontiac dream car for 1954 was the four-passenger Strato-Streak (SO 1953). Pontiac called it a "spectacular sports car," but it is best defined as a luxury sports sedan.

### Bonneville Special

As with the Le Sabre, the futuristic styling of the Bonneville Special was largely influenced by rocket and airplane designs of the day. The name, which is credited to Harley Earl, was strongly associated with speed due to the records set by racers at Utah's Bonneville Salt Flats. Even a special set of Utah license plates was issued by the state at the request of Earl for display on the original Bonneville Special.

Inspiration for the Bonneville Special's design came from Eddie Miller's Pontiac-powered racer, which was used to set a number of records at the Salt Flats in 1950. Overall responsibility for the design of this car was assigned to Paul Gillan and Homer LaGassey. They styled the car using extremely few Pontiac styling cues: the so-called silver streaks on the hood, the taillights, and the taillight bezels.

*Engine Decision*
Although the Bonneville Special's name and styling projected a race car theme, its engine was somewhat of a contradiction. Under the hood of the dream car sat a 268-ci straight-8 with four side-draft carburetors and other unspecified modifications said to produce a peak horsepower of 230. That figure was nearly a 100-percent increase over the engines powering Pontiacs in production. However, it was still the old straight-8 rather than a V-8, which was a much more popular engine among performance enthusiasts.

The decision to install a straight-8 rather than a prototype V-8 may have been made so as not to reveal to the

*The red Corvette with a prototype hardtop, built from 1953 Corvette E53F1001260, was shown in Canada: twice in Toronto in the late winter or very early spring of 1954 and at the GM Wonderama in August/September 1954. It was also shown in other cities in Canada. (Photo Courtesy CNE Archives, Alexandra Studio, MG5-5891-32)*

## CHAPTER FOUR: THE GM MOTORAMA OF 1954

The two-passenger 1954 Pontiac Bonneville Special had almost nothing in common with the mass-produced Pontiacs of the day. Apart from the so-called silver streaks across its hood and its straight-8, it was unlike any Pontiac ever built. Its namesake was the Bonneville Salt Flats in Utah where many land speed records had been set. The car signaled that Pontiacs were about to become exciting automobiles. (Photo Courtesy Hillary Hess Collection)

Four side-draft carburetors were installed on the Pontiac straight-8 to boost the horsepower of the engine of both Bonneville Specials. (Photo Courtesy Don Keefe)

general public the still somewhat secret V-8 scheduled for 1955. Any hint that a V-8 would soon be offered may have negatively impacted Pontiac's sales (which proved to be low enough as it was); some potential Pontiac buyers no doubt would have waited for the more powerful engine. However, the V-8 was really an open secret by the latter part of 1953, at least for enthusiasts who read the trade journals. In fact, the chassis of the 1953 Pontiacs was designed to accommodate the new V-8, but the engine was rescheduled for the 1954 model year.

Finally, the problems with engine development were resolved in time for the 1955 debut of the Pontiac V-8.

### Body Styling

The racy lines of the Bonneville Special were achieved in part through a low height (just 48½ inches) and the proportions of its long hood and short deck. The long hood was made necessary by the choice of the straight-8 engine. The car's short deck ended with a built-in, functional Continental kit, although it was not included in the design at first. At the direction of Bill Mitchell, it replaced the central blade first proposed.

Over the two-place passenger compartment was a plexiglass roof with only a minimal amount of framing and flip-up panels to ease entry and exit. According to a news release from Pontiac regarding this feature, "Hinged at the center, the canopy raises at each side on counter-balanced springs at the touch of a release catch. The doors are then opened from the inside. There are no outside door handles."

The fiberglass body was painted a metallic red-copper and had many other features not found on everyday cars, such as no grille, but rather a wide opening roughly the size and shape of the Corvette's grille opening. Underneath this opening, six thin bumper guards were mounted in sets of three per side. Two chrome-trimmed air vents were located along the leading edge of the hood. Pontoon-like fenders were fitted with thin, crescent-shaped bumpers and the recessed headlights were enclosed with transparent covers. Scoops located on the cowl at the end of the silver streaks funneled air into the interior for ventilation.

The interior of the Bonneville Special is still impressive. From its 120-mph speedometer, array of gauges in chrome-plated pods, and its red-copper leather upholstery, the interior of this dream car is as it was when it appeared on a turntable at the 1954 GM Motorama shows.

In 2008, the Bonneville Special was displayed at the Pebble Beach Concours d'Elegance along with several other dream cars of the GM Motorama. This Bonneville Special still retains its GM-applied paint and even its original tires. It may be the most original dream car in existence. (Photo Courtesy Bortz Auto Collection)

The second Bonneville Special was given a color scheme consisting of a metallic green exterior with a green and pewter interior. Other than the color combination, there were few differences between it and the first car. It was fully restored more than a decade ago. (Photo Courtesy Don Keefe)

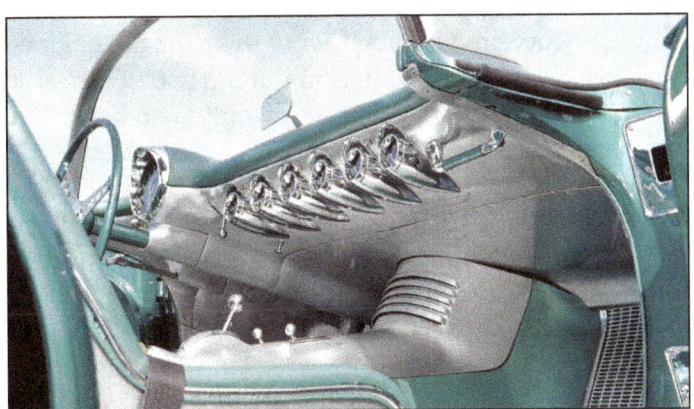

The competition-style interior of the Bonneville Special included bucket seats, console, and instrumentation said to be backlit from a source mounted on the canopy center panel. Various tachometers, clocks, and altimeters obtained from an aircraft salvage yard were used to create the sophisticated-looking instrumentation. This avoided the time-consuming tasks of actually designing and building this equipment. (Photo Courtesy Don Keefe)

Special albums for each of the 1954–1956 GM Motoramas were created for GM company president Harlow Curtice. These albums comprised an artist's rendering along with color chips and upholstery samples of each. Shown here is the page dedicated to the 1954 Pontiac Strato-Streak. (Photo Courtesy GM Global Design via GM Media Archive)

## CHAPTER FOUR: THE GM MOTORAMA OF 1954

*The Bonneville Special was so popular that a second one was built. Both were displayed all over the country. This newspaper advertisement promoted the appearance of one of the Bonneville Specials at a Syracuse, New York, Pontiac dealership.*

These could be independently opened and closed via levers inside the car.

Simulated oil coolers machined from solid aluminum (or billet aluminum) were mounted on the front fenders behind the wheel openings. The recessed rear license plate mount was offset to the left of the functional Continental kit. Twin exhaust outlets exited through cutouts in the lower valance, although in reality the engine had only a single exhaust; the second outlet was for appearance only. Wheel covers were brushed-aluminum discs with turbine-like impeller fins for brake cooling and a two-bar spinner to simulate knock-off hubs.

### Interior Features

The two-toned interior of the Bonneville Special fit the race car theme, as did its bucket seats, console, 120-mph speedometer, tachometer, competition-style spring-steel steering wheel, and instrumentation said to be backlit from a source mounted on the canopy center panel. A clock and compass were installed in the windshield header; however, this instrumentation was non-functional.

According to an article written by Michael Lamm for a 1988 issue of *Automobile Quarterly*, Vol. 26 No. 3, LaGassey and Gillan went to an aircraft salvage yard in Detroit to buy various tachometers, clocks, and altimeters to create the complex-looking instrumentation for the car. This clever shortcut did away with the time-consuming tasks of actually designing and building these components.

Adding to the competition car look of the largely metallic red-copper interior (with its contrasting pewter-colored lower dash, console, and door panels) was a set of chromed levers protruding from the console. The center lever served as the gear selector for the 4-speed Hydra-Matic transmission; the other two opened and closed the air scoops on the cowl. The car's ignition switch was also mounted on the console. In addition, a substantial tool compartment was included behind the seats, a brushed-aluminum floor covering with non-slip rubber strips was applied through slots, a set of lap belts was added, and door panels were recessed for additional elbowroom.

### The SO 2026 Provenance

After the national tour ended, the Bonneville Special used on the GM Motorama circuit went into storage in a warehouse for a few years before it was slipped out the door. An article written by Jay Lamm for the December 1991 issue of *Corvette Fever* stated this car "was sold to an anonymous engineer in 1959 who was taking stock of what GM Styling [by then renamed GM Design] had ferreted away in its many warehouses.

"One day he came across a warehouse filled with dusty, forgotten dream cars. The Pontiac Strato-Streak was there, along with a number of others; the Chevrolet Corvair (Corvette fastback) *wasn't* there, or the engineer would have gone after that one, too. He had to 'settle' for the Bonneville Special and he won't say how he even managed that."

A short time later the car was sold to a Michigan collector who, in 1959, loaned it to the Detroit Historical Society Museum. Twenty-one years later, museum officials put the car back into storage. When the owner learned of this, he reclaimed the Bonneville Special, and soon thereafter, offered it for sale. Auto restoration specialist Fran Roxis informed his friend, Joe Bortz, about the opportunity to buy the dream car. Bortz soon became its next owner and has owned it ever since.

This Bonneville Special is likely the most original dream car in existence. It is completely original right down to its lacquer paint and even "the 1954 air in the tires" according to Bortz. He is aware of a small amount of air being added to the original tires on only two occasions so he is not joking.

## The Second Example

The Bonneville Special was very popular with the public. In the aforementioned *Automobile Quarterly* article, Paul Gillan was quoted as saying, "People were spellbound by the fact it was a Pontiac . . . Everyone liked it." Due to the car's popularity and dealer demands for it to appear at dealerships across the country, a second example was built about two months after the original version debuted at the Waldorf-Astoria.

The second Bonneville Special was given a different color scheme consisting of a metallic green exterior with a metallic green and pewter interior. Other than the color combination, it was virtually identical to the first car. Minor alterations included two extra air vents (a total of four) in the leading edge of the hood (but without any chrome trim), a chrome-plated radiator core support, and a cylinder head painted red instead of being chrome-plated like that of the first car.

Reportedly, after this Bonneville Special's show car duties were completed, it was sent to a GM dealership in Michigan and was quickly forgotten by most people. Supposedly, this is when the car was made drivable. A pair of holes was bored into each of the lift-up plexiglass panels of the canopy for improved ventilation. It was repainted white at some point, too.

The car was, at one time, rumored to have been seriously damaged and subsequently scrapped. Perhaps there is a grain of truth in the story, as it's possible that it was damaged, then repaired, and that is when the color was changed to white. Decades had passed since the green Bonneville Special had been in the spotlight. Then in 1990, Joe Bortz received a phone call asking, "Why do you claim to own the Bonneville Special when I have it?!" Joe understandably doubted the caller's claim believing instead the car must be one of the many Corvettes customized over the decades and this one happened to resemble his Bonneville Special. Bortz had been assured by a GM official that only one Bonneville Special was built and obviously the caller believed there was only one, also.

Despite the assurances and his expectations, Joe was curious so he requested some pictures of the car. Later, he received some photocopied photographs through the mail, which surprisingly showed another Bonneville Special really did exist. Joe then tried to contact the owner, but was unsuccessful after many attempts. Two years passed, Bortz tried contacting the owner again, but was told he had passed away shortly after their only conversation. Joe was able to purchase the second Bonneville Special from the deceased man's estate. Although the odometer read only 700 miles, the obscure show car needed a thorough restoration due to neglect. After deciding not to pursue a restoration of the car, Joe sold it to Roger Willbanks, a well-known collector in Denver. He took on the bold task of having the dream car restored to its original specs (with the exception of the flip-up plexiglass panels, which retain the small holes bored into each of them years ago although they were plugged with plexiglass). The dream car's restoration was completed in time for it to be displayed at the 2000 Meadowbrook Concours d'Elegance.

Some years late, Willbanks decided to part with his Bonneville Special and consigned it for sale at the January 2006 Barrett-Jackson auction in Scottsdale, Arizona, where it sold for $2.8 million plus commission, to collector Ron Pratte of Arizona. While the bidding was ongoing, one of the car's designers, Homer LaGassey, watched the action from the stage. When invited to make a few comments about the metallic green show car he noted that the Bonneville Special was one of the cars that set the stage for Pontiac's entrance into the youth market in the 1950s and 1960s. The second Bonneville Special is scheduled to be sold at the 2015 Barrett-Jackson Auction in Scottsdale, Arizona.

## Strato-Streak

Gillan and LaGassey designed the Strato-Streak. Like the Cadillac Orleans, which preceded it, the Strato-Streak was a pillarless four-door hardtop with reverse-opening (suicide) rear doors.

### Exterior Innovations

The frames around the windows did not roll down with the windows, thus with the doors closed the Strato-Streak actually had the appearance of a four-door

*Buick adopted the Strato-Streak's three-piece backlight for its 1957 cars. This photo was taken at the GM Motorama in Chicago.*

# CHAPTER FOUR: THE GM MOTORAMA OF 1954

*The metallic green 1954 Pontiac Strato-Streak appears in the background to the right sitting on its turntable platform during the GM Motorama in Miami. Note the dressed-up Picador Red convertible in front of it. (Photo Courtesy GM Media Archive)*

sedan! A special latching mechanism for the doors was built into the rocker panel sill because there was no pillar post present. Because the rear doors opened into the direction of the air stream, the locks were designed to allow the doors to open only when the car was stopped and the Hydra-Matic gear selector was in neutral.

The 54.7-inch overall height of this experimental car was 8.7 inches lower than a production Pontiac. The Star Chief chassis was modified as required for use on the Strato-Streak; the wheelbase measured 124 inches. The Star Chief was a new model for 1954 and had a 2-inch-longer wheelbase than the lower series models offered by Pontiac.

The frontal design of the car included a concave, egg-crate grille and oblong headlight bezels. Beneath the grille was a distinctive gull-wing-style bumper foretelling the general appearance of the one designed for 1956 Pontiacs. A projectile-shaped bulge on the side of the front fenders contained engine compartment cooling vents. The pattern of the vent continued across the front doors. Flow-through ventilation for the passenger compartment was provided through a pair of cowl air intakes and elliptical air outlets above the backlight.

Despite fins being very much in vogue at the time, this Pontiac did not have them. Instead, the rear profile of the upper quarter panels tapered into a projectile shape similar to that of the quarter panels of the 1957 Cadillac, although the latter had tail fins.

The Strato-Streak also featured windsplits along the roof, which continued across the rear deck and were flanked by vertical twin taillights, a wraparound windshield, and a large glass area to provide all-around vision. The windsplits continued uninterrupted across the backlight resulting in a three-piece window. (This concept was adopted for production on the 1957 Buicks and Oldsmobiles, but it was not a popular feature.) Roof-pillar posts were as narrow as possible to maximize visibility for the driver without sacrificing structural integrity.

### Interior Details

Leather upholstery with fabric inserts covered the chrome-framed individual seats of the Strato-Streak. The front seats swiveled 90 degrees for easier entry and exit. A full-length console housed the radio, selector levers for controlling the air vents and heater temperature, and ashtray.

*Four gauges were individually mounted at the center of the Strato-Streak's padded dash. From left to right are the fuel gauge, oil pressure gauge, coolant temperature gauge, and ammeter. Note the console-mounted radio. This photo is of the "retrimmed" Strato-Streak II according to GM Archive records. (Photo Courtesy GM Media Archive)*

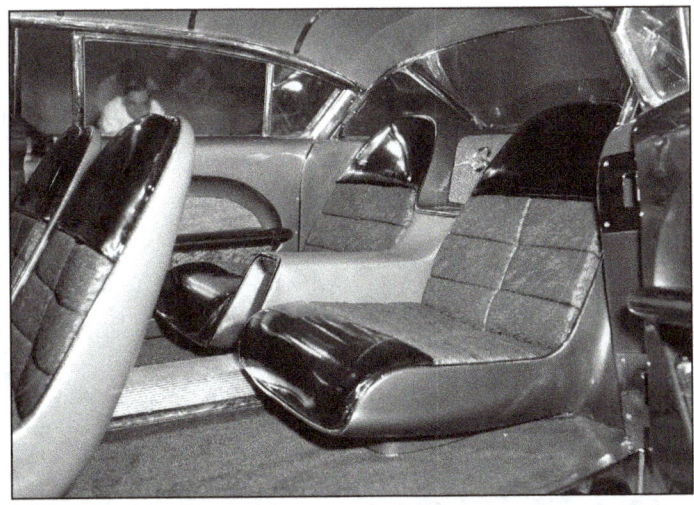

This photograph dated November 21, 1955, shows the interior of the "retrimmed" Strato-Streak. The show car was repainted in a brilliant metallic red and reupholstered to match (probably red and black). In this scheme, it was rechristened the Strato-Streak II. I think it was literally the second of two Strato-Streaks built. (Photo Courtesy GM Media Archive)

This rarely seen color photograph from the files of GM Media Archive shows a 1954 Pontiac Strato-Streak in metallic blue. I suspect this is the show car, which became the metallic red Strato-Streak II. (Photo Courtesy GM Media Archive)

Spanning the area from the front to the rear of the console, which ended as an armrest for rear-seat passengers, was a chrome-plated ribbed section. The dream car's dash was padded along its leading edge and contained a large round speedometer directly ahead of the driver; to the right was a set of four round gauges.

## Strato-Streak II

The Strato-Streak, shown during the 1954 GM Motorama tour, was painted light metallic green (similar to a couple of Cadillac colors offered two years later) with a beige leather and nylon upholstery intertwined with metallic gold threads; the dash was body color. During 1955, this car (or more likely, another Strato-Streak) was repainted metallic red and reupholstered with a two-toned interior (possibly red and black) with a different pattern for the nylon inserts. In the latter guise it was referred to as the Strato-Streak II.

Like the other dream cars of GM's Motorama, the Strato-Streak went on tour across the country. For instance the metallic green car was shown at Nearhoof Pontiac in Altoona, Pennsylvania, August 1–2, 1954, according to an article in the *Altoona Mirror*. A brief article about the Strato-Streak appearing in the July 12, 1954, issue of *Automotive News* stated that it was scheduled to appear along with the Pontiac Bonneville Special at dealerships in 70 locations across the country during the summer.

The 1954 Strato-Streak II was shown in Canada. It was distinguished by a two-tone interior scheme and a metallic red exterior.

This photograph from an unspecified auto show is of the metallic blue Strato-Streak. Note the beige interior with the swivel front seats.

# CHAPTER FOUR: THE GM MOTORAMA OF 1954

*The 1954 Cutlass had, among many other features, an unusual headlight treatment. A vertical central "fin" was fitted over the upper half of each headlight. Note the driving lamps.*

The story did not mention, however, that more than one Strato-Streak had been built. Considering a show schedule of that magnitude and the fact that two Bonneville Specials were built, there is good reason to believe more than one Strato-Streak was constructed, too.

Pointing strongly to at least one more Strato-Streak is a color photograph and a special promotional postcard showing a metallic blue version also with a beige interior. Moreover, according to an article in the May 23, 1955, edition of the *Abilene Reporter* newspaper, the *metallic green* Strato-Streak was scheduled to be on display at Manly Pontiac on May 25 and 26.

Because the green and blue cars appear to have existed simultaneously, I firmly believe that two Strato-Streaks were built and the blue car is the one that was changed into the so-called Strato-Streak II.

Presumably these cars were scrapped, but the possibility of at least one them still being in existence is not an unreasonable thought.

## Oldsmobile Cutlass and F-88: Sleek Sports Cars

The two-passenger, iridescent copper 1954 Cutlass (SO 1981) was one of the more unusual dream cars built by General Motors. The Oldsmobile F-88 (XP-20 SO 1939) was a legitimate two-seat sports car that was built on the Corvette chassis and carried a fiberglass body.

## The Cutlass

Named to honor the U.S. Navy's unconventional F7-U Cutlass jet fighter plane, the Cutlass dream car was also unconventional. (Surprisingly, the only places Cutlass script appeared were on the car's steering wheel hub and on a rear license plate plaque when the car was on display.) Inspiration for some aspects of the styling of the Cutlass was actually sourced from its namesake.

*The pretty model appears pleased with the styling of this 1954 Cutlass. Note the show car's louvered backlight, canopy-like roof, and rectangular exhaust outlets. (Photo Courtesy Carter Ross collection)*

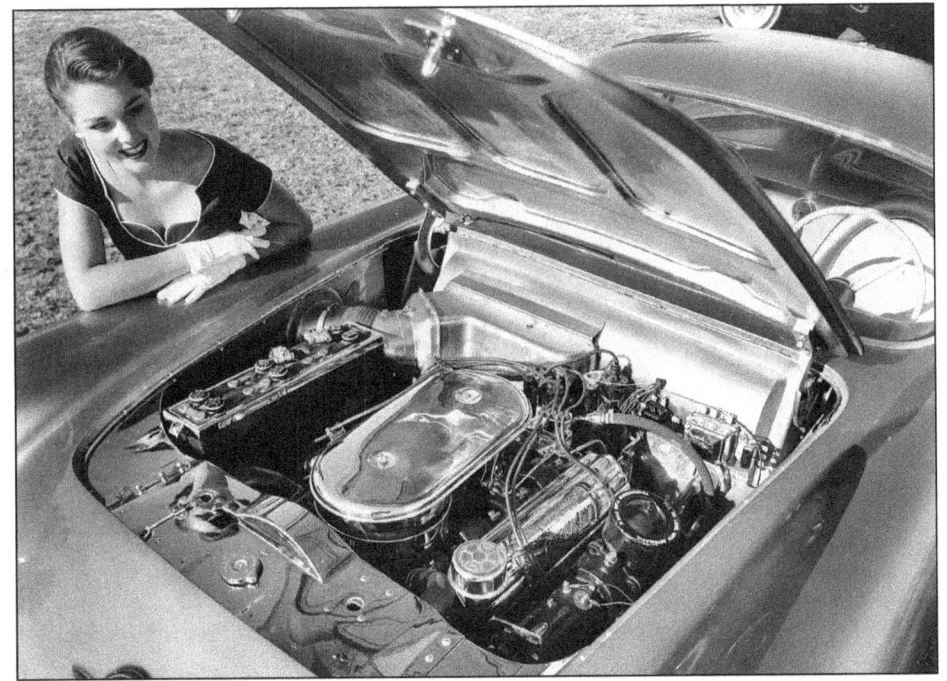

*The engine for the Olds Cutlass was the same as that of its companion, the F-88.*

black sidewall tires. The dream car's spare tire was stowed in a compartment behind the fold-down center section of the rear bumper. Because the Cutlass had no deck lid, access to the luggage compartment was through a panel in the body-colored filler assembly behind the seats.

### Similarities to the F-88

Various press reports stated the Cutlass was powered by a 250-hp 324 V-8 and Hydra-Matic, exactly the same as its companion F-88.

Because this dream car had so many characteristics in common with the shorter F-88, the Cutlass was simply called "the long-wheelbase F-88" before it was formally named, which, incidentally, may account for the "88" numerals mounted in back. Its frame was probably made from a modified Corvette version stretched to give a wheelbase of 110 inches. Other pertinent measurements included an overall length of 188.5 inches and an overall height of 51.5 inches.

### Exterior Design

Most would probably agree the most distinctive features of the Oldsmobile Cutlass were the car's aircraft canopy-like roof and louvered backlight, but neither was adopted for production. However, a similar-looking combination bumper grille was fitted to the 1956 Oldsmobiles. For the Cutlass, split-grille inserts with a set of driving lamps were installed. A pair of stylish, hood-mounted scoops was used to funnel air to the heater. Teardrop-shaped wheel openings with polished stainless steel inner fenders and engine compartment heat vents were also prominent features on the front of the Cutlass.

In back, modest tail fins appeared and blade-like quarters were decorated with small "88" numerals. Flattened dual-exhaust outlets integrated into each end of the rear bumper were each divided into four segments to simulate one exhaust per cylinder. Deeply recessed, split tail lamps were set into the chrome-plated quarter-panel extensions. The Cutlass' lower quarters panels were either detachable or hinged to swing upward like those of the Buick XP-300 to allow removal of the rear wheels. A formed-in body-side windsplit fitted with a slim bright molding almost completely concealed the seam of the lift-off (or lift-up) panel.

As on the F-88, the 13-inch wheels on the Cutlass were fitted with an identical set of wheel covers as well as

*The Cutlass' many features included swivel bucket seats, as demonstrated by the model.*

MOTORAMA 91

# CHAPTER FOUR: THE GM MOTORAMA OF 1954

*The sleek profile of the iridescent copper 1954 Oldsmobile Cutlass is evident in this photograph taken on the beach near Miami's Dinner Key Auditorium.*

Another similarity that the Cutlass shared with the F-88 was its instrumentation layout; they were identical. Also, cutouts in the bulkhead behind the seats allowed for a few more inches of additional fore and aft adjustment. Copper and white leather upholstery covered the seats, which swiveled to facilitate entry and exit. Conventional rearview mirrors were not provided, but instead rearward vision was provided with dual, wide-angle mirrors mounted on the central control panel. A console between the bucket seats carried a radio-telephone, a very forward-thinking innovation.

*This rendering by stylist Irv Rybicki shows an alternative design for the 1954 Oldsmobile Cutlass. (Photo Courtesy GM Media Archive)*

### Style versus Function

*Auto Age* offered an interesting comparison between the production Starfire and the experimental Cutlass in the February 1955 issue. The report presented speculation on the contribution the Cutlass might make to the future of styling from General Motors: ". . . while the Cutlass, in its present form, is for the most part an entirely impractical vehicle, it does furnish us with the basis for an interesting comparison.

"Let us return, for a moment, to the Starfire. This car is . . . one of the largest on the road, a fact that is its very selling point to many people. But while the Starfire is long, powerful, and impressive, it is by some standards rather clumsy and even impractical when it comes to garage or parking space, especially in the crowded city. What is the alternative? Smaller (but not necessarily skimpier or less stylish) cars.

"This is where the Cutlass fits into the picture perfectly. It represents a trend toward the smaller, and presumably more maneuverable, automobile of the future. True, the Cutlass is only a two-seater, but it is really much smaller than the Starfire and yet has at least as much if not more room for each passenger. Its utilization of space is definitely reminiscent of certain current Italian designs, which are based on balance and beauty of line coupled with utility . . . The Cutlass design, or one like it, could easily be extended just a bit to make room for more passengers and additional luggage."

The Cutlass was converted into a functional car at some point, probably just after that year's GM Motorama concluded in Chicago. Judging by photographs, this is evident. One photo from July 1954 shows the car with a Michigan license plate and another of the car in a parade with the F-88. Other such cars in the past had been made operable, so for the Cutlass to have also become functional is not unusual. The car went on to be shown across Canada in 1955.

What became of the Cutlass? Bill Warner, the founder of the Amelia Island Concours d'Elegance, believes it may have been sold. He has an old *CARtoons* magazine with a drawing of the car with a caption stating that the car was sold to a New Jersey resident.

### The F-88

For all intents and purposes, the F-88 was Oldsmobile's version of Chevrolet's Corvette. But there was not to be a divisional competitor to the Corvette even though the F-88 could easily have gone from dream car to production car in short order; General Motors decided not to take that step. Ironically, Oldsmobile was better suited to offering the sports car at the time as they already had a powerful V-8, but Chevrolet closed this gap the following year with the introduction of the 265 V-8.

#### *Exterior Concepts*

The design of the F-88 was the responsibility of Art Ross, head of the Oldsmobile Studio.

The fiberglass body of the original F-88 was painted metallic gold with contrasting dark green wheel wells. Chrome trim was applied sparingly, at least by 1950s standards. A simple bright molding ran atop the quarter panel to the dip in the beltline near the door opening, turned downward, then turned rearward, and finally terminated at the rear wheel opening. An oval-shaped honeycomb grille filled the opening of the combination bumper/grille surround. Large chrome-plated "88" numerals were mounted over the engine heat vents on the front fenders.

Another visual cue associated with Oldsmobile was the "around the world" emblem affixed to the nose and deck lid. At the rear of the quarters, vertical, oval openings outlined with a chrome-plated surround provided the exits for the dual-exhaust system. Also in back were seven chromed bumper guards across the body-colored bumper. A set of conical tail lamps was employed on the F-88 and these appear so similar to those used on the 1959 Cadillacs that they likely served as the inspiration for their design.

*The metallic gold F-88 made its public debut at New York City's Waldorf-Astoria in January 1954. It was essentially an Oldsmobile version of the Chevrolet Corvette, but with a V-8 engine. The F-88 was one of the most production-ready show cars exhibited at a GM Motorama, but a divisional competitor to the Corvette was not to be. (Photo Courtesy GM Media Archive)*

*Like the F-88s, the Cutlass was made into an operable car. An F-88 and the Cutlass led a parade of new 1954 Oldsmobiles in early July of that year, but the venue is unknown. (Photo Courtesy GM Media Archive)*

## CHAPTER FOUR: THE GM MOTORAMA OF 1954

Wheel covers for the 13-inch wheels resembled a turbine with a three-blade spinner, or "flipper." The wheels were fitted with black sidewall tires throughout the GM Motorama tour, but were later changed to a set of wide whites.

Not surprisingly, the F-88's convertible top folded into a well that was covered with a flush-fitting, hinged lid just as on the Corvette. The fuel filler was placed just behind the top well along the fore/aft centerline of the car, and the deck lid opening cut around it. Because trunk space was limited, the spare tire was located under the trunk floor and accessed with a drop-down, center bumper section. This concept was adopted the following year for the Chevrolet Cameo and GMC Suburban pickups.

### The Engine

The 324 Rocket engine, with a single 4-barrel carburetor and coupled to a Hydra-Matic transmission, was boosted to 250 hp for the F-88. This was a 65-hp increase over the rating of the 185-hp engine, which powered the Eighty-Eight and Ninety-Eight series. The compression ratio was bumped up to 10:1 and as a result a label was applied to the fuel filler cap specifying that 94- to 100-octane fuel must be used.

*The spare tire for the F-88 was stored inside a compartment accessed through the opening center section of the rear bumper. (Photo Courtesy Steve Wolken Collection)*

Writers for *Motor Life* magazine (April 1954) speculated that the top speed of the experimental car was approximately 150 mph. Despite the hoopla attributed to the F-88's performance capabilities, it reportedly did not run during the time of the GM Motorama tour. After

*The gold F-88 was a somewhat frequent attraction in downtown Lansing, Michigan. In addition to parades, it was on exhibit on the 100 block of S. Washington Avenue as part of the festivities of Lansing's Second Annual Automotive Industrial Show. The four "Community Queens" standing around the F-88 are (from left to right): Miss Dimondale, Miss Potterville, Miss Fowler, and Miss DeWitt. All are names of small towns surrounding Lansing. The "Queen" in the F-88 is Miss Holt. (Photo Courtesy GM Media Archive)*

A 250-hp version of the Oldsmobile 324 Rocket V-8 was said to power the F-88. Note the special low-profile air cleaner and the use of chrome plating to dress up the engine compartment. (Photo Courtesy Steve Wolken collection)

This photo from December 1953 shows the fold-down armrest of the F-88. When the armrest was not needed it could be folded up to fit flush with the door panel. This car was used for the GM Motorama show circuit. (Photo Courtesy GM Media Archive)

it was retired from the show circuit, a complete electrical system was installed and it was made functional. During the summer of 1955, this car was driven in a Shriners Parade in downtown Lansing, Michigan. It was scheduled to be driven again in the annual parade the following year and is probably the car that experienced an engine compartment fire prior to or maybe after its appearance there.

The F-88's body sat on a Corvette frame modified to accept the Rocket V-8. This car's wheelbase remained the same as the Corvette's at 102 inches. Overall length of the car was stretched to 167.25 inches and its overall height with the peak of the windshield frame was a low 45 inches.

### Interior Design

The interior of the F-88, designed by Jack Humbert, was quite spectacular. It featured bucket seats and a steering wheel covered in pigskin. A set of competition-style instruments was arranged in an upside-down "L" layout across the driver's position then extending vertically to the transmission tunnel.

The vertical stack of gauges was fabricated from the 1953 Oldsmobile parts bin, and was mounted within three round housings. At the top was an odometer combined with a 150-mph speedometer and a 6,000-rpm tachometer laid out concentrically; the center housing was divided into the amp (above) and temperature gauges (below); the bottom housing contained the fuel gauge (top) and the oil pressure gauge (bottom). The console, finished in chrome and textured metallic gold hardware, had a full complement of equipment: chronometer, shifter, radio, and radio controls. A bulkhead behind the bucket seats had cutouts around the seats' backrests to provide additional room for fore and aft adjustments. A radio speaker grille was placed on the bulkhead between the seats.

Fresh-air vents in the cowl and along the cowl edge of the dash and in the kick panels as well as flip-up air scoops in the windshield header helped provide flow-through ventilation with the top raised.

The original F-88 show car (SO 1939) had air scoops built into the windshield frame, which could be opened for ventilation when the top was in the up position. Not all F-88s had this feature. (Photo Courtesy Steve Wolken Collection)

As originally built, the dash, upper door panels, instrumentation stack, and carpeting were a golden color. Later, the dash, upper door panels, center instrument pods, forward console, and carpeting were dark green.

### Four F-88s?

According to the Oldsmobile Engineering Logbook, three XP-20 F-88s were constructed. Listed in it were the show car for the GM Motorama (SO 1939), one for Harley Earl (SO 2292), and another for Sherrod E. Skinner (SO 2264), GM vice president of the accessory group and the former general manager of the Olds division.

Despite the Olds logbook, enough configurations are shown in photographs for me to suspect four were actually completed. Indeed, this belief was justified with the inspection of the Shop Order books in the possession of the GM Heritage Center. Listed are four XP-20 F-88s: SO numbers 1768, 1939 (the Motorama display car), 2292, and 2264.

A yellow car with black interior (SO 2292) appeared at the 1954 Chicago Auto Show and other venues. It also served as transportation for Harley Earl and underwent numerous modifications over the years. It was equipped with side-mounted oil coolers, which resembled the side-mounted exhaust pipes found on some Corvettes in

These photos at an unknown event show an F-88 (SO 2292) with its side-mounted oil coolers. It must be the same car shown at the 1954 Chicago Auto Show, a car that is known to have been painted yellow. At this time the car lacked the body-side molding like that of the metallic gold car shown on the GM Motorama circuit. The steering wheel on this F-88 differs from that of other F-88s.

This Oldsmobile F-88 appeared at the 1954 Chicago Auto Show. Note the side pipes and the body-side molding just visible on the open door. (Photo Courtesy Chicago Automobile Trade Association)

This black Oldsmobile F-88 is probably SO 2292, which was originally painted yellow. Note the presence of side-mounted oil coolers. This F-88 underwent numerous mechanical and cosmetic changes. (Photo Courtesy Media Archive)

Harley Earl's restyled F-88 (SO 90020) included scalloped wheel openings and a new grille. This one was painted metallic blue. It was built from his previous F-88 (SO 2292). The car could be equipped with a removable hardtop, which had the appearance of a convertible top. According to GM documents, the special chrome-plated wheel covers were installed prior to the body modifications. (Photo Courtesy GM Media Archive, Steve Wolken collection)

later years. The body-side molding on this F-88 was later deleted, as were the simulated vents on the lower rear quarter panels.

In approximately June 1954, this car was repainted black, the seat inserts were changed to yellow, a new windshield assembly without cowl vents was ordered, and a frame header without vents was ordered. In addition, the lower dash was modified to provide more footroom. Also, cutting vents into the fiberglass panel separating the engine compartment from the front fenders to correct the problem of vapor lock in the fuel pump was recommended.

In July, General Motors specified 35 other changes for SO 2292, including a reworked honeycomb grille, new hood with a different scoop, new seat tracks, new door panels, reinforced lock pillars, new backup lights, the Autronic Eye relocated to inside the hood scoop, etc. Finally, a new transmission, the Whirl-Away, built by the Detroit Transmission Division was installed.

In January 1955, Harley Earl ordered that SO 2292 undergo various styling modifications. That car became SO 90020 and was ready in the latter part of 1955. It was painted metallic blue, and featured distinctive scalloped wheel well openings and a new split grille similar

Harley Earl's restyled F-88 was equipped with a supercharged, twin-carb Oldsmobile V-8. Its top speed must have been quite high! The 4,550-pound car could run 0–60 mph in 8 seconds. (Photo Courtesy Steve Wolken collection)

Harley Earl's F-88 (SO 90020) was repainted white before it appeared in a July 1956 Shriners Parade. A Bahama Blue strip was added across the hood. The car was later stripped of its layers of paint and repainted in white (again) as seen here from September 1956. (Photo Courtesy GM Media Archive)

MOTORAMA 97

# CHAPTER FOUR: THE GM MOTORAMA OF 1954

*This letter to Bill Mitchell reported on the planned use of two Oldsmobile F-88s a July 1956 Shriners Parade, the original show car used for the Motorama (SO 1939) and Harley Earl's "XP-20 Car Number Two" (SO 90020). The letter went on to state that Earl's car was to be repainted white and that upon its "return to Styling, approximately July 16, it will be restored for use by Mr. Earl." The body was stripped of its layers of paint and repainted white. The original F-88 had already been repainted white by this time. This is most likely the parade in which "F-88 Number One" was damaged by an engine compartment fire. (Photo Courtesy GM Media Archive)*

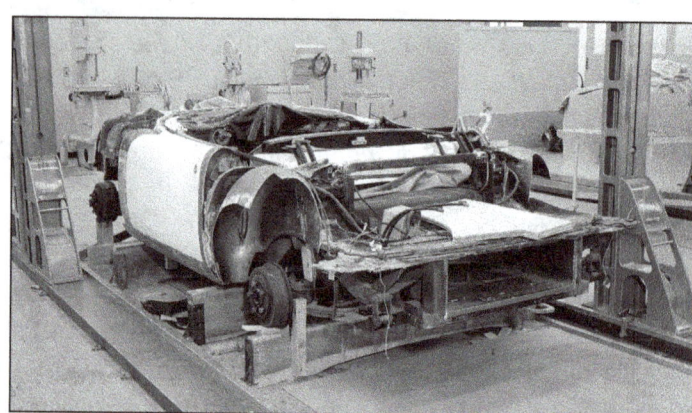

*This F-88 (SO 90020) had the front and rear portions of its body cut away in order to update the car to the Mk. II. Past references have said the car was "rebodied," which implies a total body replacement. (Photo Courtesy GM Media Archive)*

*Here are Harley Earl's freshly restyled F-88 Mk. II and his Le Sabre. The occupants' names and the occasion are not known. (Photo Courtesy GM Media Archive)*

in design to that of the 1954 Cutlass. The exposed oil coolers were deleted and a standard rocker panel was installed. It also had a hardtop that resembled a convertible top with a wraparound rear window for use in cold weather. It was powered by what must have been an awesomely powerful engine for the day: a supercharged twin-carb Rocket V-8.

This car continued to undergo various changes, such as the addition of a white stripe across the hood along with various grille changes. It was later repainted white prior to appearing in a 1956 Shriners Parade in Lansing along with the original F-88 (also repainted white) in July 1956. (During this time, the F-88 displayed on the GM Motorama circuit reportedly was damaged by an engine compartment fire and was subsequently salvaged.)

Next, SO 90020 was partially rebodied as the 1957 F-88 Mk. II. It was given a monotone color scheme of metallic blue. Its front end (which resembled that of a 1958 Corvette) featured quad headlights and a blacked-out grille with OLDSMOBILE in individual chrome-plated letters spread across it. At the rear were tail fins that were low in height and stopped well short of the rear of the car. It was never shown at a GM Motorama. The final disposition of this rendition of the F-88 remains unknown. However, an enthusiast has built a virtually perfect replica of this unique car.

Harley Earl also used another F-88 (probably SO 1768) painted bright red for personal transportation. It does not appear to have served as a major show car although it did appear at various public events such as the SCCA road races at Andrews Air Force Base and Atterbury Air Force Base in May 1954 according to a story published in the October 2003 issue of *Collectible Automobile*. Apparently no documentation exists regarding this particular F-88 at the GM Heritage Center. The fate of this car is unknown.

Sherrod Skinner's metallic blue 1954 F-88 (SO 2264) was built in the middle of 1954. It lacked the looping quarter-panel molding and quarter-panel vents installed on other F-88s as well as the vents in the windshield header and cowl. It also had upholstery with wider pleats and engineering refinements incorporated into

*Here is a rare color photo of Harley Earl's red F-88, which was on display at the "Dome Show," (year unknown) a reference to the domed GM Design building that was formally dedicated in May 1956. That provides a rough estimate for when this photograph could have been taken. (Photo Courtesy GM Design Center)*

# CHAPTER FOUR: THE GM MOTORAMA OF 1954

*This photo of Sherrod Skinner's F-88 posed with a curved-dash Oldsmobile is interesting because, according to GM Media Archive's records, this photo was taken in 1957 and represents the latest known date for which his car was still in existence. (Photo Courtesy GM Media Archive)*

it. Like Harley Earl's car (SO 2292), Skinner's received the Whirl-Away transmission. This F-88 appeared several times on the Parade of Progress tour (in 1955 and 1956) and at dealerships, too. Its fate is not known.

### And . . . SO 90388

Harley Earl received one more F-88 (XP-88/SO 90388) as a farewell gift when he retired as GM design chief. The 1959 F-88 Mk. III was the ultimate version of the series. The fiberglass-bodied car was equipped with a stainless steel retractable top, wraparound windshield, tubular frame combined with a 1959 Olds front suspension, 1958 Olds engine with a special intake and twin Solex side-draft carburetors, cross-flow aluminum radiator with twin cooling fans, new Saginaw variable-ratio power steering gear, and experimental automatic transmission.

*Sherrod Skinner, GM vice president of the accessory group (and the former general manager of the Olds division) received this F-88 (SO 2264). The metallic blue car was used as a show car for a time. It appeared on the Parade of Progress tour in 1955 and 1956. (Photo Courtesy GM Media Archive)*

The transmission was a modified Hydra-Matic with six forward speeds made possible by a 3-speed automatic gear set combined with a 2-speed rear axle. The experimental transmission proved to be troublesome and was replaced with a regular Hydra-Matic. Prior to the carburetor setup being installed, an experimental Rochester fuel-injection system was fitted. However, it too, proved to be troublesome. The dealer near Harley Earl's Palm Beach, Florida, home did not have the expertise needed to work on these complex systems, which likely led General Motors to retrofit more conventional components.

After Harley Earl died (April 10, 1969), his F-88 Mk. III was reportedly intended to be displayed in an as-yet-to-be-built NASCAR museum. (Earl and NASCAR founder, Bill France, had known each other for years.) Ultimately, though, Bill Mitchell allegedly asked NASCAR officials to return the Mk. III to General Motors. Some time later it was trucked back to Warren, Michigan, and the car was ordered to be scrapped by Irv Rybicki or Bill Mitchell, reportedly due to its deteriorated condition. Whether it really was scrapped or not remains a controversial matter.

### The Mystery of SO 2265

This does not conclude the subject of the F-88, though. GM Styling ordered one more, XP-20/SO 2265. This car is actually the subject of a well-written award-winning story by Michael Lamm for the October 2003 issue of *Collectible Automobile*. His research was based on interviews of those who were with General Motors during the years of the GM Motorama. Unfortunately, their decades-old recollections have since proven to present a somewhat inaccurate account of this car and the other F-88s.

Lamm's article ended with the conclusion that the only known F-88 to still exist is probably the GM Motorama display car, but carefully noted, "We will likely never know with certainty unless some documentation exists and can be found at General Motors to confirm this supposition." Supporting Lamm's conclusion in part was the presence of green paint in the wheel wells and floorpans (just as the original show car had) according to one of the car's past owners. The most important clue seems to be the presence of cowl vents; the original F-88 show car had this feature while the others did not.

With the assistance of former Olds engineer John Perkins, collector Joe Bortz, vintage home movie film shot by Oldsmobile enthusiast Don Baron, Ed Lucas (a former owner of this car), Michael Lamm's story, and some surviving GM documents, I am able to present the following brief history of SO 2265. To say the least, it is a unique car.

*Although there are two lovely models in this Photo, only the F-88 can be identified. The car built for Sherrod Skinner got extensive use as a show car on the Parade of Progress tour in 1955 and 1956. This location was likely Stockton, California; the date was March 1956. (Photo Courtesy GM Media Archive)*

*The subject of this May 1958 letter issued by the GM Tech Center and in the files of the GM Heritage Center is about "F-88 Number One," which was also referred to as the Motorama show car in earlier documents. Perhaps this car still exists. (Photo Courtesy GM Media Archive)*

## CHAPTER FOUR: THE GM MOTORAMA OF 1954

Harley Earl received one more F-88, the red Mk. III version shown here with the Le Sabre and 1959 Cadillac Cyclone. His 1959 F-88 Mk. III was equipped with a fuel-injected Olds V-8 and a retractable hardtop. (Photo Courtesy GM Media Archive)

In March 1955 a set of crates with unusual contents sent from GM Styling arrived at the home of E. L. Cord, who founded the Cord Corporation, which among other things produced the Cord 810/812 and the Auburn Speedster. The crates contained nearly all of the parts necessary to assemble a 1954 Oldsmobile F-88 along with almost enough spares, including extra doors and deck lids, to build a second one (minus a body). Many of the parts, according to later owners, showed signs of having been installed on another car at one time (i.e., remnants of caulking on retainer spikes). The only components Cord needed to complete the car were a Corvette frame and an engine.

A plausible theory as to why Cord received the crated F-88 is that he likely saw the gold car when it was shown in Los Angeles at the Pan Pacific Auditorium (a rental facility that he owned) and probably inquired about the possibility of obtaining the car. It was of course not for sale, so Harley Earl arranged a compromise. Also included with the parts were scores of blueprints needed to properly assemble the F-88. No one at General Motors, as general rule, would have been allowed to remove such blueprints from GM's control; it was an offense subject to dismissal. Only Harley Earl could have done such a thing; he seemed to be able to do almost anything he wanted. Success and rank has its privileges.

Cord, who died in 1974, never did assemble his F-88. Instead, the crated components went to the second private owner, a California resident, and then on to a third owner, also of California. Soon thereafter, classic car dealer Leo Gephardt bought the unassembled car. By this time a Corvette chassis with a Blue Flame Six came with the crated parts.

Gephardt then sold the F-88 to an Oldsmobile dealer in Ohio who reportedly was going to assemble the car and use it to publicize his dealership. That never happened

The only F-88 known to exist was sold for $3.24 million at the 2005 Barrett-Jackson Auction in Scottsdale, Arizona, and is the car originally sent to E. L. Cord in crates. Cord (and later owners) did not assemble it; it was finally put together in the 1990s. (Photo Courtesy GM Media Archive)

and the car was purchased next by Ed Lucas who later traded it back to Leo Gephardt for a Duesenberg chassis. Gephardt sold the car again, this time to Lon Krueger who finished assembling it.

In December 1990 Krueger sold it to Don Williams of the Blackhawk Museum who quickly resold it at the 1991 Barrett-Jackson auction in Scottsdale, Arizona. The high bidder, collector Bruce Lustman, kept the car for about six years and during that time showed it at Pebble Beach.

In 1997, Lustman placed the F-88 on consignment with Don Williams who placed it in the Blackhawk Collection until it was sold to collector Gordon Apker of Washington state. His F-88 gained fame as the car that sold for a hefty $3.2 million at the 2005 Barrett-Jackson auction in Scottsdale, Arizona. The winning bidder, Discovery Channel founder John Hendricks, still owns the car, which is on display at his Gateway Automobile Museum in Gateway, Colorado.

So, is there any chance the body of this F-88 is that of the original car? Collector Joe Bortz inspected the "Cord" F-88 prior to it being assembled in Arizona. He saw a body that had not yet had its panel openings (hood, doors, trunk lid) cut out. In fact, the suggestion has been proposed that the body of the car sent to Cord was a backup rather than one molded exclusively for him.

A copy of an interoffice memorandum sent to Bill Mitchell, and in the possession of former Olds engineer John Perkins, is revealing. The memo details the use of a pair of F-88s for an upcoming Shriners Parade. The June 6, 1956, memo begins, "It is our understanding that Mr. A. Ross has arranged for Mr. Earl's F-88 Oldsmobile XP-20 Car Number Two to be used with the Oldsmobile Division XP-20 Car Number One (1954 Motorama Show Car) in the Shriner's [sic] convention for the week of July 6 to 14." The date of this memo is almost fifteen months after E. L. Cord received his F-88 in crates.

My interview with Ed Lucas backed up Bortz' statement that the body had not had the doors, hood, or trunk openings cut out. Also according to Lucas, one of the three different combination bumper/grilles included in the crates of F-88 parts showed clear evidence of having been subjected to high heat, such as a fire, although it was repairable. (The scorched one was the correct one. One of them, which was not chrome-plated, was clearly a spare for the 1954 Cutlass. The other one appeared similar to a

**The fold-down armrest in the center of the rear seat of the 1954 Landau contains a cocktail shaker and goblets. These had been separated for several years before they were restored and reunited with the car.**

The 1954 Buick Landau has had several owners since General Motors sold it for $700 in 1959. Bill Warner, the founder of the Amelia Island Concours d'Elegance, performed a partial restoration of the unique car. Houston attorney John O'Quinn (now deceased), owned the car in 2008, when this photo was taken. It is currently owned by Bob Coker who has since replaced the wire wheels with a set of turbine-style wheel covers nearly identical to the unique set that was stolen in the early 1960s.

The passenger compartment of the Landau is upholstered in tan leather with cloth inserts while the front section is upholstered in dark blue leather. A limousine-style, retractable glass partition divides the front and rear compartments. The original leather upholstery of the front seat has since been replaced.

## CHAPTER FOUR: THE GM MOTORAMA OF 1954

later configuration of the F-88.) Also scorched was one of the two windshield frames supplied by GM Styling. This suggests the original F-88 (XP-20/SO 1939) was salvaged and those parts were forwarded to Cord.

Therefore, the bumper/grille of the only known F-88 in existence is the one originally installed on the Motorama display car. Regardless of what components compose the only F-88 currently known to exist, it is a fascinating automobile with a unique and fascinating history.

According to Joe Bortz, who over a span of many years, has spoken to numerous people associated with the GM Motorama cars, has also heard the story of an F-88 catching on fire. Ed Lucas, however, provides stronger evidence.

Many years ago, GM stylist Jack Humbert showed to Lucas (they shared a storage facility along with GM stylist Dave Holls) a set of photos of an F-88 on fire! They were taken by the passenger in the car who was the son of the driver after it was immediately driven off the road and parked in a driveway or next to the curb at the first sign of the fire. According to Lucas, the blaze was extinguished before it completely engulfed the F-88, but not before serious damage had been done. Lucas spoke to other GM employees over the years who confirmed the original F-88 was damaged by a fire and that it was indeed salvaged.

Based upon these facts, SO 2265 could not be the original F-88 dream car nor could it have that car's body.

### What About SO 90456?

There is one more mystery surrounding the F-88 Motorama show car. Documentation at the GM Heritage Center makes reference to "F-88 Number One," which was also referred to as the Motorama show car in prior work orders. Work orders from the summer of *1958* detail a "refurbishing" program for F-88 Number One, but as SO 90456.

Assuming that F-88 Number One is the car that caught on fire (and all indications seem to prove it was), it was not simply salvaged and its remains scrapped. These work order memorandums seem to show that the car was refurbished in the late 1950s. Therefore, it must be assumed to have an unknown fate.

## Buick Landau and Wildcat II: Going Retro and Going Wild

Buick was represented with a retro design on one of the two dream cars for the 1954 GM Motorama: the four-door Landau (SO 2308). The Cobalt Blue (a 1953 Cadillac color) Landau began as either a pilot line or early production 127-inch-wheelbase Series 70 Roadmaster. The elegant Landau's most distinctive features included a folding rear roof section and a padded, detachable trunk.

The Wildcat II (SO 1940) was a radical departure for Buick and once again General Motors used the Corvette as inspiration to create a bold, new, two-seat sports car for another division. The Wildcat II was indeed an all-new car and it had virtually nothing in common with the Wildcat I, which had been shown during the preceding GM Motorama tour.

### The Landau

The passenger compartment of the Landau was upholstered in tan leather with cloth inserts while the front section was upholstered in dark blue leather. A limousine-style, retractable-glass partition divided the front and rear compartments. The car was equipped with power windows, power brakes, power steering, radio, and Dynaflow automatic transmission. Furthermore, a fold-down armrest in the center of the rear seat contained a cocktail shaker and goblets. The spare tire was stored in a compartment accessed via a fold-down, center section of the rear bumper. Special turbine-style wheel covers with red, white, and blue centers were fabricated for this unique show car.

Because of space limitations, the Landau was not shown at the opening venue of the 1954 GM Motorama, the Waldorf-Astoria, but did join the circuit with the next show in Miami.

### Life after the Motorama

The Landau was used as an executive courtesy car in New York City after it was no longer needed as a show car. Around mid-1954 it was actually fitted with its folding landau top.

While using the Landau as a courtesy car, Harlow Curtice complained of its ride qualities and Buick engineers made appropriate adjustments. Such matters were listed in a logbook maintained on the car. This story was confirmed in a 1980s *Automobile Quarterly* article about dream cars in which the Landau was detailed: "After the show circuit ended, Buick kept the Landau and used it as an executive courtesy car in New York City. Its original turbine-style wheel covers were stolen during this time. A logbook was updated regularly, which detailed the maintenance history and changes Buick made to the car over time. Harlow Curtice complained of the ride qualities of the car and Buick engineers made appropriate adjustments.

*The elegant Buick Landau's most distinctive features included a folding rear roof section and a padded, detachable trunk complete with functional leather hold-down belts reminiscent of the landaulets of the early classic era. (Photo Courtesy GM Media Archive)*

*The Wildcat II and the Skylark made a spectacular pair at the 1954 GM Motorama. The Skylark shown here was reportedly painted Lido Green. (Photo Courtesy GM Media Archive)*

CHAPTER FOUR: THE GM MOTORAMA OF 1954

*The 1954 Buick Wildcat II was originally built with Roto-Static front wheels similar to those of the 1953 Wildcat I. However, before it was shown at the GM Motorama, Skylark-type wire wheels were fitted. (Photo Courtesy GM Media Archive)*

"Around 1959, a GM executive in Flint, Michigan, convinced General Motors to let him have use of the car, which they did with the proviso that it be returned to them. The executive believed that if he ever returned it, the Landau would be scrapped so he kept it and later sold the car to a Clauson, Michigan, resident. This owner kept the Buick for about a year and a half then sold it to American Motors engineer Del DeRees. That was in 1965. DeRees sold it in 1982."

Most of that story is correct, but not quite all of it. A more revealing history came to light as the result of a magazine article I wrote for Hemmings Classic Car (HCC). The two-part article appearing in the March and April issues of HCC caught the eye of Robert K. Blair, the son of the "GM executive" mentioned above. Specifically, the small photo of the Buick Landau appearing on page 73 of the April issue brought back a flood of memories to him. He wrote a letter to HCC about the article and the Landau, which was printed in the magazine's "Recaps" column in the June issue. That in turn led to details about the show car that were known to very few and finally to Robert being reunited with the Landau for the first time in more than 45 years.

Robert's letter began, "I am a big GM fan and the son of a former Buick executive, R. F. Blair. Dad served as both district and regional manager for Buick in the mid-1950s. So I was surprised to see a car we owned in the Motorama article in HCC #43, the Landau."

The rest of his letter revealed some post-Motorama history about the Landau: "My dad was promoted to assistant general manager of the Eastern Region in 1956. His office was on 57th Street in Manhattan and when he was in town, he drove his company car to the office . . . One day he drove home a very special car . . . it [had been] used to chauffeur Harlow Curtice around New York when he was in town.

"The car languished in Buick's midtown garage and my dad asked about it in 1957. He was told to sell it and bought the car for $750 with only 700 miles on it!"

Robert wrote that he got to drive the special car on several occasions including his senior prom and noted, ". . . what a stir the car caused!" It also led to another "stir" when the unique wheel covers were stolen during the evening of his senior prom! A set of stock Buick wheel covers were purchased and substituted. When his father was transferred back to Flint in 1961 he elected to sell the Landau; that was the last time Robert saw the car until October 10, 2008.

*Ownership Trail*

The Landau eventually became part of the Bortz Auto Collection before being sold to Bill Warner, the founder and chairman of the annual Amelia Island Concours d'Elegance. A partial restoration begun by Warner in 2004 was completed in time to be shown at Pebble Beach in 2006. A set of Skylark wire wheels was installed during the restoration. Missing at the time were the cocktail shaker and goblets kept in the rear fold-down armrest.

In another twist of fate, these items were listed on the Internet auction website eBay.com in early 2008. The high bidder, the late Charles D. Barnette of Texarkana, Texas, had, at the time, already arranged for the Landau to be displayed in October at the Four States Antique Auto Museum located on the Arkansas side of the city. Barnette had these items restored before returning them to the Landau at a special ceremony at the museum where Robert K. Blair spoke about his experiences with the car.

Furthermore, Barnette discovered that the wheel covers used for the 1959 DeSoto were remarkably similar to those that were custom-made for the Landau. Therefore, he had a set modified to more closely resemble the long-lost originals and donated them as well.

At the time this book was written, Bob Coker of the Coker Tire family owned the one-of-a-kind Buick. Coker installed a set of steel rims with the modified DeSoto wheel covers and installed the Skylark-type wire wheels on another Buick from the 1955 GM Motorama. (More information on that car appears in Chapter Five.) The odometer showed the Buick had logged only 24,000 miles with nearly all of them occurring after General Motors sold the car. The car was sold not long after this book was published.

## Wildcat II

One of the objectives of this dream car's design, according to Ivan Wiles, the general manager of Buick and vice president of General Motors, was to make a sports car that was typically American, completely free of any European influence." Hence, the Wildcat II was billed as "an American Adventure in Tomorrow's Design."

Buick had an established reputation as a builder of upscale luxury sedans and rather conservative styling; the

*Four side-draft carburetors were installed to feed the fuel/air mixture to the combustion chambers of the Wildcat II's 220-hp 322-ci V-8.*

*The interior of the 1954 Wildcat II was upholstered in white leather. Brushed-aluminum inserts and chrome trim decorated the door panels. A gauge cluster housed within twin pods sits on a pedestal atop the transmission tunnel.*

*Headlights were located more traditionally on the Wildcat II after the 1954 GM Motorama ended. The car was titled to Harlow Curtice for a few years, after which it was donated to the Alfred P. Sloan Museum in 1976. Note that the leaping Wildcat hood ornament is missing. It was probably broken and discarded long ago.*

# CHAPTER FOUR: THE GM MOTORAMA OF 1954

*Here is a rare view of the 1954 Buick Wildcat II with its convertible top in the "up" position. The convertible top was not installed until after that year's GM Motorama tour was completed. (Photo Courtesy Steve Wolken Collection)*

Wildcat II broke that mold and showed the car-buying public what was possible. Buick's chief designer, Ned Nichols, headed the Wildcat II project. He created a genuine sports car; it was the only one with the Buick name built in the 1950s. He began with the specifications laid out in an experimental order submitted by the Technical Data Section of the Buick Engineering Department on May 19, 1953, which gave the basic design criteria of a wheelbase of 100 inches, a front tread of 59 inches, and a rear tread measurement of 57 inches. The general description of the Wildcat II was that it would be, "a special sport type car to be shown at the Waldorf show in January 1954."

## Body Styling

A special paint color, Electric Blue, adorned the sporty fiberglass body of the 1954 Wildcat II. For the 1956 model year, Electric Blue was among the color choices offered for all Buicks.

The radical Wildcat incorporated such distinctive features as biplane bumpers similar to those on the 1934 Cadillac. The headlamps were mounted on the front edge of the fender cowl that resided under the hood/fender combination. It had free-standing parking lamps, and "flying-wing" fenders with polished inner fenders and engine compartment heat vents, as well as hidden fuel fillers beneath the tail lamp assemblies. Nerf bars were used in back rather than a conventional rear bumper.

Skylark-type wire wheels added a refined and dignified style to the Wildcat II; the use of these wheels was decided upon later in the design process. Initially, GM Styling was to install a set of newly designed Roto-Static hubcaps; these were solid hubcaps in front and nearly smooth discs covered the rear wheels. Why the switch was made (prior to the car's debut at the Waldorf-Astoria) is unknown.

The hood lifted from the front and was hinged at the back. But the Wildcat II had its hood and fenders

*In January 1955, the 1954 Wildcat II appeared at the Los Angeles Auto Show held at the Pan Pacific Auditorium. This publicity photo shows actress Jayne Mansfield sitting on the show car. (Photo Courtesy Los Angeles Public Library archives)*

integrated into one unit and lifted as a single piece. The front fenders were open so the suspension components. Therefore, many of the suspension parts were chrome-plated for cosmetic reasons. Ned Nichols' "ventiports" had become nearly traditional by 1954 and a set was placed on the upper portion of the Wildcat's front fenders.

The modified 220-hp, 322-ci V-8 featured four side-draft 2-barrel carburetors with flame arresters, and powered the 3,770-pound car. It was coupled to a twin-turbine Dynaflow transmission; rear-end gearing had a ratio of 3.6:1. Exhaust exited through a dual system 2 inches in diameter with a crossover pipe, dynamic flow mufflers, and 1¾-inch tailpipes. The Wildcat II's suspension consisted of four coil springs, direct-acting shocks, and an 11/16-inch-diameter front stabilizer bar. Brakes were 12-inch cast-iron drums with an effective area of 207.5 square inches.

## Interior Comfort

The Wildcat II interior was upholstered in white leather, including the bucket seats and dash pad. A speaker for the remotely controlled, trunk-mounted radio was mounted between the seats on the rear bulkhead. Brushed-aluminum inserts and chrome trim decorated the door panels. The Wildcat II's body-colored carpeting and lower dash contrasted nicely with the largely white interior. A gauge cluster housed within twin pods sat on a pedestal atop the Wildcat II's transmission tunnel. Additional instrumentation was provided on a small console between the seats, which also carried the gear selector lever.

As a Buick, the Wildcat was well appointed including the convertible top, which was a fully automatic electric unit. The automatic top, however, was installed after the Motorama tour came to an end. It was operated via a single switch on the dash. When the side power windows were up, they interfered with the closing of the power top. So the convertible top system automatically lowered the side windows when the top was raised. Then the side windows were raised. A set of limit switches mounted underneath the door glass mechanisms ensured that the top did not operate unless the windows were lowered.

## By Any Other Color . . .

A second Wildcat II was reportedly built. This possibility was even suggested in the experimental order submitted by the Technical Data Section of the Buick Engineering Department. At the end of the first page was the directive to build the Wildcat II as "runable, so that Mr. Curtice and Mr. Wiles might decide whether or not a Number Two is to be built for their use." Assuming a second car was actually built, the likelihood exists that it was destroyed in a highway crash. Automotive writer Terry Boyce heard a story to that effect while interviewing a long-retired GM Styling executive several years ago. The source, who had been a junior stylist at GM Styling when the original Wildcat II appeared, said the second car was painted gold, with a white interior.

The accident happened somewhere "out West," the interviewee recalled. "There was absolutely nothing left of it," he added. However, Boyce noticed the former executive seemed to be experiencing a failing memory. Furthermore, after intensive research, I have yet to discover GM documentation related to a second Wildcat II, or an accident involving such a car. Therefore, the preceding anecdotal report must be considered unproven as long as solid evidence supporting the story is lacking.

However, there is one comment in a shop order memorandum dated September 22, 1954, that implies the existence of another Wildcat II Concerning the construction of a removable hardtop for Harley Earl's F-88, S.O. 2292:

*General Motors' dream cars were quite substantial, as shown by this photo of the nearly completed interior of the 1954 Cadillac Park Avenue. Note the steering shaft sticking through the steering column, the sliding door handles. Even a dimmer switch was included; far from the myth of the cars being just "shells."*

"Approved design drawings were turned over . . . for the roof including the latest windshield frame (similar to the procedure followed on Mr. Curtice's Wildcat #1)."

Why specify "Number One" if only one of the cars was constructed? Perhaps the phrase "Curtice's Wildcat #1" was a reference to his 1953 Wildcat with the hardtop. The blue Wildcat II was registered to Harlow Curtice for some years, and even an operations manual was printed for him with his name on the front cover. His daughter is reported to have had use of the car at the Curtice Florida home during the summer of 1955.

The Wildcat II was repainted a metallic tan or rose-beige color during the time it was titled to Curtice. The car was still this color when it was donated to the Alfred P. Sloan Museum in Flint, Michigan, in 1976. Many years later it was restored to its original color scheme. Photographs of the Wildcat II in the tan/beige color often lead to claims of two cars having been built, but these are unquestionably the differing color schemes of one car.

Another interesting anecdote related to the Electric Blue color of the Wildcat II is that it appears to be the same exclusive shade Harlow Curtice specified for several other GM cars he allegedly drove, including a special-order 1940 Buick Roadmaster convertible now owned by Terry Boyce.

### Cadillac Park Avenue, La Espada and El Camino: Links in the Chain

Three dream cars bore the prestigious name of Cadillac for the 1954 GM Motorama: Park Avenue (SO 1930), La Espada (XP-27, SO 1928), and El Camino (SO 1929). The Park Avenue was similar in concept to the 1953 Cadillac Orleans and was a link in the chain leading to the 1957–1958 Eldorado Brougham while the other two dream cars were each akin to the 1953 Cadillac Le Mans.

### Park Avenue

The Park Avenue, which sat on a Series Sixty Special frame, was described in a GM-issued press release as "Seizing the imagination of even the most conservative" Cadillac owner. Its dark Antoinette Blue lower body was trimmed with bright chrome and had a hand-brushed aluminum roof. The sedan dream car measured 230.1 inches in overall length, 58.3 inches in overall height, and 80 inches in overall width. Essentially, it was the second rendition of a series of prototypes, which culminated in the limited-production Eldorado Brougham of 1957–1958.

Not all of the ideas exhibited in the Park Avenue's design, though, went into that of the Eldorado Brougham. Below the rear deck lid of the Park Avenue was a compartment housing the spare tire, which could be removed by lowering a bright chrome-trimmed door that also served as a bumperette and license-plate mounting. Most of the dream cars of the 1954 GM Motorama had this feature, but it appeared only in production on the Chevrolet Cameo and GMC Suburban Carrier pickups, which went into production the following year.

The Park Avenue's tiered drive, stop, and park lights were not put into production, but its fin shape (without the forward taper of the trailing edge) was adapted to the 1957 and 1958 Cadillacs. However, the design of the twin exhaust ports was used on the 1955 Eldorado.

Upholstery for the interior of the Park Avenue consisted of monotone gray leathers, including imported English calf with an unusual grain and suede-like nap texture for the inserts. Brushed and bright chrome trim provided additional styling accents. Instrumentation was set in a gray leather-covered panel and was clustered around the chrome and brushed-aluminum steering column.

As for the 1954 Park Avenue's disposition, according to, *History of Cadillac's Motorama Dream Cars*, released by General Motors on March 28, 1956, the car "was turned over to the Cadillac Engineering Department for experimental purposes in April of 1955." Presumably it was later scrapped. Its latest auto show appearance that I found was at the 1955 Los Angeles International Automobile Show in late January. There was no mention of the car's appearance in any references beyond the date it was sent to the Cadillac Engineering Department.

*The 1954 Cadillac Park Avenue was painted Antoinette Blue and had a hand-brushed aluminum roof. This dream car was another stepping stone in the creation of the limited-production 1957–1958 Eldorado Brougham. (Photo Courtesy GM Media Archive)*

*Except for being a convertible, the La Espada was identical to the El Camino. Two of these dream cars were built; this one was painted Apollo Gold, a stock Cadillac color. (Photo Courtesy GM Media Archive)*

Incidentally, the Buick Motor Division adopted the name Park Avenue years later, but only after Cadillac used the moniker for a short-deck version of its 1962 and 1963 four-door hardtop models.

## La Espada and El Camino

The nearly identical sporty, two-passenger La Espada and El Camino were a convertible and a closed coupe, respectively. They each had a wheelbase spanning 115 inches and an overall length of 200.6 inches, and both were said to be powered by a 1954 Cadillac 331-ci V-8 of 230 hp. Like the Park Avenue, these two dream cars had dramatic fins, aluminum alloy turbine-blade wheels designed to aid in brake cooling, air conditioning, and a spare tire compartment concealed by a chrome-trimmed door underneath the deck lid. (The general design of the turbine-blade wheels was used in the form of wheel covers in 1961 and 1962.)

*The aircraft-inspired turbine-powered 1954 Firebird I occupied a turntable for that year's GM Motorama. In the background are the 1954 Oldsmobile Cutlass (left) and the 1954 Cadillac El Camino (right). (Photo Courtesy GM Media Archive)*

CHAPTER FOUR: THE GM MOTORAMA OF 1954

The rear-end styling of the 1954 Park Avenue appears similar to that of the 1955 Eldorado. As with the El Camino and La Espada, the center section of the rear bumper dropped down for access to the spare tire.

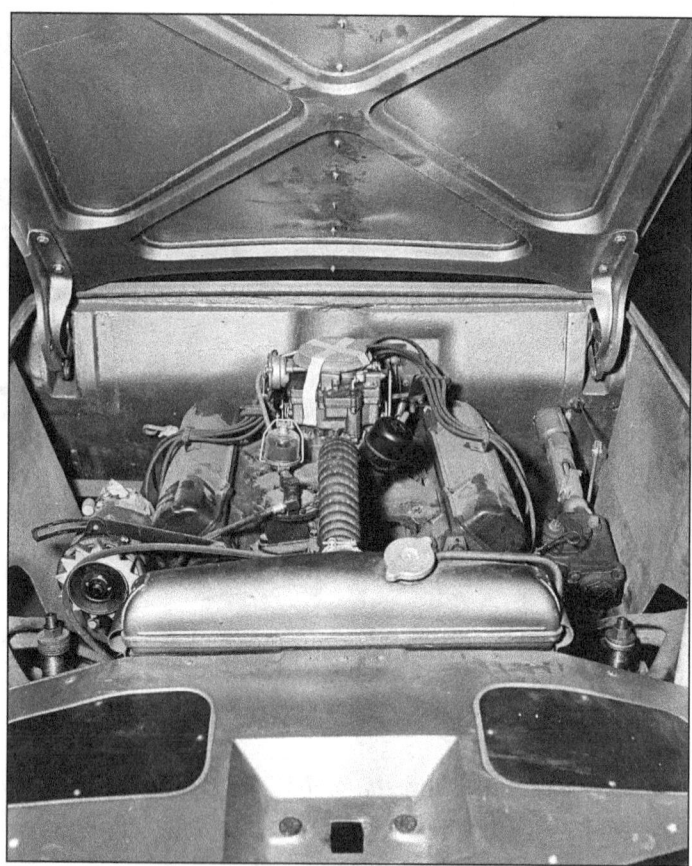

A persistent myth exists that GM's dream cars typically did not have an engine installed. This photo of the engine compartment of the Cadillac El Camino (or possibly of the silver La Espada) should help put an end to that tale. (Photo Courtesy Detroit Public Library Automotive History Collection)

A trio of stainless steel tumblers and a stainless steel thermos were stored in the center armrest of the back seat of the Park Avenue. (Photo Courtesy GM Heritage Center)

The interior of the La Espada (as well as that of the El Camino) shows aircraft-inspired features. Note the design of the gear selector lever. Controls for the air conditioning/heater and the radio, along with a cigarette lighter, armrest, and glove box were integrated into the console.

The 1954 Cadillac El Camino (Spanish for "the royal highway") was painted a distinctive pearlescent silver-gray and the bubble-type aircraft canopy-shaped roof was brushed aluminum coated with clear lacquer. Note the saber-spoke wheels. (Photo Courtesy Hillary Hess Collection)

This photograph of one of the La Espadas in the shop at GM Styling offers an excellent view of the car's rear-end styling design. The spare tire was stored behind the center section of the rear bumper, which dropped down for access; this was a feature of some European cars of the era. (Photo Courtesy GM Media Archive)

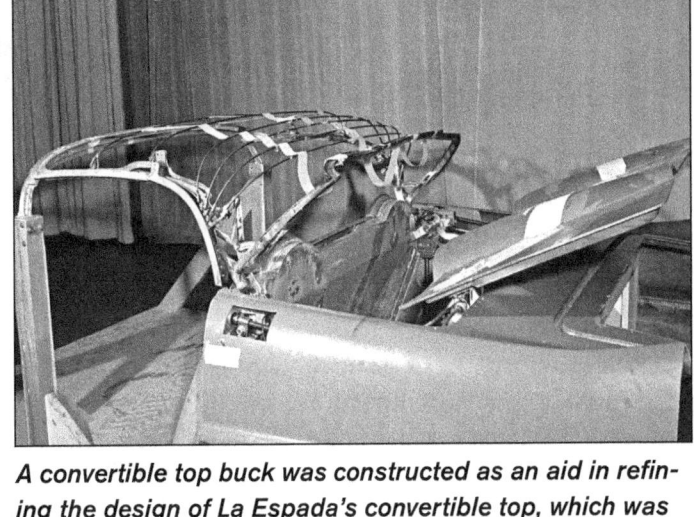

A convertible top buck was constructed as an aid in refining the design of La Espada's convertible top, which was said to produce a perfectly curved surface when in the up position. (Photo Courtesy GM Media Archive)

The Sword Silver La Espada was displayed at the GM Motorama at Chicago's International Amphitheatre. Some weeks earlier, the Apollo Gold car was shown at the same facility during the annual Chicago Auto Show. (Photo Courtesy GM Media Archive)

Both Cadillac La Espadas continued to be shown after the 1954 GM Motorama ended. Shown here is the Sword Silver example (SO 2136) on display at the Parade of Progress in Rochester, New York, on August 31, 1954. (Photo Courtesy GM Media Archive)

# CHAPTER FOUR: THE GM MOTORAMA OF 1954

*The Apollo Gold La Espada was shown concurrently with the Sword Silver car at separate venues on the Parade of Progress. This photograph was taken at a show in October or early November 1954, probably in Kentucky or Tennessee. An early curved-dash Oldsmobile is in the background. (Photo Courtesy GM Media Archive)*

Cadillac's press release regarding the La Espada stated the car was "a compact, well integrated, personalized type of car containing the traditional luxury, conveniences, quality of finish and fineness of materials traditionally identified with Cadillacs."

The interior of the La Espada and the El Camino was well appointed. The fuel, temperature, and oil gauges; ammeter; and clock were, according to Cadillac press releases, "scientifically engineered for perfect visual control."

The gear selector for both cars was an aircraft-style joystick mounted on a machine-ground, stainless steel trimmed tunnel between the seats. Controls for the air conditioner/heater and the radio, along with a cigarette lighter, armrest, and glove box, were integrated into the console. The air conditioner/heater system was high-tech for the day as it was operated through spectrum-lighted rheostatic controls, which was claimed to be a first for automotive use. The advanced setup allowed warmer temperatures to be indicated with shades of red while cooler settings were in shades of blue.

Other special features of the La Espada included a tachometer, Autronic-Eye automatic headlight dimmer (first offered on Cadillacs in 1952 then later for other GM cars), and convertible top. However, no photos with the top raised seem to have been taken, so whether or not a top was ever fitted is unknown. A functional convertible top buck (a wooden mockup) was constructed and tested, though. The convertible top well was concealed under a flush-fitting lid. The El Camino coupe was also equipped with tachometer and Autronic-Eye.

At one time, only one La Espada was thought to have been built and to have first appeared in Apollo Gold (a stock Cadillac color) with a black and yellow interior; it was then later repainted Sword Silver and reupholstered with a black and silver interior. However, these are clearly two separate cars as they appeared concurrently during the 1954 and 1955 Parade of Progress.

*General Motors continued to show the 1954 El Camino at least into 1956. This photograph shows the car on display at Kerrisdale Arena in Vancouver, British Columbia, in April 1955. (Photo Courtesy Vancouver Public Library)*

At least one La Espada was displayed into 1956 and included showings at the CNE (silver example) and major cities in Europe. What became of the two cars remains unknown. The Sword Silver car must have been functional based on an entry in the Shop Order book at the GM Heritage Center stating that it was for "H. Earl."

Designed by Dave Holls under the direction of Ed Glowacke, the El Camino was a two-seat fiberglass-bodied sports car that featured a bubble canopy and dramatic fins. It was very much like the La Espada; the major difference was its aircraft-inspired canopy formed of brushed aluminum and coated with clear lacquer.

The El Camino's exterior was painted pearlescent silver-gray and its interior was upholstered in gray leather (seats, door panels, and upper instrument panel). The headliner was perforated gray Naugahyde with sound-deadening qualities. The high-back bucket seats had integrated headrests that resided near the rear window. Gray nylon cord covered the El Camino's steering wheel. A brushed-aluminum insert added beauty and a sporty flavor to the instrument panel in front of the driver. In fact, brushed aluminum was used in abundance elsewhere in the interior just as it was on the La Espada.

The La Espada and the El Camino each had a recessed cellular grille guarded by massive sweeping front bumpers with resilient vinyl to cushion shocks and prevent scuffing of the chrome plus a double-humped rear deck flaring into the bucket seats. Another prominent feature shared by both cars was a special insignia on the quarter panels. The insignia on the driver's side served as the fuel filler door. The red, white, and blue insignia was the same as that of the GM Air Transport Division and served to underscore the aircraft-inspired styling of these two dream cars.

Neither the La Espada nor the El Camino went into production, but some of their styling attributes did appear in production on the 1955 and 1956 Cadillacs, such as gull-wing bumpers, wheels, etc. The quad headlight setup took a little longer (1957) as some state laws had to be changed to make it legal in all states.

The El Camino was shown in the United States and Canada into 1956 and perhaps longer. Reportedly, this masterpiece of the 1954 GM Motorama was crushed. The name lived on when Chevrolet applied it to its car-based truck starting in 1959. Only one El Camino is known to have been built, although the possibility remains that a second identical car could have also been built.

Both the La Espada and the El Camino drew a lot of attention, but just as was the case with the Le Mans, people who were serious about buying a Cadillac were more interested in owning a car similar to the Park Avenue rather than a sporty Cadillac.

## GM Firebird I: Turbine Research

Although some Motorama concept cars subtly integrated aircraft cues and styling into the overall design, the Firebird series of cars boldly looked like aircraft with wheels. The 1954 GM Firebird (XP-21, SO 1921) was later renamed the Firebird I after its successor, the Firebird II, was built. But these cars didn't just resemble jet-powered fighter planes, they used the same type of engines: turbine jet engines.

### *Styling Cues*

The delta-winged F4D Skyray interceptor substantially influenced the shape of the Firebird I. While on an airline flight, Harley Earl read a magazine story about the F4D, and that inspired him to build the vehicle. Incidentally, General Motors originally intended to use the name "Thunderbird" for its XP-21, but Ford trademarked it first, thus another name had to be chosen.

Styling for the Firebird was not simply about getting noticed and underscoring the fact that a turbine engine was in place. The Firebird was expected to provide a chance to test the little-understood concept of aerodynamics for land vehicles. A nearly exact, scale model of the research car was sent to the California Institute of Technology for extensive wind tunnel testing to refine the shape of the Firebird's body as well as find the most favorable brake flap angles and the best amount of negative angle of attack for the wings.

*This photograph provides a good look at the speed brakes that were to be used to assist in slowing the Firebird from high speed. (Photo Courtesy GM Media Archive)*

# Other Notable Show Cars of the 1954 GM Motorama

Several specially prepared production cars were among the sights of the 1954 GM Motorama. One was a two-toned Chieftain four-door sedan X-Ray Car. See-through plastic panels allowed viewers to see the inner mechanical and structural details of a Pontiac. A large board behind this car carried the banner, "Inside Story of Pontiac Quality." At the push of a button visitors could see various moving parts of the car light up via fluorescent and black lights.

Another show car was an Oldsmobile Super Eighty-Eight Holiday painted in highly iridescent turquoise with a blue-white top. Its upholstery was ivory leather with a dark blue nylon waffle-weave insert.

Also making appearances at some or all of the venues for the 1954 GM Motorama were a few regular-production Buicks with non-standard features. One of them was a pearlescent green (lower body) and pearl white (top) Super Riviera with gold-plated interior hardware (door handles, instrument paneling, and roof bows) and gold brocade tapestry upholstery with yellow pearlescent leather inserts. The Super Riviera's instrument panel was in matching yellow with a dark green insert.

A Coupe de Ville (left, foreground) and a Sixty Special (left, background) were dressed up in non-production color schemes and posed with the La Espada inside the "Cadillac room" at the Waldorf-Astoria. (Photo Courtesy GM Media Archive)

It was also equipped with the optional power windows and 40-spoke wire wheels that were standard issue on the Skylark A Century sedan. The Skylark was yet another special display. It was painted in pearlescent yellow with a metallic green top and had seats covered in pearlescent yellow leather with green nylon inserts and a yellow leather headliner.

A Buick Century was painted in the stock combination of Titan Red with an Artic White top. The interior reportedly consisted of dark green, Swiss-dot nylon upholstery combined with light green metallic pleated bolsters.

A Roadmaster sedan was painted an attractive turquoise on its lower body and white on its top. It had a special interior consisting of turquoise nylon for the seats, turquoise leather for the door panels, and a headliner of white leather. Other features of this car included power brakes, power steering, power front seat, special thick carpeting, and a turquoise instrument panel insert.

Three special Cadillacs were on exhibit. One of them, which was shown at the Waldorf-Astoria and perhaps elsewhere, was a Fleetwood Sixty Special painted pearlescent gold and equipped with an off-white long-grain leather landau top. This car's interior was upholstered in white leather and gold fabric. A GM press release noted this particular car as having a pearlescent gold ring edging the whitewall tires.

Another special Cadillac at the show was a Series 62 Coupe de Ville with pearlescent Peacock Green paint applied to its lower body and a lighter shade of green on its top. This car had an interior of Peacock Green leather and light green nylon silver-threaded fabric employing a block "V" and Cadillac crest pattern for the seat inserts.

A Fleetwood Sixty Special painted iridescent Caprice Blue on its roof and Jordan Gray (a Buick color) on the lower body was also shown. Upholstery on this car's seat bolsters was dark blue broadcloth combined with light blue nylon inserts. This model also had the block "V" and Cadillac crest pattern for its inserts.

*The 1954 GM Firebird I is shown here being prepared for testing. Three-time Indy 500 winner Mauri Rose was hired to do the test-driving of the car; it was expected to reach 200 mph. Note the logo on the nose of the experimental car. A similar design resurfaced two decades later on Pontiac's Trans Am. (Photo Courtesy GM Media Archive)*

*The GM turbine-powered Firebird I was shown at the 1954 Paris Salon.* Autosport *magazine (left) showed it on the front cover of the October 15, 1954, issue, which reported on the experimental car's presence at the auto show. At right is a promotional poster in French about the event.*

# CHAPTER FOUR: THE GM MOTORAMA OF 1954

*Other venues for showing the Firebird I included the Parade of Progress. (Photo Courtesy GM Media Archive)*

The unconventional appearance of the car was also intended to imply that practical turbine engines for automobiles were considered by GM engineers and managers to be years in the future. Even so, it represented the beginning of learning about whether or not a turbine engine could be used to provide economical and satisfactory performance in an automotive application.

## Engine Basics

Soon after practical jet engines emerged at the end of World War II, exploration of the idea of adapting the technology for automotive use began. The British had already built and tested the world's first turbine-powered car, the Rover J.E.T., beginning in 1950.

In 1953, after turbine engine research (with the GT-300) had been underway at the GM Research Laboratories Division for several years, Harley Earl decided General Motors should proceed with the construction of an actual experimental turbine car; thus began the Firebird series. However, it was originally expected that the engine would be tested in heavy-duty trucks and buses. The Firebird I's GT-302 Whirlfire Turbo-Power engine and its chassis design were the responsibility of GM Vice President Charles McCuen and General Manager of GM Research Laboratories Division William Turunen who had performed extensive research on the subject. Bob McLean, a Cal Tech graduate with an aeronautical background, was placed in charge of the Firebird's overall design. The nose of the Firebird contained a 35-gallon fiberglass fuel tank. Just behind the cockpit sat the two-part gas-turbine engine consisting of the gasifier and power sections connected by a flexible shaft. The gasifier section was analogous to the engine and torque converter pump of a conventional automobile; the power section substituted for the torque converter turbine, transmission, and rear axle gears. A jet engine compresses air and adds fuel; then the mixture is electrically sparked. This produces thrust to propel an aircraft, and hot exhaust gas is expelled.

The turbine engine of the Firebird, had to have its exhaust gases funneled through a power turbine connected directly to the car's rear wheels via a transmission. The gasifier section comprised the compressor rotor and a gasifier turbine wheel, each attached to a common shaft. Air entering the compressor was pressurized to 3½ times atmospheric pressure (14.7psi at sea level) before entering the two combustion chambers where the gas temperature soared to 1,500 degrees Fahrenheit. The hot gas blasting from the gasifier turbine ran the second turbine (the power section turbine) connected to the Firebird's rear wheels through a 2-speed planetary transmission.

## Top Speed Goals

The GT-302 produced 370 hp at 26,000 revolutions per minute with the gasifier turbine and 13,000 rpm with the power turbine. Its relatively low rotational speed reduced the stresses imposed on the moving parts, thus increasing reliability. Even so, the stresses applied were plenty high; a gasifier turbine blade tip speed could be as high as 1,000 mph, placing a 3,000-pound pull on each lightweight blade. The 775-pound weight of the GT-302 turbine engine accounted for 31 percent of the Firebird I's total weight of 2,500 pounds.

These numbers pointed to a theoretical top speed beyond 200 mph! According to the website conklinsystems.com, the Firebird had "only two speeds: fast and faster" and its 2-speed transmission could be overwhelmed by the torque. During a test drive, the Firebird test supervisor, Emmett Conklin, shifted into second gear at about 100 mph, and "the tires broke loose at that speed." Emmett decided, "I am too old for this . . ." and turned it off. This is when three-time Indy 500 winner and engineer Mauri Rose was hired to do the test-driving.

The suspension system of Firebird I had a double wishbone and torsion bars in front while the rear received a de Dion type. Split brake flaps on the trailing edges of the wings controlled with switches on the steering wheel activating aircraft-type actuators helped to slow the Firebird from higher speeds. Eleven-inch-diameter brake drums were mounted outside the wheels rather than inside them to help dissipate the heat from braking.

*The 1954 GM Firebird I is a part of the GM Heritage Collection and is still shown at various events across the country.*

Furthermore, a total of 16 gauges provided important performance data to the driver.

### Test Drive Results

Mauri Rose was expected to test drive the Firebird at GM's test track in Mesa, Arizona. Engineers believed the car would easily surpass the record set by the experimental Rover J.E.T. However, before Rose could put the Firebird through high-speed runs, Charles McCuen decided to perform some tests himself and almost got killed doing so.

The Firebird accelerated slowly, but once its turbine engine reached high RPM, it began to accelerate quickly. As McCuen approached the far turn in the test track, the Firebird was accelerating at a high rate, and he attempted to slow for the corner. However, letting off the accelerator did virtually nothing to slow the speeding car because the turbine engine did not provide engine braking as in a conventional automotive engine.

There was very little time to apply the brakes either. The car skidded underneath the 41-inch-high guardrail and tumbled several times. McCuen survived only because of the Firebird's built-in headrest and safety harness. He recovered from his injuries just enough to return to work for a while, but then took an early retirement in 1956.

The fiberglass-bodied Firebird was repaired in time for the opening of the 1954 GM Motorama at the Waldorf-Astoria. Although Mauri Rose did test drive the Firebird I, high-speed trials were not attempted again, thus leaving the true top speed as nothing more than an educated guess.

In a GM film on the Firebird, Rose said, "Fellas are always asking me what it's like to drive the Firebird. With 375 hp, it's the smoothest car I have ever driven . . . For my money, the Firebird is a mighty good example of the important kind of job the stylists, as well as the engineers, are doing to make the world a better place to live; now and in the future."

However, all was not perfect. The Firebird was somewhat noisy, extremely fuel thirsty, and the exhaust temperature was very high (roughly 1,000 degrees Fahrenheit). These problems were to be addressed in the next Firebird turbine car.

## Oldsmobile Skylark and Eldorado: Updated

For 1954 the Oldsmobile Fiesta was dropped from production; it was replaced by the Starfire. The Skylark and Eldorado, however, remained in production, but each was substantially altered.

The Skylark was based on the revived Century, last produced in the war-shortened 1942 model year. Buick's Century combined the relatively light weight of the Buick Special body with the 200-hp engine, which was standard equipment for the senior-level Buicks.

The heavily restyled and distinctive Skylark was given body panels unique to the model. These included deeply scooped wheel openings that, in some cases, had their inner surfaces painted a contrasting color, unique quarter panels with chrome-plated fins/taillight housings, and a sloping deck. Unlike the previous model year, the new Skylark had a wraparound windshield, which was standard issue on the 1954 Buick line.

A Roadmaster version of the V-8 Dynaflow transmission, leather upholstery, power accessories, and 40-spoke wire wheels remained part of the package for the Skylark. All Buick models this year received an updated instrument panel patterned after that of the Wildcat I, although revised to include the Redliner speedometer, a red and black drum that pushed a red line across the speedometer (instead of a needle) as speed increased.

At least two 1954 Skylarks were exhibited for the GM Motorama: one was painted Lido Green (a color exclusive to this model) with a two-tone green interior and occupied a turntable at the show. The other was painted Condor Yellow with a yellow and black interior and sat on the floor where people could see it up close. Only 836 of the 1954 Skylarks were built and the special model was discontinued afterward.

This time, the Eldorado shared the same body shell with the other 1954 Cadillac models greatly reducing its price tag that, not surprisingly, resulted in higher production.

## Chapter Five

# THE GM MOTORAMA OF 1955

In 1955 the GM Motorama toured five cities: New York City, Miami, Los Angeles, San Francisco, and Boston. Boston was added due to dealer demand in the Northeast and Chicago was dropped as it already had a dealer show. In all, two million spectators visited these venues setting a record for the GM Motorama.

The theme for this year's stage presentation was "Looking at You." Richard and Edith Barstow once again choreographed the staging.

This year marked the first use of a giant swinging arm mounted on a turntable to present a car from each of GM's automobile divisions. Called the "Flying Saucer," it was loaded with a car backstage behind the curtain and then burst through while being raised and pivoted toward the crowd of onlookers. On stage, a narrator described all the wonderful attributes of the car appearing before the amazed spectators.

Costs of producing the spectacular show appear to have begun escalating by this point as General Motors reduced the number of dream cars compared to the previous year. Only about half as many were constructed and evidently only one of each.

Prior to the official opening of the 1955 GM Motorama at the Waldorf-Astoria, company president Harlow Curtice said that the eight dream vehicles on display were, "the most impressive group of experimental cars to appear on the automotive scene since General Motors introduced the dream car idea to the industry 17 years ago."

*Both LaSalle IIs were illustrated on the front page of the GM Motorama section of the March 5, 1955 edition of the* Los Angeles Examiner. *When the big show came to town, newspaper coverage of the event was extensive.*

*The GM LaSalle II sedan (center) was designed as a six-passenger four-door pillarless hardtop. This photograph shows the dream car at the Waldorf-Astoria along with the (left to right) Buick Wildcat III, Chevrolet Biscayne, and Oldsmobile 88 Delta. (Photo Courtesy GM Media Archive)*

CHAPTER FIVE: THE GM MOTORAMA OF 1955

## Chevrolet Biscayne: From Show Car to Junk to Show Car

For 1955, the Chevrolet dream car was the Biscayne (XP-37, SO 2249), a four-passenger, pillarless four-door hardtop described by GM as "an exploration in elegance . . . a superlatively luxurious experimental car that illustrates an entirely new way of thinking about automotive design." This was not just advertising speak. The head of the Chevrolet studio, Clare "Mac" McKichan, is credited with the styling of the Biscayne, which went against the styling norms of the day. The trend was tail fins and lots of chrome, but, of course, the purpose of the Biscayne's styling was to counter the current style. Advanced ideas moved the art of styling forward. Some of the Biscayne's forward-thinking concepts were incorporated into cars over the following several years.

The Atlantic Green fiberglass-bodied Biscayne previewed numerous styling cues that were applied to various cars over the next few years such as the side coves of the 1956 Corvette. The side coves of the Biscayne, though, were reversed (compared to the Corvette) and wrapped around the back of the body. Its taillight panel and taillight design appear to have inspired the design for the 1961–1962 Corvette as well as the compact Corvair of the 1960s. The slim rear bumpers of the Biscayne likely influenced the design of those for the C2 Corvette.

To most people, the frontal design of the Biscayne was its distinctive exterior feature. The Biscayne's headlight and grille design were most likely inspired by the Kurtis sports car. Long fairings for the headlights, which stretched across the hood, ended just ahead of an inlet for interior ventilation. Nine vertical chrome bars sat over the fine-mesh-filled frontal opening where a grille is typically placed. Parking lamps were fitted into the end of the projectile-style front fenders. An anodized gold "V" was mounted here, too, which noted the presence of Chevrolet's new small-block V-8. A "Stratospheric" wrap-around windshield curved upward into the roof panel. The upper portion of the compound curved windshield was tinted to reduce glare from the sun. Another feature of this dream car was its touch-type fuel filler cap, located just behind the rear window.

The body of the Biscayne was mounted on a mostly custom-fabricated frame. Only the frontal part, which was taken from a stock 1955 Chevrolet, made use of

*For 1955, the Chevrolet dream car was the Biscayne (XP-37, SO 2249), a four-passenger, pillarless four-door hardtop described by General Motors as "an exploration in elegance . . . a superlatively luxurious experimental car that illustrates an entirely new way of thinking about automotive design." (Photo Courtesy GM Media Archive)*

off-the-shelf components. The custom-built frame was a perimeter design. This allowed the floor of the body to drop below the frame and allow sufficient head room in a car with a relatively low roof height of 52½ inches.

Interior features included an instrument panel with a padded leading edge and a conventional-looking 110-mph speedometer along with a fuel gauge and clock in round pods underneath. For seating, the Biscayne offered thin-shell, swiveling front bucket seats to aid entry and exit for the driver and front passenger. The bucket-type rear seats were separated with a small console serving as a storage area and armrest. Chrome-plated brass trim framed the green and white leather-covered seats.

Underneath the hood of the Biscayne was Chevrolet's new small-block Turbo-Fire 265 V-8. A claimed rating of 215 hp was reportedly attained through a high-lift camshaft, 4-barrel carburetor, and dual-exhaust system. Such ratings were likely theoretical and seldom included where peak horsepower was developed (e.g., 215 hp at 4,400 rpm). Their purpose, though, was to indicate that there would be much more horsepower in future versions of the new small-block. For 1955 the standard 265 produced 162 hp at 4,400 rpm or 180 hp at 4,600 rpm with the optional 4-barrel carburetor. Silver engine enamel and numerous chrome-plated components, including the special low-profile air cleaner, made the Biscayne's engine a showpiece.

### Saved from the Crusher

After the Biscayne was no longer needed as a show car, General Motors stored it in a warehouse until late 1959. At that time, some within the company decided storing this car and other obsolete show cars was a waste of money. Several cars including the Biscayne were ordered to be scrapped. That job was left to the nearby salvage yard Warhoops Used Auto & Truck Parts in Sterling Heights, Michigan. However, fate stepped in and kept the Biscayne and at least three other cars from being completely lost to history.

According to the story told to collector Joe Bortz, on December 23, 1959, General Motors sent the LaSalle II roadster and the Biscayne, along with a representative of the company, to Warhoops. GM's rep was there to witness the destruction of these cars, which were to be cut apart and their remains crushed. GM's witness, as the story goes, stayed just long enough to see these two cars cut into pieces. He reminded the yard owner, Harry Warholak, Sr., to crush the pieces when he finished cutting them apart and then left because he simply wanted to go home. For whatever reason, Warholak never followed that last part.

On the 24th, Christmas Eve, two more dream cars, the LaSalle II sedan and the 1956 Eldorado Brougham Town Car, were hauled into the yard with the same instructions for Warholak. This time the man charged with watching the two cars get cut apart and crushed also decided to go home. As he left, he told Warholak to "just cut 'em up and crush 'em and I will mark down I saw everything." Instead, these two cars were pushed aside out of the way and sat in the yard for about three decades.

Over the years, rumors began to circulate about some of GM's dream cars being in a salvage yard in Sterling Heights. In fact, some GM employees had actually seen the cars there. In 1989, Joe Bortz' son, Marc, read an article in *Automobile Quarterly* that mentioned the persistent story about some of GM's dream cars sitting at the Warhoops salvage yard and he suggested to his father that he call the salvage yard. Joe's reply to his son's suggestion was, "If those cars were ever there, they would be gone by now."

Marc made that phone call anyway. After he introduced himself over the phone and inquired about the Motorama cars, the man on the other end of the phone, Harry Warholak, Sr., immediately connected the name Bortz with a well-known collector who owned a few

*A slightly modified 1955 passenger car steering wheel was used for the Biscayne. Note the 110-mph speedometer and the round pods underneath the speedometer, which house the fuel gauge and a clock. Also note the padding on the leading edge of the dash. (Photo Courtesy GM Media Archive)*

# CHAPTER FIVE: THE GM MOTORAMA OF 1955

*The Biscayne's reversed-form side coves soon appeared on the 1956/1957 Corvette. Rear-end styling resembles the yet-to-be-conceived Corvair of the 1960s. (Photo Courtesy GM Media Archive)*

dream cars, including the 1953 Wildcat. When Marc confirmed that his father was the same man, Warholak issued an invitation for Joe to call. Joe's subsequent call resulted in a flight from Chicago to Detroit and, ultimately, the purchase of all four dream cars at Warhoops.

### Road to Reassembly

At first, Bortz was not interested in the Biscayne or the LaSalle II roadster, as they appeared to be beyond saving. (In fact, the Biscayne's body was cut into ten pieces!) Bortz' mechanic talked him into taking everything. Fortunately, after a lot of digging in the dirt, nearly every unique piece of exterior trim for these cars was found. The engine, transmission, seats, (simulated) instruments, and console of the Biscayne were missing, though. What became of these parts is unknown, although an unconfirmed report claims that Harry Warholak, Sr., may have donated the chassis to an area tech school.

The Biscayne's mutilated body and its trim, along with the other three dream cars, were loaded for transport back to Bortz' warehouse near Chicago. The 10 fiberglass body panels were piled up in a corner with no apparent way to ever reassemble them and there was no chassis upon which to place the body even if it could be reassembled. Also absent were blueprints and photographs to use as a guide in crafting a replacement of the unique chassis. Over time, however, a series of unexpected events occurred that ultimately led to the complete restoration

*Most of the Biscayne's original custom-made interior was missing when Joe Bortz bought it in pieces from Warhoops Used Auto & Truck Parts. The missing components, including the seats, had to be fabricated. Most of that task was left to Marty Martino. Ruben Collazo handled the upholstery work using the correct color and grain material. (Photo Courtesy Marty Martino)*

*Fortunately, the special air cleaner crafted for the low-profile hood of the Biscayne was found at the salvage yard where the Biscayne's many other pieces lay for three decades. The original engine installed in the dream car was missing so it was replaced with an early 1955 265 V-8. (Photo Courtesy Marty Martino)*

Less than five years after its public debut at the Waldorf-Astoria, the 1955 Biscayne lay in ruins at Warhoops. This dream car and three others (including the LaSalle II roadster, remnants of which can be seen underneath the Biscayne) were taken there in late 1959 to be cut up and crushed. Only two of the cars were cut apart, but none of the pieces were ever crushed. Nearly three decades later, collector Joe Bortz purchased all four cars.

of the Biscayne. Bortz said that the Biscayne's restoration "was saved by accident and in increments."

About two years after Bortz' acquisition of the four dream cars, he mentioned the group of cars to Chicago fiberglass display expert John Bucci, who asked to visit the warehouse so he could examine the Biscayne's separated body components. After looking over the body parts, Bucci said he could reassemble the body and Bortz agreed to let him try. The task of reconnecting the fiberglass parts consumed about three years. Afterward, the reassembled body was mounted on a cart to facilitate moving it around in the warehouse. At that point, Bortz thought his Biscayne had at least become a "curiosity instead of a pile of body parts." However, that was not the end.

Eventually, GM personnel, including Dave Holls and Larry Faloon, found blueprints and photographs of the Biscayne's chassis and passed them along to Bortz. Later, he met famed street rod builder Kerry Hopperstead, who was confident he could recreate the chassis from the GM photographs and indeed he did. When the chassis was completed the Biscayne's body was lowered onto it, which revealed an unexpected problem: The body was "out of square," as evidenced by the positioning of the wheels relative to the wheel openings. The only way to remedy this was to cut apart the body again!

### A Restoration Project

Bortz went to Mel Francis, to "square" the body and to also fabricate a new roof panel. The original was simply too warped to repair. After many years, the Biscayne had advanced from a "pile of parts" to a "curiosity" to a full restoration project. Additional parts also had to be made including one of the cast brass wheel covers, the right rear door skin, the rear bumperettes, and almost the entire interior.

To continue the restoration effort, two more restorers were hired for the project. Bortz' personal restorer for the past four decades has been the renowned Fran Roxas, who is considered to be one of the best restoration specialists of American classic cars in the United States. Roxas assisted Bortz in recreating several missing components of the car. Among them were cast and billet hinges, the one missing hubcap (recast in brass), as well as the intricate clock-like mechanisms to operate the door latches.

Marty Martino was hired to complete the final steps of the Biscayne's restoration. Bortz approached him about working on the Biscayne after seeing Martino's impressive recreation of another GM Motorama car, the 1956 Pontiac Club de Mer. Martino's tasks included detailing the car's undercarriage and engine compartment, making its power windows operable, and essentially replicating the largely incomplete interior.

The electric window switches of the Biscayne were never functional. In fact, no provision for a battery was

With the help of many people, including Marty Martino, the Biscayne is today as show ready as it was on the opening night of the 1955 GM Motorama at the Waldorf-Astoria. (Photo Courtesy Marty Martino)

# CHAPTER FIVE: THE GM MOTORAMA OF 1955

built into the dream car. The position of the windows could only be changed by removing the door panels, loosening some bolts, placing the windows in the up or down position as desired, and reinstalling everything. After some experimentation Martino was able to make the front windows functional by using components from an early-1970s Cadillac, but the geometry of the rear doors precluded doing the same for those windows. To make these and other electrical systems functional, a battery was installed in the Biscayne's trunk.

The non-functional instrumentation, seats, and console were constructed by using original factory photographs. A fragment of one seat frame recovered from Warhoops was useful in creating the external frame surrounding the seats. They were created from fiberglass (even though they were originally brass) and coated with an electrical conduction material to make it possible to chrome plate them. Luckily, traces of the original upholstery material remained in the Biscayne. New leather upholstery of the same grain and color was obtained through Bill Hirsch Automotive Products. The dream car's Daytona carpeting with binding that matched the upholstery was sewn to match the original pattern by the talented upholster Ruben Collazo.

Because a structural brace behind the dash left no room for such things as a speedometer cable and real gauges, a set of modern gauges was mounted inside the glove box for monitoring oil pressure and coolant temperature.

Applying paint to the Biscayne was left to the talented staff of Page Customs. When stripping away the original nitrocellulose lacquer finish from the show car, a discovery was made: It had been repainted once by General Motors. Use of a spectrophotometer made it possible to match the custom-mixed, Atlantic Green color, but this time using R-M Diamont urethane clear coat/base coat.

### Second Showing

In 2010 (about five decades after being left for dead) the completed Biscayne was ready to be shown. Its first venue was The Concours d'Elegance of America at Meadowbrook. It was attended by designers from the past including the late Chuck Jordan and Wayne Cherry, both former heads of GM Design. Also present was the current leader of GM Global Design, Ed Welburn.

After an unexpected 22-year effort beginning with an "accident" and progressing for a time simply by "increments," the Biscayne in every way is again the impressive show car it was in 1955.

## Pontiac Strato-Star: A Radical Design

The 1955 Strato-Star (XP-36, SO 2250) was designed by a team led by Paul Gillan. General Motors claimed it to be "The most daring new design ever displayed."

Powering the Strato-Star was the Strato-Streak 287 and 4-barrel carburetor said to produce 250 hp, 50 more than the production version with the optional 4-barrel carburetor. In reality, the car was likely never operational. Even so, the advertised output of the Strato-Star's engine hinted at higher performance engines in Pontiac's future.

But the engine was only one aspect of the interesting six-passenger sedan. One of its primary features was an unusual roof design that utilized two slim-section cantilever pillars growing upward from the flat rear deck and extending forward as windsplits through the roof section and gradually tapered to join the windshield bar. These same rear pillars also flowed back across the deck to form fins. Panoramic quarter glass in the rear along with the Panoramic windshield provided a nearly unobstructed view in all directions.

Because of the dream car's low overall height of 53.1 inches, flip-up panels in the roof approximately 6 inches deep opened and closed automatically via an electric circuit to assist with entry and exit of the driver and passengers. The other basic dimensions of the Strato-Star were an overall length of 202.5 inches and an overall width of 75.6 inches.

The Strato-Star was painted Dark Silver Metallic with contrasting vermillion paint covering the deeply extended wheel wells in front. The shape of the front wheel openings was probably inspired by a Bertone-bodied Abarth designed by Franco Scaglione four years earlier. The elongated wheel openings resulted in some of the front suspension components being exposed so these pieces were

*A clay mockup was made from which the molds for the fiberglass body of the Pontiac Strato-Star could be formed, a typical process for the fiberglass dream cars. (Photo Courtesy GM Media Archive)*

*One of the primary features of the 1955 Strato-Star was its unusual roof design, which used two slim-section cantilever pillars growing upward from the flat rear deck and extending forward as windsplits through the roof section and gradually tapered to join the windshield bar. These same rear pillars also flowed back across the deck to form fins. Panoramic quarter glass in the rear, along with the panoramic windshield, provided a nearly unobstructed view in all directions. (Photo Courtesy GM Media Archive)*

*Because of the Strato-Star's low overall height of 53.1 inches, flip-up panels in the roof approximately 6 inches deep opened and closed automatically via an electric circuit to assist with entry and exit of the driver and passengers. Its gull-wing-style dash strongly resembled that of the yet-to-be designed second-generation Thunderbird.*

The Strato-Star's conventional-looking latticework grille resembled that of the new Chevrolet, but a divided gull-wing bumper with pod-mounted parking lights hanging underneath was certainly unconventional for an American car. Hooded, round taillights were aligned with the tail fins and underneath each of them was a chrome-trimmed vertical slot from which the exhaust exited.

chrome-plated. Another unusual styling feature of this dream car was its protruding headlight fairings, which extended back to the cowl. A wide air scoop sat on top of them to funnel air into the interior.

Even the wheels for the Strato-Star were experimental units formed as a deep-draw section of chrome with a brake-cooling air intake styled like a turbine impeller.

MOTORAMA 127

# CHAPTER FIVE: THE GM MOTORAMA OF 1955

The 1955 Pontiac Strato-Star was painted Dark Silver Metallic with contrasting vermillion paint covering the deeply extended wheel wells in front. The shape of the front-wheel openings was probably inspired by a Bertone-bodied Abarth designed by Franco Scaglione four years earlier.

The Pontiac Strato-Star was shown at the GM Wonderama in Dayton, Ohio, in May 1955 along with other 1954 and 1955 GM dream cars including the Buick Wildcat III in the foreground. (Photo Courtesy H. B. Stubbs, Co.)

After the 1955 GM Motorama show circuit ended, the Strato-Star went to Canada for various auto shows including the 1956 GM Canada Motorama where it was known as the Strato-Chief.

(You could argue that these were effectively prototypes of the popular eight-lug aluminum wheel Pontiac offered in the 1960s.) Red-painted rectangular recesses surrounded the wheel hub.

The six-passenger Strato-Star's bench-seat interior glowed with its vermillion red leather upholstery. Its gull-wing-style dash strongly resembled that of the yet-to-be designed second-generation Thunderbird, which might not have been a coincidence! The door and rear side panels were sculpted with a concave projectile form upon which projectile-shaped armrests were mounted. A gray padded headliner with pleats running lengthwise covered the inner roof panel.

After the 1955 GM Motorama show circuit ended, the Strato-Star appeared in Canada at various auto shows including the 1956 GM Canada Motorama where it was known as the Strato-Chief. What became of this dream car after making the rounds of the Canadian auto show venues is unknown, although presumably it was scrapped by the late-1950s.

## Oldsmobile 88 Delta: Daring Departure

The Oldsmobile 88 Delta dream car (XP-40, SO 2251) was another bold change from traditional Oldsmobile style, although, like the models in showrooms, it did without tail fins. It featured teardrop wheel wells and had a refined front fascia that featured stacked headlights and a twin-pillar bumper. A two-toned blue paint scheme graced this four-passenger two-door hardtop that stood only 53.1 inches high. According to a GM-issued brochure detailing the dream car, it was said to have a "Supersonic Shape."

Powering the 88 was an Oldsmobile 324 V-8 that had a 10.0:1 compression ratio and dual exhausts. This particular package produced 250 hp at 4,600 rpm and torque was 350 ft-lbs at 2,800 rpm. (Only rarely was the torque rating provided for dream cars.) For comparison, the highest output stock engine (that of the Super Eighty-Eight and Ninety-Eight) was rated at 202 hp at 4,000 rpm and peak torque was 332 ft-lbs at 2,400 rpm. The high-output Rocket engine was mated to a Hydra-Matic Super Drive automatic transmission.

Wide-set vertical ovals housed the headlamps and parking lights in addition to scoops used to cool the front brake drums. Between the wide ovals was a bumper/grille combination with a set of thin horizontal bars divided centrally with a chrome vertical bar. The hood spanned the entire width from fender crown line to fender crown line and the hood cut-lines were neatly concealed with chromed trim.

A jeweled around-the-world emblem in front and back let onlookers know this was an Oldsmobile. It was one of the few visual cues (other than the rear end-mounted individual chrome letters spelling out OLDSMOBILE) on the 88 Delta to suggest which division of General Motors it represented.

GM stylists certainly embraced a theme of blue for this particular model. All glass received a light blue tint to blend with the

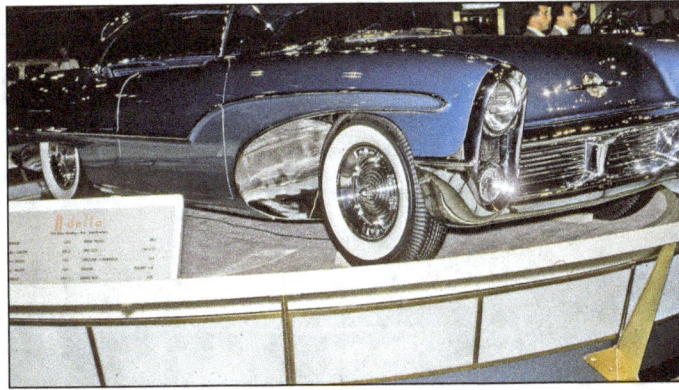

*The Oldsmobile 88 Delta dream car was a two-toned blue, four-passenger, two-door hardtop standing only 53.1 inches high with a "Supersonic Shape" according to a GM-issued brochure detailing the dream car. (Photo Courtesy GM Media Archive)*

*This photograph of the Oldsmobile 88 Delta taken at the Waldorf-Astoria provides a good view of the teardrop-shaped wheel well openings. Those in front swept back and were fitted with polished stainless steel inner fenders. (Photo Courtesy GM Media Archive)*

# CHAPTER FIVE: THE GM MOTORAMA OF 1955

*The 88 Delta's wide-set vertical ovals housed the headlamps and parking lights in addition to scoops used to cool the front brake drums. Between the wide ovals was a bumper/grille combination with a set of thin horizontal bars divided centrally by a vertical chrome bar. The body-side molding wrapped around the rear and formed a thin rear bumper. Its taillights also wrapped around the dream car's body.*

highly metallic two-tone paint scheme and blue-tinted brushed-aluminum roof. However, the backlight received a darker tint to give the impression that it was a continuation of the roof panel. Vent windows, standard equipment on cars of the day, were deleted on the 88 Delta. The slim, vertical A-pillars were blended into the frame of the wraparound windshield.

Interestingly, the roof design of the 88 Delta evidently was not planned this way in the beginning. A July 23, 1954, "Engineering Progress Report" from GM's Convertible Top Group revealed assignments given to two engineers that indicate a convertible top was originally considered for the dream car. The section of the memorandum related to this car read as follows:

OLDSMOBILE CONVERTIBLE HARDTOP
WALDORF SHOW – SO 2251
1. Convertible top linkage     Husko
2. Power drive for top         McClue

The 88 Delta's profile included a dropped beltline from just inside the windshield to the rear roof pillars.

*Clearly seen in this photo of the clay mockup of the 1955 Oldsmobile 88 Delta's interior is the unique "floating" strut upon which the instrumentation was mounted. The oval pods housed a 130-mph speedometer and a 5,500-rpm tachometer. Note the side-mounted emergency brake pedal at the driver-side kick panel. (Photo Courtesy GM Media Archive)*

*The 88 Delta was equipped with swivel bucket seats in front. Tires were 7.60x15-inch-wide whites mounted on six-lug wheels; the exposed brake drums had integral concentric cooling fins and exposed acorn-style lug nuts.*

Door handles were a flush oval design, which stayed depressed so you could pull the door open.

All wheel well openings were a teardrop shape although the rear wells were cut much lower than the front ones. Those in front swept back and were fitted with polished stainless steel inner fenders. Tires were 7.60x15-inch-wide whites mounted on six-lug wheels with exposed brake drums with integral concentric cooling fins and exposed acorn-style lug nuts.

Side trim for this dream car provided a dividing line for the two-tone paint scheme. Colorful two-toning became a major styling trend and Oldsmobile offered 89 two-tone combinations for 1955; 14 new paint colors were added as well.

The rear-mounted around-the-world logo served as the fuel filler door for the 88 Delta. Both quarter panels carried a 15-gallon fuel tank. Wraparound taillights sat just above the thin rear bumper, which was actually a continuation of the body-side trim. As with many dream cars of 1954, a central drop-down door in back provided access to the 88 Delta's spare tire. Flanking this access door were chrome-trimmed vertical slots, which served as both bumper guards and exhaust ports.

The fiberglass body of the 88 Delta was bolted to a modified Oldsmobile frame with wide side rails to permit the rear floor to drop down thus giving adequate head room for rear-seat passengers.

Following the multi-tint blue theme of the glass and paint, the leather interior featured multi-blue shades and four individual seats. Entry and exit for the driver and passengers was made easier with swiveling front seats, which could also be folded and pushed forward in one motion for smoother transition to and from the rear seats. A pair of oval pods mounted on a detached, horizontal leather-padded support bar, which gave the appearance of a floating strut, housed a 130-mph speedometer and a 5,500-rpm tachometer. This full-width support bar, positioned about 4 inches ahead of the firewall, also served as a structural tie-bar; the lower two-thirds of it could be pulled out to serve as a tray or small desk.

As on the 1954 Oldsmobile Cutlass dream car, the 17-inch steering wheel of the 88 Delta had exposed rivets and the model identification on the hub. Detached from and forward of the main instrument panel was a full-width grille containing the air and heater outlets, radio speaker, and drum clock. The linkage for the 88 Delta's emergency brake pedal concealed by the driver-side kick panel and a map pocket was included on the right-side kick panel.

The console between the front seats contained the radio (or at least a simulated radio dial) and radio controls, an ashtray, and a waste container with a disposable wax paper liner plus storage for refills. An armrest dividing the back seats contained a glove box, ashtray, and power window switches for the rear windows. The model identification was embossed on the vertical bulkhead between the rear seats. Garnish moldings for the interior of the 88 Delta were of blue anodized aluminum.

In addition to a radio and power windows, the 88 Delta was equipped with power brakes and power steering.

The 88 Delta's wheelbase was 120 inches, 2 inches shorter than that of the Eighty-Eight and Super Eighty-Eight series. Other measurements provided for this dream car included a ground clearance of 6.2 inches, overall length of 201 inches, overall width of 74 inches, and curb weight of 4,078 pounds.

What became of the Oldsmobile 88 Delta after it turned into an obsolete dream car is unknown. Presumably, it was shown at least into 1956, but to date I have found only three showings after the end of the 1955 GM Motorama. Those were at the GM Wonderama in Dayton, Ohio, in late May; in the lobby of the upscale Edgewater Beach Hotel north of Chicago in early June; and the Powerama (also in Chicago) during August/September 1955.

### Buick Wildcat III: A Man's Car

Following the evolution of the Wildcat series of dream cars, the fiberglass Wildcat III (XP-35, SO 2252) was the most conventional of these three concept cars.

*This photograph, taken at an unidentified auto show, reveals the unusual instrument panel of the 1955 Oldsmobile 88 Delta that comprised a detached, horizontal leather-padded support upon which the instrumentation was mounted. The console housed the radio, ashtray, and a waste container. Note the extended pullout tray.*

# CHAPTER FIVE: THE GM MOTORAMA OF 1955

The 1955 Buick Wildcat III was painted Kimberley Red in honor of race car driver Jim Kimberly. It was styled with more Buick themes than the previous Wildcat I and Wildcat II. Two of them clearly visible in this photograph (probably taken in Los Angeles or San Francisco) are the so-called sweepspear molding and radiused rear wheel openings. (Photo Courtesy Hillary Hess collection)

According to Buick's general manager, Ivan Wiles, "The unique styling of the new Wildcat, with its bold, clean lines and its high-powered engine, suggests that this car was designed strictly for a man."

Homer LaGassey was given overall responsibility for its design after he had moved up to Buick from the Pontiac studio following his involvement with the Strato-Streak and Bonneville Special dream car projects. The Wildcat III went in a different direction in terms of styling. It was considerably more conservative than the Wildcat II, but was much more Buick-like in appearance. The name of the car's color, Kimberly Red, was chosen to honor race car driver and SCCA member Jim Kimberly, who was well known for his wins at Sebring, Road America, Watkins Glen, etc. Unlike the previous Wildcat dream cars, this one could seat four.

### Exterior Features

Most Motorama cars were low-slung and the Wildcat III was no different. It was obviously significantly lower in height (51.75 inches) and shorter (110-inch wheelbase) in length than any production model built by the division. But the profile sweepspear molding was a familiar Buick styling cue. Also obvious in the profile view was the dream car's compound curved Panoramic windshield, which provided improved protection from windblast when the top was down. The beltline gently sloped downward, and then kicked up just behind the door. Outer door handles were a pullout type. A cooling slot in the quarter panels for the rear brakes sat at an angle immediately above the dip in the sweepspear molding.

The Wildcat III's hood sloped in front to improve visibility immediately ahead of the car and was also recessed beneath the cowl where an upright air intake for passenger compartment ventilation was located. The frontal

A Buick theme was reflected in the frontal design of the Wildcat III, but close observation revealed special styling characteristics, such as the dream car's fine-screen grille, roll pan with paired air intakes for brake cooling on each side underneath the front bumper, and the sloped hood designed to improve visibility immediately ahead of the car; it was recessed beneath the cowl where an upright air intake for passenger compartment ventilation was located. (Photo Courtesy GM Media Archive)

This stylist's rendering of a proposed design for the 1955 Buick Wildcat III appeared in the GM-prepared booklet, *The Look of Things*. The booklet provided details of the stages of styling an automobile by using the Wildcat III as an example.

*The dash of the Wildcat III received plenty of chromed housings for its instruments. The steering wheel looks similar to that of the following year's Corvette. Note the Wildcat III's swiveling front bucket seats.*

*The Wildcat III's chassis included a high-quality finish even for components that were not easily seen by the public. This frame appears to be the same color as the engine block. (Photo Courtesy GM Media Archive)*

design carried a Buick theme with special styling characteristics. These included the dream car's fine-screen grille and roll pan with paired air intakes for brake cooling on each side underneath the front bumper. Other frontal elements included parking/directional lights mounted in the bumper "bombs" and headlamps embossed with the Buick insignia.

When the convertible top was retracted, the entire trunk lid opened from the front to accept the convertible top assembly. On the other hand, the Wildcat I and Wildcat II had a small flush-fitting lid that opened to house the convertible top. The deck lid and the upper portion of the quarter panels were a single unit. Incorporating the upper quarters allowed greater access to the trunk. At first glance, the integrated upper quarter panels and deck lid made the Wildcat III appear to be a four-door, although with very small rear doors.

Despite the sophisticated top stowage arrangement, the Wildcat III never actually had a convertible top installed. According to Homer LaGassey, the seats were not adjustable so there was no way to get adequate headroom with the top raised. During an interview with me several years ago he gave a humorous account of Harley Earl sitting in the car on one occasion. The 6-foot, 4-inch Earl sat in the driver's seat with his head and shoulders positioned higher than the top of the windshield frame! Of the sight, LaGassey remembered, "We all laughed." But he quickly noted, "But not for long!" (The stylists knew too much laughter at their boss' expense was unwise.)

Even though this show car did not receive a convertible top, according to a September 1, 1954, memorandum from GM's Experimental Mechanical Department, one was, at the very least, partially designed. Regarding the Wildcat III it stated:

*Instead of a small, flush-fitting lid to cover the retracted convertible top as on the preceding Wildcats, the entire trunk lid opened from the front on the Wildcat III. The deck lid incorporated the upper portion of the quarter panels thus improving access to the trunk. Note the recess with the groves in the central trunk. All three members of the Wildcat series from 1953 to 1955 had this feature. (Photo Courtesy Bill Warner collection)*

- The geometry of this top is almost 75-percent completed; however, the Riviera-type rear window still presents a problem to get it between the frame in the down position. The studio suggests making it narrower, similar to the present production convertible rear window. A layout using this type rear window will be made upon the return of Dana Waterman.
- Two methods for operating the rear deck lid have been completed.
- Power-operated rear quarter window being changed to incorporate lowered D.I.O. layout, 70-percent completed. Top surface lines, 75-percent completed. (Author note: The reference to "D.I.O." was probably a typographical error and should have been D.L.O., meaning "Daylight Opening," the area bounded by the window opening.)

The Wildcat III's dual exhausts exited through rectangular outlets in the rear roll panel; above them were the reverse lights. The rear bumper consisted of only a nearly conical cap at the bottom end of each quarter panel.

### Interior Styling

Inside the Wildcat III, four round dials across the central dash in chrome-plated surrounds housed the Selectronic radio, combination fuel/oil gauges, 6,000-rpm tachometer, and clock. Most likely, all of the instrumentation was simulated. The Sovereign Red interior had swiveling bucket seats in front and a bucket-styled bench-type seat in back, all covered in leather and trimmed in gleaming chrome. A padded vinyl covering with a fine checkerboard pattern was used instead of the traditional carpeting.

Sporty touches included positioning the shifter lever for the Dynaflow transmission between the front seats on the flattened transmission tunnel and a new steering wheel design similar to that of the all-new 1956 Corvette.

The 322-ci V-8 under the hood of the Wildcat III was modified with four 2-barrel carburetors mounted on a special intake. It was said to produce 280 hp, 44 more than a stock engine with a single 4-barrel carburetor. However, this dream car was probably like most of the others: lacking an electrical system and therefore non-operational.

### An Uncertain Fate

Not surprisingly, the Wildcat III did not lead to a production version of the car. The name, however, was selected for the sporty, Buick Invicta-based two-door hardtop that came equipped with bucket seats and a console. It made its debut in the middle of the 1962 model year.

The Wildcat III continued to be shown at least into 1956. This car may have met its end in the late-1950s at a wrecking yard. Eldorado Brougham enthusiast and Michigan resident Larry Muckey said he became acquainted with the owner of the first Detroit-area salvage yard to get a car crusher. During a telephone interview many years ago with me, Muckey recounted a conversation he had with the salvage yard owner.

According to the story, GM officials required first-hand knowledge of how effectively the new car crusher did its job so a test was arranged. Reportedly, the test car was a "Motorama Buick," which was hauled to the salvage yard, placed in the crusher, and destroyed. Muckey also recalled the yard owner saying he really hated to crush the car.

The process of elimination leaves one of the 1953 Wildcats or the Wildcat III as the only possibilities for the car that was crushed, assuming the yard owner correctly remembered it as a Buick. However, author Don Keefe was told that General Motors bought a car crusher and first used it to crush the Wildcat III.

Tantalizingly, though, is the comment made to me by the late Homer LaGassey. As he recalled, an actress who saw the Wildcat III commented on it favorably and soon afterward, the car disappeared!

### Cadillac Eldorado Brougham: Steel-Bodied Prototype

The design of the 1955 Eldorado Brougham (XP-38, SO 2253) commenced in May 1954 when the preliminary specifications were established and authorization was given to fabricate a full-scale clay model and a seating buck. Unlike most GM dream cars, the *steel-bodied* Eldorado Brougham represented a much more serious design proposal. In fact, it was a prototype of the limited-edition 1957–1958 Eldorado Brougham. A number of features of the preceding Cadillac show cars (Orleans and Park Avenue) were carried forward in the design of this car, such as a brushed-aluminum roof, reverse-opening rear doors, no center pillars, and no vent windows. (Including an integral air conditioner/heater system in the Eldorado Brougham meant vent windows were no longer considered necessary equipment.) Another idea carried forward from other Cadillac showpieces, the La Espada and the El Camino, was the quad headlamp design. Quad headlamps were illegal in some states at the time, but legislation was passed to legalize them in all states for 1958.

*The rear end styling of the 1955 Eldorado Brougham appears to have evolved from that of the 1954 Cadillac Park Avenue. (Photo Courtesy GM Media Archive)*

Ed Glowacke, the head of the Cadillac studio from 1952 to 1957, had his team prepare the clay model of the Eldorado Brougham for viewing by their boss, Harley Earl, and other managers within three months after the go-ahead decision. By August 10, the specifications were far enough along to press forward with the clay and plaster mockups. The design review resulted in the rear overhang being reduced several inches to achieve "more compact proportions and improve handling and parking," commented Harley Earl. Aircraft-style air intakes were added to the upper front fenders with outlets in the rear doors for pressurized ventilation.

After a review of the revised mockup, it was moved to the Cadillac Studio for additional refinements. The interior model was completed during September and October, and assembly of the actual prototype began on November 6 when the chassis and underbody was delivered.

Despite the long hours put in by everyone involved in the Eldorado Brougham project, the car was not painted until just days before it was to go on display at the opening of the 1955 GM Motorama at the Waldorf-Astoria. However, after being delivered the prototype fell from its transport dolly causing damage to its front and rear. With mere hours left before the preview night (held for dignitaries, GM personnel and their families, and other VIPs the day before the official opening), workers hurriedly repaired the damage well enough that the admiring crowds never knew anything had gone amiss.

A GM press release about the Eldorado Brougham said it was "Completely functional in every detail . . . the grace and sleekness of the car is augmented by its extremely low over-all height of 54.4 inches . . ." (suggesting that the car was actually a running, driving prototype). Also mentioned in this press release was the highly iridescent exterior color called Chameleon Green, which was developed solely for the Brougham. A GM-prepared brochure detailing the car noted its "special high-powered" engine, the specially designed lounge seats for four passengers, vanity case, and unique padded instrument panel. Other equipment included an Autronic Eye automatic headlight dimmer mounted at the top of the windshield, leather and silk interior, pivoting front seats, map light, and storage compartments in the dash and between the front seats.

The Eldorado Brougham's body was mounted on a modified Cadillac Series 62 frame with a wheelbase of 124 inches, 5 inches shorter than that of a stock version. An Eldorado version of the 331 V-8 coupled to a Hydra-Matic transmission was installed in the car, although it was claimed to produce 280 hp, which was 10 more than that advertised for the production Eldorado.

The final resting place of the 1955 Eldorado Brougham is not known, although it certainly could have been scrapped.

**The pillarless design of the four-door hardtop Eldorado Brougham meant the doors had to latch into the rocker panel sill.**

# CHAPTER FIVE: THE GM MOTORAMA OF 1955

## GMC L'Universelle: A Practical Cargo Vehicle

Until the 1955 GM Motorama, GMC was represented only with a lineup of trucks. Before that, trucks were meant to be more utilitarian than stylish. However, that attitude began to change in the 1950s. At the 1954 GM Motorama, GMC unveiled its all-new pickup, which was the first to receive passenger car styling. In 1955, GMC's only dream vehicle for the GM Motorama was very much ahead of its time. It was dubbed the L'Universelle (XP-39, SO 2280), a kind of all-purpose vehicle. By modern definition, GM had developed a panel van, and this advanced panel delivery prototype was equipped with front-wheel drive, a mid-mounted Pontiac V-8 rated at 180 hp, two-way radio-telephone, torsion-bar front suspension, and fold-up cargo doors.

### More Than Function

When General Motors developed the XP-39 prototype, few vehicles were in the same class. Only a handful of small and underpowered import models were somewhat similar. The Volkswagen Bus was one of those similar models and it was the only one to sell in significant numbers. At that time, General Motors offered the Chevrolet Carryall and the GMC Suburban but neither was comfortable due to their harsh ride qualities, or even especially easy to load with a ground-to-floor height of about 30 inches.

The L'Universelle served as a prototype for a vehicle designed for comfort and ease of loading. This dream truck eventually led to the Chevrolet Corvair-based Greenbrier/Corvan.

The concept of the L'Universelle is credited to GM Truck & Coach Division head Phillip Monaghan, who at the time was 40 and the youngest vice president at General Motors. According to Monaghan, car design had far outpaced truck design. Harley Earl shared his assessment and thought a dream truck for the 1955 Motorama would help in changing the way trucks were made, plus persuade the public that trucks or vans could be much more than simple utility vehicles.

Not surprisingly, Earl (who was always thinking ahead) had actually sketched some van-like trucks in the 1930s. Earl's ideas had even featured fold-up doors similar to those that appeared on the L'Universelle.

Chuck Jordan was on the fast track at General Motors and rising through the ranks. In April 1954, he headed up the Experimental Styling Group so he was in the ideal position to conceptualize and develop a bold new truck design. This was as an extension to his job as assistant chief designer in the Chevrolet truck studio, where he had designed the Chevrolet Cameo and its companion GMC Suburban Carrier.

Jordan and Bill Lange of the GMC Truck and Coach studio and the rest of his team set out to design the new panel delivery truck, to integrate cutting-edge styling

*The 1955 GMC L'Universelle almost went into production, but it would not have had the jackknife doors as seen here.*

*Unlike most GM dream cars, the steel-bodied Eldorado Brougham represented a much more serious design proposal. In fact, it was a prototype of the limited edition 1957–1958 Eldorado Brougham. A number of features of the preceding Cadillac show cars, the Orleans and Park Avenue, were carried forward in the design of this car, such as a brushed-aluminum roof, reverse-opening rear doors, no center pillars, and no vent windows. Its color was iridescent Chameleon Green, a color specially developed for this car. (Photo Courtesy GM Media Archive)*

and innovative features for a utilitarian application. The vehicle had to incorporate passenger comfort more than previous trucks had while allowing full access to the load and offer easy loading. It was also to use side panels adaptable to glass inserts so station wagon, taxi, and "sportsman" versions could be made at low cost.

The L'Universelle also had much more complete engineering than most GM Motorama vehicles. Charles Chayne supervised the engineering team. Early research on the project by Jordan and his team centered on driving a Chevy Carryall and a Volkswagen Microbus to learn the most favorable aspects of the most popular vehicles having any similarity to the XP-39 concept.

### Practicality with a Flare

Styling was a vital element to creating a successful show truck. To avoid a boxy look, a sharp crease wrapped around the front to the sides and curved downward to the rear wheels resulting in a forward-leaning edge. Styling was further enhanced by forward-leaning roof pillars that were similar to the 1955 Nomad. The prow of the L'Universelle was slanted just enough to avoid appearing bus-like. The front fascia was distinctly different than the Suburban's and other trucks of the era. It featured frenched headlamps and a slatted grille that followed the curve of the headlamps. The styling of the quarter panels and taillights reflected those of the 1955 Chevy.

*Passenger car styling (an important design goal for the show vehicle) is evident in this view of the GMC L'Universelle.*

# CHAPTER FIVE: THE GM MOTORAMA OF 1955

*A low ground-to-cargo floor height was a major consideration in the design of the GMC L'Universelle.*

The interior layout placed the driver directly over the front wheels, a position not generally beneficial in terms of ride comfort. So, to meet the requirement of comfortable ride qualities, torsion bars were adopted for the front suspension. To achieve the ideal steering wheel placement, an L-shaped steering shaft that turned bevel gears was installed so the driver had the best angle to the steering wheel.

*The low height of the cargo floor and overall height of the L'Universelle is evident in this photograph taken at an unspecified auto show.*

When the design work began, the team started at the rear of the vehicle. Because the design focused on full access to the interior and ease of loading, a low floor height was required. A drop axle fit well with the need for the low height, and that led to a front-wheel-drive system. For better vehicle weight bias, the 180-hp Pontiac 288 V-8 (GMCs used Pontiac engines) was placed transversely behind the driver and connected to a Hydra-Matic transaxle mounted ahead of it.

But this proved to be problematic for the positioning of the radiator, as it needed a steady supply of air to flow through it. After some false starts, the situation was resolved by placing the radiator behind the driver angled forward, installing a grille in the roof, and having fans pull air through the grille to the radiator.

Another problem the team encountered was that the engine cover did not clear the distributor. A hole was drilled into the water pump housing and the distributor shaft placed there! Because the transaxle was no more than an empty shell, the distributor placement did not matter as the L'Universelle was not intended to be drivable.

Eventually the design team arrived at a 13-inch floor height, 1,000-pound load capacity, and 173 cubic feet of cargo space in a van with a compact 107-inch wheelbase, 71-inch overall height, 78-inch overall width, 188-inch overall length, and 60/40 unloaded weight distribution

A 1955 GMC pickup appears in the foreground and in the background is the GMC L'Universelle. (Photo Courtesy GM Media Archive)

Passenger car comfort was one of several factors considered by the L'Universelle design team. A radiotelephone was included in the L'Universelle, but of course would not have been standard equipment on the production version had it gone forward. Note the two-tone steering wheel and the different seat inserts shown in this pair of photos.

# CHAPTER FIVE: THE GM MOTORAMA OF 1955

(54/46 fully loaded). This prototype was nearly 1 foot lower than conventional panel trucks, but could carry more cargo and do so with the comfort of a standard passenger car.

The "jackknife" loading doors used for the sides and at the rear of the L'Universelle lifted on a four-bar hinge system. Its side doors rose to provide an opening 46 inches high and 48 inches wide, while the rear-loading door was somewhat smaller at 38¼ inches high and 44 inches wide. These doors extended no more than 20 inches away from the body as they swung upward.

A "floating" instrument cluster stood out from the concave, copper-plated dash panel. Its lower center section contained a compartment with a fold-down door behind which was stored the radio-telephone. The split front bench seat was designed to accommodate three comfortably. Taxi, bus, and station wagon versions of the L'Universelle would have added two facing, three-passenger seats and side windows instead of the side panels.

The clay mockup of the XP-39 was completed during October 1954, and was followed by fabrication of the fiberglass molds. The body was then constructed, the trim pieces were hammered out over wood forms, and castings were formed in brass and then chrome-plated. The completed vehicle was painted an iridescent copper tone. The car was initially named Expedier during the drawing-board stage, and then Livraison in the clay stage. Ultimately, the name L'Universelle (meaning "all-purpose") was selected.

## Production Halted

The public's acceptance of the prototype panel van was so strong that GM president Harlow Curtice announced at the GM Motorama in San Francisco the vehicle would go into production as soon as possible. Two test "mules" dubbed T-1443 and T-1478 were cobbled together and a press to stamp out the roof panel was bought for what was to be a steel-bodied vehicle. This is as close to production as GMC's compact van got. As the work progressed, the higher the production costs went; so high that the vehicle would have had a price greater than that of a Cadillac, which was clearly impractical. Even cost-saving measures, such as substituting sliding loading doors for the complex folding doors, did not cut costs enough.

GM managers and designers realized that they needed to go in a different direction with the panel van idea. Less than one year after the L'Universelle program was aborted, the first sketches were done of the Corvair Greenbrier/Corvan. This was one of the last projects Harley Earl directed before his late-1958 retirement from General Motors.

The new, much more practical design went into production for the 1961 model year. The L'Universelle had served to influence the design of the first compact passenger vans from Chevrolet and provided valuable experience on how to build such a vehicle.

Despite its uniqueness and wonderful styling, the L'Universelle was evidently not saved from being scrapped. With the expectation that a toned-down version was about to be placed into mass production, GM officials probably had no interest in keeping it. Those jackknife doors were no doubt heavy and may have soon led to stress cracks around their mounting points; these fiberglass dream vehicles were not necessarily built with structural strength in mind. If true, this alone probably would have doomed the L'Universelle to scrap.

## GM LaSalle II: Advanced V-6 and a Story of Recovery

The GM LaSalle IIs seemed out of step with the times in spite of the spectacular styling of the roadster and sedan. The pair was named after the first car Harley Earl designed for General Motors: the 1927 LaSalle. (Cadillac's companion marque, LaSalle, was last produced in 1940.) These cars were built and shown at the time when V-8s were all the rage. Each new model year more horsepower achieved through increased cubic inches, higher compression ratios, multiple carburetion, etc., was promoted. Thus this was seemingly not an era to test public reaction to a V-6 engine. Furthermore, both dream cars

*Carl Renner was given responsibility for the design of the 1955 GM LaSalle II roadster. Shown here is one of his original sketches showing one the proposals for its styling. (Photo Courtesy Joe Bortz Auto Collection)*

*In the 1950s, General Motors had a serious V-6 program that led to a production-ready engine to be offered by Chevrolet. It was canceled before its planned 1955 release. The LaSalle IIs served as a showcase for a more advanced version of the engine. Shown here is the restored mockup V-6 in the LaSalle II roadster. (Photo Courtesy Lea Lenz-Dunham)*

were quite small for the day, which also went against established norms at the time. Regardless, this is how the LaSalle II project broke new ground.

### Exterior Styling

The rather compact six-passenger four-door pillarless hardtop LaSalle II sedan (XP-32, SO 2217) had a wheelbase of 108 inches (just 6 inches longer than that of the Corvette) and an overall length of 180.2 inches, which was about the same length as some alternative sports cars of the day. The roadster (XP-34, SO 2220) was even more compact with a wheelbase of 99.9 inches and an overall length of 151.7 inches.

Both cars were quite low in height: The hardtop stood 49.8 inches high and the roadster, just a mere 42.8 inches high. Each used a drop-floor construction made possible by offsetting the transmission downward with a consequent lowering of the driveshaft and driveshaft tunnel.

Frontal styling for both LaSalle IIs featured vertical grille openings very similar to those of the canceled 1941 LaSalle. The side coves of the pearlescent white cars were painted Bahama Blue on the roadster and Le Sabre Blue on the sedan. This feature gave a preview of the styling for the upcoming 1956 Corvette.

Carl Renner, who was placed in charge of designing the LaSalle IIs, also worked on the restyled Corvette for 1956. (He even proposed a 1957 Corvette design based primarily upon the LaSalle II roadster's styling.) The LaSalle II sedan's windshield was an "astra-dome" type much like that of the Biscayne. The exhaust exited through a port in each lower quarter panel for the sedan while the roadster's exhaust pipes, mufflers, and ports were housed in the rocker sills.

### Engine and Suspension

The 60-degree V-6 engines for both LaSalles were nonfunctional castings without provisions for internal components, but represented aluminum (heads and block), fuel-injected, double-overhead (DOHC) cam power plants that were expected to produce a maximum horsepower of 150 in finished form. Even though these particular V-6 prototypes were simulated, General Motors had had a serious V-6 research program over the preceding seven years.

Phillip Frances, Jr., was one of the engineers assigned to the V-6 project by GM Engineering Power Development Manager John Dolza. Frances had previously designed a 120-degree V-6 for Pontiac, although it was completely different. He believed that the concept for the 6-cylinder program was initiated by Charles Chayne and that the motivation for it was its more compact size. According to him, this engine was not originally intended to be a fuel-injected aluminum DOHC design, but a conventional cast-iron block and heads with a single cam; the more advanced aspects were seen as prospects for the future, though.

As work progressed, the LaSalle II project began concurrently and Dolza asked Frances to change the design into a DOHC type. That task, however, could not be completed in time to use real engines in the LaSalles. Work continued on the V-6 until it was actually ready for production as a Chevrolet engine, but GM managers evidently reconsidered the idea of releasing it because of production cost considerations as well as the fact that the division had just released its new V-8 and a virtually all-new Chevrolet.

CHAPTER FIVE: THE GM MOTORAMA OF 1955

*The LaSalle II roadster's small size is evident in this publicity photo. The wheelbase is only 99.9 inches, its overall length measures only 151.7 inches, and the height is a mere 42.8 inches. It was recovered from Warhoops Used Auto & Truck Parts in Sterling Heights, Michigan, by collector Joe Bortz about 25 years ago and is now fully restored. (Photo Courtesy GM Media Archive)*

*The LaSalle II sedan is shown here at an unknown venue receiving a close inspection. Note that the roofline and C-pillars appear to be similar to those of the 1958 Chevrolet Impala. (Photo Courtesy GM Media Archive)*

*The 1955 GM LaSalle II roadster is shown here in an advanced state of construction. (Photo Courtesy GM Media Archive)*

Both cars were given 13-inch wheels with exposed brake drums cast with radial blades for heat dissipation. The bimetal brake drums bolted to the wheel hub to form a brake chamber designed to inhibit the entrance of moisture and dirt. Removal of the drums for servicing was said to take only seconds.

The suspension for the sedan consisted of torsion bars in front and coils in back while the roadster employed coil springs all around.

The LaSalle IIs actually sort of predicted of the future; the compact car emerged in the 1960s and Buick offered a V-6 (though quite different from the 1950s design) starting in 1962. It was an engine that became very important to Buick two decades later.

### Roadster Restoration

As mentioned earlier in this chapter, the LaSalle IIs were taken to Warhoops Used Auto & Truck Parts where they were supposed to be cut apart and crushed. Only the roadster was cut apart and the pieces stayed there for nearly three decades until Joe Bortz purchased all four dream cars present at the salvage yard. Like the Biscayne, the LaSalle II roadster seemed to be beyond saving and was missing some parts that would have to be made. Also like the Biscayne, it became a long-term project.

Marty Martino was employed to complete the LaSalle II roadster's restoration. Using numerous contemporary photographs, he was able to correctly and precisely recreate the original sculpting of the front end of the dream car. GM Heritage Center Design Director and retired GM Design Director Larry Faloon was instrumental in providing important copies of a treasure trove of original documents, which had been discovered at the Center some years earlier. Even with all these valuable assets, Martino still needed to call upon his creative thinking abilities for some tasks, such as reproducing the missing dual instrumentation nacelles. These were ultimately molded by using an ideally shaped iced-tea pitcher he had in his shop.

As with the Biscayne, just enough of the original upholstery remained intact to use as a guide to restore the seats. Some small trim parts also had to be made from scratch, such as the LaSalle script and rear emblem. Martino's girlfriend, Sue Adams (who is a jeweler), recreated these special pieces from sterling silver using original blueprints and photographs.

As with the Biscayne, the LaSalle II roadster was made operational, something it was not when originally built. In this case, though, Bortz could not simply rebuild or acquire an engine to put in the unique car as there are no 1950s 2.5-liter, aluminum, fuel-injected, DOHC Chevrolet V-6s to be found. This problem was solved by making the LaSalle II roadster run by using a custom-designed electric motor hidden in the car's trunk compartment. (The simulated engine was restored to show condition.) Pioneer Conversions of Lemont, Illinois, was hired to fabricate the system, but with the stipulation that as little modification to the body as possible was an absolute requirement. To that end, already existing mounting holes were used to secure the electric motor and associated hardware.

CHAPTER FIVE: THE GM MOTORAMA OF 1955

Marty Martino handled much of the fiberglass bodywork and interior restoration on the LaSalle II roadster. Here, Marty is in discussion with the car's owner, Joe Bortz. (Photo Courtesy Lea Lenz-Dunham)

This trunk ornament on the LaSalle II roadster was carefully recreated using original photographs and blueprints.

A full set of gauges along with a 140-mph speedometer and 5,500-rpm tachometer were included in a compact instrument cluster for the LaSalle II roadster. A power switch for adjustment of the driver's seat is mounted on the console. Power window switches are on the door panels. All of this was simulated since this dream car was not built as a functional vehicle.

The braking system of the LaSalle II roadster presented another set of problems to overcome. Not ever being operational, some creative thought had to go into making the system work. The Vair Shop (a Corvair specialist) in Frankfort, Illinois, performed the cosmetic restoration of the brake drum and wheel assemblies. They also added a master cylinder and the necessary hydraulic lines to get the unusual brakes to function. A rotating drum and backing plate assembly completely surrounds the brake shoes and wheel cylinders, which are of course stationary. Brake fluid flows to the wheel cylinders via a stationary center that holds the bearings for the rotating drum and wheel carrier assembly.

The chassis of the little roadster was originally finished to the same high standards as the rest of the car. Therefore, it was restored accordingly. Chrome plating was applied to the front lower control arms, idler arm, and support members for the rear axle driveshafts.

The completely restored LaSalle II roadster made its second debut as a show car approximately six decades after its first debut at the 2013 Amelia Island Concours d'Elegance. Sitting next to it was the unrestored LaSalle II sedan, which is expected to undergo a complete restoration in the near future.

*The restored 1955 LaSalle II roadster made its post-restoration debut at the 2013 Amelia Island Concours d'Elegance.*

Appearing almost the same as it did when it was found nearly 30 years ago at Warhoops Used Auto & Truck Parts, the LaSalle II sedan was shown at the 2013 Amelia Island Concours d'Elegance. This one is expected to be under restoration in the near future and is to receive an electric motor to make it easier to move.

# Other Notable Show Cars of the 1955 GM Motorama

General Motors' 50-millionth automobile, a 1955 Bel Air two-door hardtop, occupied a turntable at that year's GM Motorama. The car, painted gold, was adorned with hundreds of gold-plated parts, which otherwise would have been chrome-plated.

The 1955 Bel Air-based Nomad was inspired by the 1954 Corvette-based Nomad. Its public debut was during the 1955 GM Motorama. (Photo Courtesy GM Media Archive)

Spinning on a turntable at the 1955 GM Motorama was GM's 50-millionth production automobile, a Chevrolet Bel Air two-door hardtop painted Anniversary Gold and adorned with a reported 716 gold-plated trim parts. The car, which was assembled on November 23, 1954, appeared on the GM Motorama circuit that year and also at other special events such as the "Golden CARnival" in Flint, Michigan. The keys to the special Bel Air were ceremoniously handed over to Harlow Curtice as part of the festivities. Chevrolet also built a reported 5,000 Bel Air sedans painted in the limited-edition Anniversary Gold color.

For whatever reason, this unique Bel Air left the possession of General Motors repainted black and white (but still with its gold interior and gold-plated hardware) and became privately owned. It was about to be turned into a dirt track racer when a North Carolina resident discovered the car and made a deal to buy it not knowing the significance of the former showpiece. Only after finding unusual gold plating under the tarnish, gold paint under multiple repaints, and a special plaque on the firewall did he begin to suspect there was something very different about his acquisition. A phone call to the late Tom Trainor, who had worked for General Motors for 30 years and was a Chevy hobbyist, provided the owner with the verification that his was indeed the actual 50-millionth GM car. Perhaps this car will resurface again soon.

New to the Chevrolet lineup for 1955 was the Nomad two-door station wagon, inspired by the previous year's Motorama dream car, the Corvette-based Nomad. A Cashmere Blue example was prominently displayed at this year's GM Motorama.

Other special exhibits of Chevrolet included a cutaway Bel Air as well as a Bel Air sedan with a clear plastic hood. This allowed visitors to the Motorama to view the new air conditioning unit that was completely contained within the engine

A 1955 Bel Air sedan with a clear plastic hood allowed visitors to the GM Motorama a view of the new air conditioning unit contained completely within the engine compartment; it still allowed a clean, hood-down look at the car. This was the first model year in which Chevrolet offered air conditioning as an option.

*For 1955, Chevrolet introduced yet another new vehicle, the Cameo pickup. It brought passenger car styling elements to pickup truck design. The pricey vehicle featured a wraparound windshield, hooded headlights, egg-crate grille, and a fiberglass bed with fenders that fit flush to the cab; chrome molding covered most of the gap between the two units. (Photo Courtesy GM Media Archive)*

*Chevrolet's Corvette was lagging well behind its expected sales of 10,000 units per year. Even with the new 265 V-8 under the hood instead of the straight-6 of the first two model years, the car only managed to attract 700 buyers.*

compartment and yet still allowed for a clean, hood-down look at the car. This was the first model year in which Chevrolet offered air conditioning as an option.

This year Chevrolet also introduced the Cameo pickup. It brought passenger car styling elements to pickup truck design. The pricey vehicle featured a wraparound windshield, hooded headlights, and egg-crate grille as well as a fiberglass bed with fenders that fit flush to the cab; chrome molding hid most of the gap between the two units. A Cameo prototype may have been shown during the Miami exhibition at the Dinner Key Auditorium (held in February); the entire line of pickups was not introduced until March of that year. (Limited space at the Waldorf-Astoria likely precluded a large truck exhibit; the Dinner Key was much larger.) The 1954 models were carried over until the 1955s were in production. Thus, all 1955 Chevy pickups on display there may have been prototypes.

In addition, for the first time at the GM Motorama, three of GM's foreign models were shown: Opel Caravan station wagon from Germany, Vauxhall Cresta sedan from England, and Holden Special from Australia.

A new model, the Safari, Pontiac's counterpart to Chevy's Nomad, occupied a turntable at the Waldorf-Astoria. It was likely a hand-built version because the model did not become available until early spring.

Also appearing was a 1955 Star Chief Custom sedan cut transversely to reveal the "inside story of Pontiac's quality."

The 1955 model year was outstanding for the Oldsmobile division with a total of 583,179 vehicles sold, the highest output in the division's history. Boosting sales to such heights was new styling and a large number of two-tone paint selections. Oldsmobile's general sales manager, G. R. Jones, told a reporter during one of

*A new model, the Safari, Pontiac's counterpart to Chevy's Nomad, also occupied a turntable during the 1955 GM Motorama show circuit. (Photo Courtesy David McGee collection)*

CHAPTER FIVE: THE GM MOTORAMA OF 1955

# Other Notable Show Cars of the 1955 GM Motorama
### CONTINUED

*A prototype of Buick's Century four-door hardtop was displayed on stage at the Waldorf-Astoria. It was likely built from a two-door hardtop and its quarter panels were about 1/4 inch longer than those of the production version. It was labeled as a model 68, a designation used only for the prototype. (Photo Courtesy GM Media Archive)*

the Motorama stops that "Bright, attractive colors are utilized in striking fashion to enhance Oldsmobile's low silhouette appearance. Contrasting or complementary colors are used advantageously in two-tone styling that creates a luxurious effect of custom design."

In all, 89 two-tone color scheme combinations were offered for 1955 and 14 new paint colors were added as well. To underscore the availability of two-tone color combinations at the 1955 GM Motorama, several Eighty-Eights and Ninety-Eights were shown painted in such two-tones as coral and Polar White, Twilight Blue and Frost Blue, Burlingame Red and Mist Gray, as well as turquoise and Polar White.

Appearing on the stage at the Dinner Key in Miami was a Holiday Ninety-Eight sedan described as "one of the most luxurious production cars ever made by Oldsmobile." Eleven other production Oldsmobiles were on hand at the Dinner Key; among them was a Starfire painted chartreuse and ivory with dimpled light green upholstery.

Buick presented its new Century four-door hardtop in prototype form on that year's Motorama tour, at least until the production version was released. The Cherokee Red and Dover White Buick Century Riviera four-door hardtop equipped with "Skylark" wire wheels was likely built from a two-door hardtop. This car was restored a few years ago and is currently owned by Bob Coker.

In addition to the Eldorado Brougham, Cadillac was represented by three specially trimmed Cadillacs dubbed Celebrity, Eldorado St. Moritz, and Westchester.

The bright red Celebrity, with its matching red long-grain leather-covered top and sabre-spoke wheels, was a slightly modified Coupe de Ville and the forerunner of the Eldorado Seville two-door hardtop, which became available the following year. The plush interior was also upholstered in bright red leather; the seat bolsters were decorated with chrome buttons and silver welt, while the inserts were of a silver-thread V-pattern red cloth.

*This 1955 Buick Century four-door hardtop prototype was sold after that year's GM Motorama and is now fully restored. Bob Coker currently owns it as well as the 1954 Buick Landau. The body style became available at about the mid-point of the model year. (Photo Courtesy Bob Coker)*

The 1955 Cadillac Celebrity (background left) was a modified Coupe de Ville and the forerunner of the Eldorado Seville two-door hardtop that became available the following year. It was painted bright red with a matching red long-grain leather-covered top. A Sixty Special was altered into the Westchester. (Photo Courtesy GM Media Archive)

A Series Sixty Special equipped with air conditioning served as the basis for the Westchester. It was painted Korina Gold and was equipped with a padded black-leather roof covering. Driver and passenger compartments were divided with a glass partition. Black leather covered the front seat while the rear seat actually appears to have been body-colored leather surrounding black cloth interwoven with gold thread, although an official press release only mentions the black cloth with interwoven gold thread. Carpeting was black mouton fur. Back-seat passengers were treated to a 14-inch television mounted in the back of the front seat, telephone, tape recorder, and Korina Gold wood paneling.

An Eldorado convertible was converted into the St. Moritz by painting it pearlescent white and upholstering it in white ermine trimmed in pearlescent white English-grain leather. The standard carpeting was replaced with white mouton fur. Also included was a built-in vanity. Presumably its namesake was the popular ski resort in Switzerland.

A 14-inch television, telephone, and tape recorder were mounted in the rear passenger compartment of the Cadillac Westchester, a modified Sixty Special.

An Eldorado convertible was converted into the St. Moritz by painting it pearlescent white and upholstering it in pearlescent white English-grain leather trimmed with white ermine. The standard carpeting was replaced with white mouton fur. Also included was a built-in vanity.

## Chapter Six

# THE GM MOTORAMA OF 1956

The 1956 GM Motorama toured the same five cities as the prior year. At the time no one realized there would be no 1957 GM Motorama (even though GM Canada continued theirs through 1961). In the three short years since the 1953 tour, the cost of producing the show had doubled from $5 million to $10 million.

Among the dream cars shown was another turbine-powered research vehicle, the GM Firebird II, and the final prototype of the Eldorado Brougham, which went into production the following model year.

The theme for this year's stage presentation was "Key to the Future." Michael Kidd, a well-known Broadway film and stage choreographer designed the stage production.

### Chevrolet Corvette Impala: Five-Passenger Luxury Sport

An unusual Corvette-like dream car graced a turntable at the five venues of the 1956 GM Motorama. It was the Corvette Impala (XP-100, SO 2487), an automobile deliberately styled to give some sports car "flavoring" to a five-passenger luxury car. The dream car's toothy grille and rounded quarters revealed its styling was influenced by the newly restyled first-generation Corvette. A special brochure about the Corvette Impala stated that the car "incorporates wholly new considerations in fine passenger car design from the standpoint of sleekness, safety, and luxury." The claim was true.

Bob Cadaret and Carl Renner designed the experimental fiberglass car. Underneath the hood, it housed

*The Corvette-like grille of the 1956 Corvette Impala was proposed for use on the big Chevrolets for 1958, but was rejected due to cost considerations. Its lance-shaped windsplit on the side of the body was inspired by the 1954 Fiat V-8 coupe. The show car appears to have been painted a color similar to Aegean Turquoise, a color offered for the 1958 model year. (Photo Courtesy GM Media Archive)*

*The low height of the Centurion is evident in this view with the model standing alongside as a visual cue. This frontal angle shows the sloping hood and fenders; horizontally bisected, recessed grille; and turbine blade-styled bezels surrounding the recessed headlights.*

# CHAPTER SIX: THE GM MOTORAMA OF 1956

*The 1956 Chevrolet Corvette Impala (right) shared a display platform with the Buick Centurion (left). This photograph was likely taken at the show held at the Pan Pacific Auditorium in Los Angeles. (Photo Courtesy GM Media Archive)*

*This full-scale clay model of the 1956 Corvette Impala represented the (almost) final form of the actual show car. Notable is the reverse-slant C-pillar and wraparound rear windshield. Also note the thin, wraparound rear bumpers, which were divided by the recessed license plate mount. Windsplits ran down the deck lid. Styling creases were molded into the side of the fiberglass body and minimal bright trim was applied. The basic look was somewhat foretelling of the 1958 Impala. (Photo Courtesy GM Media Archive)*

a 225-hp Super Turbo-Fire V-8 engine coupled to a 2-speed Powerglide. Its horsepower rating suggested that it was equipped with the dual 4-barrel carburetor setup, but a photograph of its chassis with the engine in place shows only a single carburetor was used, presumably a 4-barrel. The stock 265 with a single 4-barrel carburetor was officially rated at 205 hp. Spent exhaust exited through a dual set of pipes passing through the driveshaft tunnel and into a transverse-mounted muffler with dual outlets projecting through the lower rear body panel.

Styling of the Corvette Impala gave the motoring public a preview of the styling for the 1958 Chevrolet Impala production model. In fact, at one point the toothy grille was proposed for use on the new model, but was dropped because of cost considerations. Even so, the integral bumper and grille theme was kept. Other styling features included a tinted "Panoramic" wraparound windshield curving up into the pale blue-tinted, brushed stainless steel roof, wraparound rear windshield, beltline dip near the reverse-slant C-pillars, and chrome-plated wire wheels with knock-off hubs. All of these, with the exceptions of the wire wheels and the brushed stainless steel roof, were adopted for the production car. Its nose emblem was very close to the production type used for the 1958–1960 Corvettes, but with the embossed name "Corvette Impala" circling the crossed flags.

*The bench seats of the Corvette Impala were upholstered in silver-blue vinyl and crosshatch-pattern nylon. A uniquely styled air-foil–shaped, padded strut emerged from the steering column. It held various controls. (Photo Courtesy GM Media Archive)*

*A fixed armrest containing power window switches, a courtesy lamp, and an ashtray was mounted on the center of the Corvette Impala's rear seat. (Photo Courtesy GM Media Archive)*

Exterior measurements of the Corvette Impala were a rather low overall height of 53.7 inches, a width of 74.4 inches, an overall length of 202 inches, a wheelbase spanning 116.5 inches, and a road clearance of 6 inches.

Designing safety into the interior was still in its infancy in the 1950s, but the Corvette Impala was certainly advanced in that regard; none of the safety features interfered in the least with the cosmetic appearance of the interior. A unique, airfoil-shaped, padded cornering bar (or strut) emerged from the steering column and angled upward before transitioning into a horizontal component extending across the entire width of the interior. Flush-fitting controls for the heater/defroster, headlights, and windshield wipers were located on the surface of the strut. Nestled above the steering column was the recessed and hooded instrumentation cluster, which consisted of a 120-mph (perhaps 130-mph) speedometer and a speed warning system of 10 circular windows spread across the instrument panel; each illuminated progressively in more intense shades of red as speed increased. Also included for safety were seat belts that were stored in the recesses between the backrests and seat cushion. A sloped, recessed package shelf and a padded rear window header served as additional safety features.

The bench seats of the Corvette Impala were upholstered in silver-blue vinyl and crosshatch-pattern nylon; the front seat, which was equipped with a fold-down center armrest fitted with a map case, slid forward when tilted to aid entry and exit for rear-seat passengers. A fixed armrest with power window switches, a courtesy lamp, and an ashtray was mounted on the center of the rear seat. (A fixed rear center armrest was included for the production version of the Impala two years later.) The floor covering material was similar to, if not the same as, that of the Corvette. Bright metal strips overlaid the carpet in front. The concave section of the door panels was fitted with blue-tinted metal inserts and long armrests for maximum comfort. Other conveniences included a radio and drum clock mounted in the center section of the padded cowl.

*A Corvette equipped with the optional dual-quad V-8 was on display at the GM Motorama for 1956. Examining the engine compartment is Betty Skelton, who established many records in aviation and at Daytona Speedweeks driving a specially prepared Corvette. She also served as a spokesperson for Chevrolet. (Photo Courtesy GM Media Archive)*

*The Corvette Impala was displayed at the 1957 Chicago Auto Show, where it appeared in this deep blue color. (Photo Courtesy Warren Kostelny)*

# CHAPTER SIX: THE GM MOTORAMA OF 1956

*The chassis of the Corvette Impala was remarkably complete and included a fuel filler and tank. This suggests this car may have been fully operable. Note the custom-built air-cleaner setup, which was virtually identical to that of the 1955 Biscayne. Also notice the temporarily installed 1953–1955 Corvette steering wheel.*

The Corvette Impala's color was similar to, if not a match to, Aegean Turquoise Metallic, a color offered for 1958 Chevrolets. However, it must have been repainted in a deep blue (assuming there were not two of them; a solid assumption judging by the evidence available) not long after the GM Motorama of 1956 came to an end. According to an article in the July 1956 issue of *Chevrolet Dealers News*, the Corvette Impala was blue. A color photo of the car taken by a visitor to the 1957 Chicago Auto Show (held January 5–13) also clearly shows it to have been blue.

Presumably, the 1956 Corvette Impala was scrapped. However, a photograph of the show car's chassis reveals that it was equipped with a fuel tank and filler (not all such cars were so equipped) suggesting this one may have been drivable. If so, rescuing it from a scrap order would have been more easily accomplished than with a non-running dream car. Its latest known appearance at an auto show was at the 1957 CNE held in August and September of that year.

## Pontiac Club de Mer: Real Potential?

The 1956 Pontiac Club de Mer (XP-200, SO 2488) was distinctive and exotic to say the least, so its French moniker, a name inspired by Miami's fashionable Surf Club, was certainly fitting. This dream car suggested Pontiac

*The nose of the Club de Mer did not have a conventional grille but rather an "air intake aperture for engine cooling." Note the silver streaks across the hood; it's the only theme suggesting that this dream car was a Pontiac. (The silver streak theme was discarded, though, the following model year.) It is shown parked next to the location of its namesake, the apartment complex of Miami's Surf Club.*

was serious about changing its image from a dull, yet dependable car to that of a performance car, an image much more appealing to the emerging youth market. Its design is credited to Paul Gillan who joined the Pontiac Studio in 1947 as a junior designer and three years later moved up to chief designer of the studio.

### Exterior Cues

This sporty and compact two-seater was very low, standing only a little more than 38 inches tall and was barely more than 180 inches long. The Club de Mer's wheelbase measured 2 inches more than the Corvette's at 104 inches and ground clearance was 5 inches. (For comparison, the last-generation Firebird stood 14 inches taller and had about 15 inches more length.) The dream

With the model standing next to the Club de Mer, its low height is very apparent. The Club de Mer stood only a fraction of an inch over 38 inches high. Its body panels rolled under to form a belly pan for improved airflow past the undercarriage. Regardless of its clean lines and racy looks, the Club de Mer was only for show; it did not even run. (Photo Courtesy GM Media Archive)

An earlier clay model of the Pontiac Club de Mer proposed a wraparound windshield; this feature was later dropped and replaced by twin-bubble windscreens. However, the central dorsal fin appears to be in its final form. (Photo Courtesy GM Media Archive)

The Club de Mer's outer body panels were made of clear, anodized, brushed-aluminum and painted translucent Cerulean blue. The Oldsmobile Golden Rocket appears at left.

MOTORAMA 155

car's outer body panels were made of clear, anodized, brushed-aluminum painted translucent Cerulean Blue. Its body panels rolled under to seal the entire undercarriage for cleaner airflow underneath. Removable panels bolted over openings throughout the underside to allow access to mechanical systems. The belly pan was an attribute of European race cars and sports cars such as the Mercedes 300SL, which had a bolt-on belly pan.

Other styling characteristics of the Club de Mer included its twin-bubble windscreens and shark-like dorsal fin. Regarding the latter, General Motors said it "not only adds fleetness to the car's appearance but also functions as a stabilizing influence during operation." The dream car's sleek nose was designed without a conventional grille, but instead had an "air intake aperture for engine cooling" as described in an official press release issued by General Motors. This opening was outlined with stainless, or more likely, chrome-plated fiberglass trim. Outlets in the forward portion of the doors, which were adorned with a set of three horizontal chrome strips, provided additional cooling for the engine compartment.

The highway and parking lights were integrated into a dual layout with one placed directly over the other outside the headlight assemblies. The latter rotated into the Club de Mer's body when not in use to reduce drag.

Familiar-looking silver streaks were similar to those of the production models although Pontiac General Manager Semon "Bunkie" Knudsen judged the silver streak theme to be out of touch with the growing youth market. The 1957 models as originally designed had the feature, which he ordered to be removed.

In back was the single fin that was shaped like those on the 1957 Eldorado. Slim horizontal taillights and back-up lights were fitted into nearly parallelogram-shaped openings. Four exhaust tips exited through the lower rear panel, which was trimmed with thin bumperettes. Another thin molding wrapped around the sides and was divided by the recessed license plate mount.

Finned, conical wheel covers and specially made U.S. Royal narrow-band whitewall tires with a single white stripe on the tread were additional fresh ideas exhibited on the Club de Mer.

### Interior Components

A rich vermillion interior contrasted spectacularly well with the exterior finish and featured chrome-trimmed bucket seats upholstered in soft-grain crush leather separated by a chrome-plated console housing the controls for gear selection, remote deck release, ignition, and radio. The console served as the tube through which the driveshaft ran to connect the engine to the rear transaxle. Other controls were within easy reach of the driver and were mounted at the forward end of the armrest,

This overhead view shows the cockpit of the Club de Mer well. Clearly visible are the competition safety harnesses, chrome frames around the seats, and console. (Photo Courtesy GM Media Archive)

Instrumentation for the Club de Mer was grouped in pods directly ahead of the driver; there was no panel for the passenger side. The dream car's steering wheel was a three-bar competition type.

*A motorized 1/4-scale model of the Club de Mer was constructed and displayed at the GM Motorama. This model was, at one time, in the Bortz Auto Collection. (Photo Courtesy GM Media Archive)*

which was set within the hollowed-out door panel on the driver's side. Brushed-aluminum inserts decorated the door panels.

Instrumentation was grouped in pods directly ahead of the driver; there was no panel for the passenger side. The steering wheel was a three-bar competition type similar to the wheel on that year's restyled Corvette. A small rearview mirror was mounted on the panel between the twin windscreens. For safety, competition-type lap and shoulder belts were installed and the entire rim of the interior was padded.

### Et Cetera

Most of the dream cars were built using an existing chassis modified as needed, but no so the Club de Mer. Instead it had a custom-fabricated steel tube chassis, even though its front suspension was a modified stock system. A de Dion suspension was employed in back with the transaxle. A 300-hp Strato-Streak 317 V-8 fitted with dual

*This full-color ad promoted the appearance of Pontiac's "Motorama Masterpieces" at the Pan Pacific Auditorium in Los Angeles.*

MOTORAMA 157

## CHAPTER SIX: THE GM MOTORAMA OF 1956

4-barrel carburetors powered the experimental sports car.

The weight of the Club de Mer is not readily available, although it was perhaps less than 3,000 pounds. Assuming this is true, the horsepower-to-weight ratio was somewhere between 9.3 and 10:1. For comparison, a contemporary Porsche Spyder 550, a car smaller and lighter than the Club de Mer, had a horsepower-to-weight ratio of about 11:1. You have to wonder about the car's potential performance capabilities, but unfortunately, we will never know. If the Club de Mer had been fully developed it could have seemingly been very competitive against European race cars. Perhaps a production version would have even been named Le Mans!

An interesting tidbit about the Club de Mer comes from Bruce Berghoff (author of *The GM Motorama*) who worked for H. B. Stubbs, the company in charge of the complex displays General Motors used for car shows. During the setup for the show in Miami, the dream car's titanium axle shaft was found to be sheared. The shaft may have been defective, although it could have simply been overstressed from the tie-down strap securing the Club de Mer inside its transport trailer. It could not be rolled out until it was repaired. I asked Berghoff if he ever witnessed the Club de Mer move under its own power; he replied that he never did and never even heard it idling.

Even though the Club de Mer was probably never seriously considered for production, its styling may have been the inspiration for the sculptured recess with three chrome-plated windsplits on the side of the 1958 Corvette as well as the Pontiac Tempest that came along in the early 1960s.

What became of the Club de Mer? This question remains unanswered. Old rumors tell of the car being in various places, such as Utah. If it still exists, it has remained hidden away for nearly six decades.

### Oldsmobile Golden Rocket: Aptly Named

The 1956 Oldsmobile Golden Rocket (XP-400, SO 2490) was certainly one of the most radically styled dream cars of the era. A more fitting name for it could not have been chosen. Its profile resembled a metallic gold rocket laid on its side thanks to its its twin-torpedo, pontoon-shaped fenders and tapering quarter panels with stubby tail fins. General Motors described the car as having "a special look of grace and swiftness."

#### *Styling Features*

That special look was almost certainly inspired by the styling of the 1953–1955 B.A.T. (Berlina Aero-Technica) series and perhaps even the experimental, turbine-powered 1954 Fiat 8001 (although the latter lacked the split rear window present on the Golden Rocket and B.A.T. series). The split backlight dates back at least as far as the Bugatti Type 57SC Atlantic of the 1930s. Harley Earl, who was no doubt familiar with all of these European cars, assigned Art Ross to the XP-400 Golden Rocket project.

The projectile-shaped nose of the Golden Rocket housed a small, upside-down, U-shaped grille. "Dagmar"-style bumpers were positioned at the ends of the front fenders. The dream car's headlights were positioned inboard of these bumpers. Air inlets just below the windshield on either side of the hood along with openings behind and beneath the backlight allowed fresh air to flow through the cockpit. Side-mounted running lights were placed at the rear of the dorsal fins.

The split backlight of the Golden Rocket ultimately was adopted for the second-generation (or C2) Corvette, although for only the first model year of the type, 1963. This was not happenstance. The split window was a favorite theme of Bill Mitchell who succeeded Harley Earl just about three years after the Golden Rocket made its national tour. Coincidentally, an earlier C2 Corvette design rendered in clay in 1955 (and intended for production for the 1958 model year) was styled very much like the Golden Rocket including its split rear window. Cost considerations likely stopped this proposal from going into production.

*Bill Mitchell, head of GM Design, and Mr. Payze, a stylist with GM's Holden of Australia, are shown here posing with the blue Golden Rocket in February 1962. Some of GM's other dream cars had been sent away to be scrapped a few years earlier, but this one ws clearly spared that fate, at least for a while. (Photo Courtesy GM Media Archive)*

*The projectile-shaped nose, pontoon-like fenders, and tapering quarter panels with stubby tail fins gave the Golden Rocket a rocket-like profile, something very fitting for a show car representing Oldsmobile, which used "rocket" as a marketing theme.*

Other styling features included a hidden fuel filler located behind the recessed license plate mounting, which was enclosed with a clear cover and white strobe stripes on the side walls of the tires.

The Golden Rocket had an overall height of only 49.5 inches. Opening and closing the doors automatically activated flip-up roof panels to ease entry and exit from the vehicle. Opening the doors also caused the bucket seats to swivel and raise 3 inches.

Tilt steering was another convenience added to the Golden Rocket. Unlike flip-up roof panels, this feature actually became optional equipment on some GM cars in the 1960s and over time has virtually become standard equipment. One difference, though, is that the lower portion of the steering wheel of the Golden Rocket could be folded away from the driver by simultaneously depressing two buttons; just another aid for entry and exit.

Other atypical features included a speedometer mounted at the base of the steering wheel and the dream car's rearview mirrors. Instead of the usual outside and inside rearview mirrors, the Golden Rocket had one mounted on each of the lower windshield garnish moldings beside the driver- and passenger-side windshield posts. Upholstery was in medium-dark blue leather and contrasting brighter blue carpeting covered the floor.

An Oldsmobile 324 Rocket V-8 was installed in the fiberglass two-seater. Output was boosted to 275 hp according to GM's press releases. (Most likely such claims were based on theoretical calculations.) For comparison, a 240-hp 324 powered the 1956 Olds Ninety-Eight. As usual, the higher output claimed for the Golden Rocket's engine hinted that greater performance was yet to come.

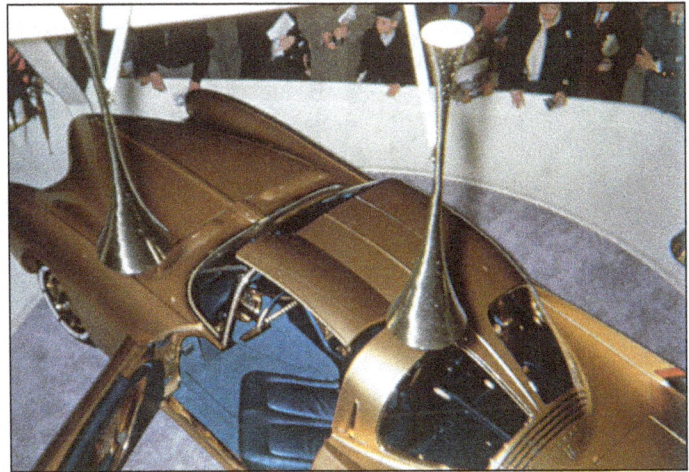

*The Golden Rocket heavily influenced this proposal for a C2 Corvette envisioned for 1958. Cost considerations probably terminated the plan. (Photo Courtesy GM Media Archive)*

*The styling of the Golden Rocket was almost certainly inspired by that of the 1953–1955 B.A.T. series and perhaps even the experimental, turbine-powered 1954 Fiat 8001. Another source was probably the Bugatti Type 57SC Atlantic of the 1930s, which featured a split backlight. The rear portion of this car's roof, with its split rear window, eventually appeared in production for an American car, the 1963 Corvette Sting Ray. The general design continued for the Sting Ray through 1967 as well as the 1971–1973 Buick Riviera. Note the swiveled driver's seat, flip-up roof panels, and folding lower half of the steering wheel. (Photo Courtesy Bruce Berghoff Collection)*

# CHAPTER SIX: THE GM MOTORAMA OF 1956

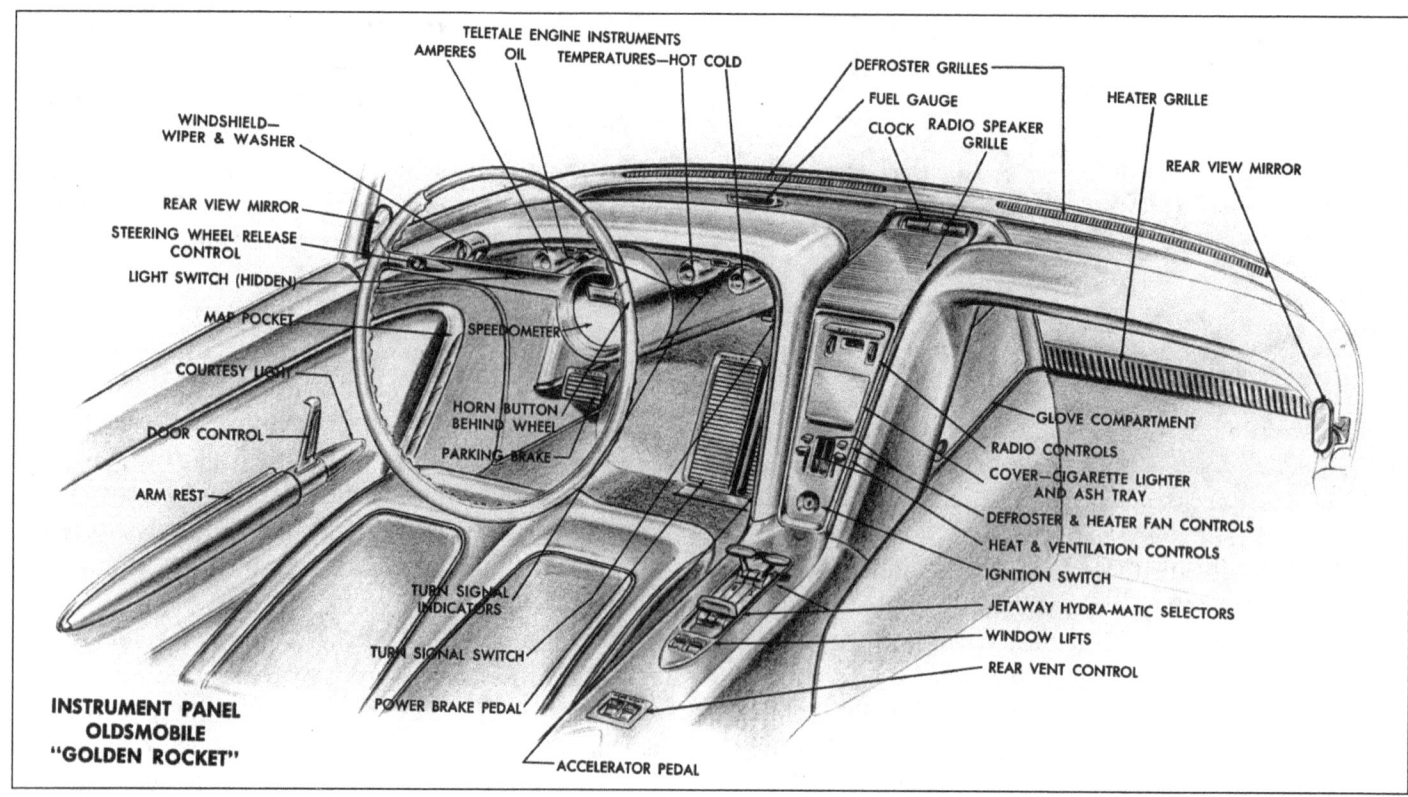

*This artist's drawing of the forward interior of the Golden Rocket reveals the special features included in the dream car. Among them was a rearview mirror placed at the far ends of the dashboard. Also present was a speedometer mounted within the deeply recessed steering wheel hub.*

*Like other dream cars of GM, the Golden Rocket appeared at dealerships across the country after the GM Motorama tour came to an end. This ad promoted the car's appearance at Larry Faul Oldsmobile in Oak Park, Illinois, in early July 1956.*

## On Public Display

The last appearance of the Golden Rocket at an event in the United States, to the best of my knowledge, was at the Oklahoma Semi-Centennial Exhibition in June 1957 where it appeared along with the Chevrolet Corvette Impala, Pontiac Club de Mer, Buick Centurion, and Cadillac Eldorado Brougham prototype.

*Unfortunately, this black and white photograph of the Golden Rocket at the 1957 Paris Salon does not reveal whether or not the car had been repainted blue by then. The strobe stripe tires had been replaced with narrow-band whitewalls. (Photo Courtesy GM Media Archives)*

*Bill Mitchell, head of GM Design, and Mr. Payze, a stylist with GM's Holden of Australia, are shown here posing with the blue Golden Rocket in February 1962. Some of GM's other dream cars had been sent away to be scrapped a few years earlier, but this one ws clearly spared that fate, at least for a while. (Photo Courtesy GM Media Archive)*

It would be interesting to know its color at this time because it was changed to blue at some point. In the digital files of GM Media Archive is a color photograph showing Bill Mitchell and a guest standing beside the Golden Rocket, which had, by then, been repainted blue and equipped with narrow-band whitewall tires rather than the strobe-striped tires it wore during the 1956 GM Motorama. According to GM records, the photo was dated February 6, 1962.

The Golden Rocket was shown at the Paris Salon in the fall of 1957 and it may have been repainted for that event. (To date, I have seen only one black-and-white photo of the car at the 1957 Paris Salon; therefore, its color at that time cannot be determined.) Interestingly, it was equipped with narrow-band whitewalls at that show.

Seemingly, the only other possibility to explain the blue Golden Rocket is that another Rocket was built. However, GM records do not support such a theory. What happened to the car after February 1962? Was it eventually scrapped or is it privately owned today? Enthusiasts are still waiting for an answer to these questions.

## Buick Centurion: Innovative Predictor of the 21st Century

For 1956, Buick was represented with the dream car (XP-301/SO 2489) formally named Centurion. This two-door, four-passenger hardtop was painted Electron Red on the upper portion of the body and white on the lower body although early press releases about the car incorrectly claimed the lower body color to be bright silver or brushed metallic finish. Most likely the mistake was the result of pearlescent white being used for the lower body that gave a metallic effect in some photos. (Today, the lower body is painted bright white.) A Roadmaster-style sweepspear molding divided the contrasting colors.

Dimensional data for this dream car includes an overall length of 213.1 inches, overall width of 73.5 inches, and overall height of 53.7 inches. Its wheelbase measured 118 inches, which was 4 inches shorter than that of the Special and Century series and 9 inches shorter than the wheelbase of the Super and Roadmaster series.

### From the Front

Other than the sweepspear and open wheels, no other outward features are associated with Buicks of the day. As was typical of GM's dreams cars, every element received careful attention from the stylists assigned to the project. In front was a sloping nose with a deeply recessed, horizontally divided grille and recessed headlights surrounded by a turbine-like bezel. The recessed grille and hood of the Centurion were built as an integral unit and hinged in front so as to lift from the rear.

Fresh-air scoops shaped like those of the restyled Corvette served as functional inlets for the air conditioner system and were located on the cowl near the front fenders. Air scoops were also incorporated into the wheel discs to help dissipate heat from the finned brake drums.

Buick's 322 V-8 and variable-pitch Dynaflow transmission was installed in the Centurion. The engine, which was adorned with chrome-plated hardware, was upgraded with four 2-barrel side-draft carburetors and possibly other modifications. Advertised output of the engine of the non-running car was claimed to be 325 hp.

### At the Rear

Rear-end styling was dramatic with a flared rear deck area that resembled the decks of 1959 Chevrolets and Buicks, thus the Centurion provided that styling element to those lines of cars. Lights were integrated into individual units with the stop and backup lights grouped behind a chrome-plated Dagmar at the end of the tail cone while the parking and directional lights were paired on the far ends and positioned just above the exhaust outlets. A license plate mount was placed on the driver's side of the tail cone.

Just above the tail cone sat a patented rear-facing television camera connected electrically to a 4 x 6-inch screen located in the center of the instrument panel. The functional camera took the place of a conventional rear-view mirror. Weighing just 6 pounds, the wide-angle-lens camera made by University Broadcasting System, was shock-resistant to prevent road bumps from interfering with the transmission of a clear image to the screen. The system provided a suitable view even at night. The TV camera, however, is no longer with the Centurion although the mounting bracket remains in place.

### Interior Imagination

Inside the Centurion were four bright red leather-covered bucket seats, each with seat belts and adjustable headrests. Entering and exiting the vehicle was made easier with an electric switch activated by opening the doors; the independent switches moved the front seat back automatically. Rear-seat passengers were assisted into and out of the car by pushing the upright portion of the front seats forward, which activated an electric switch to move the seats forward.

The Centurion's passenger compartment was covered by a transparent roof panel combined with the car's wraparound windshield and backlight. The outward view was interrupted only by the required framing around the glass.

An aircraft-type steering wheel was used instead of a conventional steering column; it was connected to

The dramatic styling of the 1956 Buick Centurion is most evident in this photograph taken in the Miami area prior to the opening of the GM Motorama at the Dinner Key Auditorium. Its bubble top, interrupted only by the required framing to support the individual pieces, allowed a nearly 360-degree view. Note the recessed grille and headlights.

Four side-draft carburetors and lots of chrome plating dressed up the engine compartment of the Buick Centurion. Note the red radiator hose. Nevertheless, the Centurion was and remains a non-functional car.

*A rear-facing television camera positioned just above the tail cone of the Centurion provided a rearward view on a 4 x 6-inch screen located in the center of the instrument panel. The functional camera took the place of a conventional rearview mirror. It was shock-resistant to prevent road bumps from interfering with the transmission of a clear image. The TV camera, however, is no longer present although the mounting bracket remains in place. (CNE Archives, Gilbert Milne Collection, MG 6-302-2)*

a cantilever arm attached at the centerline of the car. A conventional steering column was later installed, although the cantilever arm still remains. (When, as well as why, the column was added is unknown.) Other gadgets of the Centurion that were advanced for the day included a digital clock and a freestanding speedometer with a stationary indicator and revolving dial.

Surprisingly, the Centurion was not quite as finished as most of the dream cars. Some of them even had a trunk mat present. In the case of the Centurion, it did not even get a trunk floor. Furthermore, its trunk lid is represented with a scribed outline with black paint filling the recess.

In a 2006 telephone interview, I asked the late Chuck Jordan, who headed the design team for the XP-301

*Individual seating meant that the Centurion was a four-passenger car. Its pleated-leather upholstery forecast things to come in the 1960s for such cars as the Pontiac Grand Prix and Oldsmobile Starfire. Headrests did not come into vogue until the latter part of the 1960s. Note the "sweep spear" interior molding, rear-seat radio speaker, and center armrest.*

# CHAPTER SIX: THE GM MOTORAMA OF 1956

*This view of the Centurion at the Alfred P. Sloan Museum illustrates the virtually uninterrupted view provided by the bubble-top design. Although impractical for actual use in passenger cars because of interior heating from sunlight, the design gave a space-age look to the Centurion, thus creating quite an impression on those who viewed the car at the GM Motorama and other auto shows. Note the screen that received images from its rear-facing camera.*

project, if he was given any specific guidelines to follow in styling the car. He replied that there were none and went on to explain that seeing Harley Earl's Le Sabre really established what was expected from the designers at GM Styling. Jordan noted that the work environment encouraged stylists to be imaginative and he emphasized that the dream cars were meant to put forward new ideas, and in the case of the Centurion, he and his team decided "fairly quickly" that the cantilever steering arm and rear-facing camera would be included. As Jordan said, they "wanted an interior that went with the exterior."

As for the experimental car's formal name, Jordan did not know who was responsible for it and that the name "Centurion" was chosen after his work on the project was completed. He suspected the most probable explanation for the moniker was because of its similarity to the name of Buick's highly popular performance model called "Century." The Centurion nameplate did not resurface again at Buick until the 1971 model year when it replaced the Wildcat series.

The 1956 Centurion has been preserved and can be seen at the Alfred P. Sloan Museum in Flint, Michigan, when it is not on tour.

## Cadillac Eldorado Brougham: Publicity Prototype and Town Car

Another Eldorado Brougham, this time with a body of fiberglass rather than steel, was on exhibit at the 1956 GM Motorama. It served as a publicity vehicle. The fiberglass Eldorado Brougham Town Car was a chauffer-driven car with an open chauffeur's compartment separated from the passenger compartment via a divider window.

### Publicity Prototype

This Brougham (XP-48, SO 2448) was a near-final-form prototype of the production version of the Eldorado Brougham that emerged the following year. Although the car was constructed around mid-1955 and shown on the 1956 GM Motorama tour, GM documents refer to it as a 1957 prototype.

*The support bracket and wiring harness for the rear-facing TV camera of the Centurion remain in place, but the camera has long since been removed. This photo was taken from underneath the dream car and was possible because it lacks a trunk floor. The Centurion's deck lid is simulated and is represented with a scribed outline.*

164  MOTORAMA

*The 1957 Eldorado Brougham prototype was first exhibited at the 1955 Paris Salon. The four-door pillarless hardtop was very close to the production version released for sale in 1957. (Photo Courtesy GM Media Archive)*

Reportedly, photographs exist of the engine compartment and show that an engine was installed, minus a wiring harness and spark plug wires. Obviously, if true, it was not a running vehicle. The car served for publicity shots and further refinement even as the first production vehicles began leaving the assembly line. Surprisingly, it was originally built with dual headlamps rather than the quad setup seen on the previous year's prototype. The fact that such setups were not legal in all states may have caused some uncertainty as to whether or not to include it on the latest prototype. This arrangement was soon changed to the quad headlight design that made it onto the production cars. (State laws were soon standardized to allow quad headlights.)

The Eldorado Brougham was first shown at the Los Angeles Auto Show then went to the Paris Salon in the fall of 1955. It returned in time for the opening of the 1956 GM Motorama at the Waldorf-Astoria. At the end of the year it was displayed at the auto show America on the Move, held at the newly built New York Coliseum. By then the prototype was updated with the rocker panel molding and the front fender nameplate used on production Eldorado Broughams, which became available for purchase a few months into the 1957 calendar year. It is believed that this car was scrapped.

### Town Car

Ed Glowacke, who was still in charge of the Cadillac studio, is credited with the design of the Town Car (XP-500, SO 2491). It was built 4 inches longer than the Brougham prototype and its quarter panels were flush with the rear doors, unlike the prototype and production Brougham.

The Eldorado Brougham Town Car, was not seriously considered for production. Nevertheless, it was quite elaborate and very elegant. Micro-switches on the door handles at the forefinger position activated a relay for locking and unlocking all the doors at once by simply inserting the key into the lock. The process also raised any lowered windows. A lockout mechanism prevented the engagement of the switches when the car was in motion, according to an official Cadillac press release.

Two bucket-type seats covered in black Morocco leather were in the chauffeur's compartment. The

*As originally built, the 1957 Eldorado Brougham prototype was equipped with this conventional headlight setup. It was later modified to the quad system, which was used on the production version. (Photo Courtesy GM Media Archive)*

passenger compartment, which was separated by a dual-pane, horizontally sliding glass divider and a partition bulkhead, included several comfort and convenience items including a radio-telephone unit to communicate with the chauffeur, air-conditioning, vanity compartment, cigar humidor, thermos bottle, and accompanying gold-plated tumblers.

According to a GM-issued press release, "The inner doors are cloaked in black leather while beige broadcloth in a 'biscuit & button' design covers the rear seat. It blends tastefully with the deep-pile beige [mouton] carpeting and beige broadcloth headlining." The radio-telephone unit was not actually functional, but it looked convincing; the chauffeur's unit was trimmed in chrome while the passenger set was gold-plated.

The Town Car made its debut at the Waldorf-Astoria in New York City in January and continued to be shown at the remaining venues of that year's GM Motorama. It was also seen at other auto shows across the country. In October 1956, like the Brougham prototype the prior year, it was shown at the Paris Salon.

The Eldorado Brougham Town Car was to be scrapped along with three other GM dream cars brought to War-hoops Used Auto & Truck Parts in Sterling Heights in late 1959. Instead, it sat largely untouched until 1989, when collector Joe Bortz bought all four dream cars at Warhoops. Bortz later sold the Town Car to J. C. Whitney & Co. owner the late Roy Warshawsky who had planned to restore the one-of-a-kind car and also make it drivable. Over a three-year period beginning in 1991, the wood framing was replaced, rear bumperettes were constructed from steel to replace the corroded

*The 1956 Eldorado Brougham Town Car was built for show only. It was a retro design based upon chauffer-driven Cadillacs of the classic era.*

*This rarely seen photo of the Eldorado Brougham Town Car shows the cover for the chauffeur's compartment in place. It was not installed when the car was shown on the GM Motorama tour. At some point it was lost or discarded.*

*Simulated radiotelephones were installed in the chauffeur's compartment and the passenger compartment. The unit in front was trimmed in chrome and the passengers' unit was gold-plated. (Photos by the author)*

*The Eldorado Brougham Town Car was fully restored in the late 1990s by Eldorado Brougham collector Dick Baruk. (Photo Courtesy Larry Muckey)*

originals, and a 1956 Eldorado Seville engine was rebuilt, but not installed.

As Warshawsky found the Town Car, it lacked an engine and transmission, which has led to the assumption they were never present. The tale generally accepted over the years was that time had simply run out on those constructing the unique car and that the front springs were compressed to make the Town Car sit level. However, the late Chuck Jordan confirmed during a telephone interview with me in 2006 that the car did have a regular production Cadillac Series 62 365 V-8 and Hydra-Matic as intended. Just before the car was sent for scrapping, Jordan had the drivetrain removed and donated to a local high school.

Even though an engine had been present, the Town Car did not run; it lacked a wiring harness to the engine compartment, had a dash formed from solid wood without provisions for an electrical system, had only a simulated fiberglass fuel tank fitted, and the braking was via the emergency brake only. Officials from General Motors obviously never had any intent to make this car run.

Sadly, Warshawsky's health deteriorated before the restoration could be completed. His death led to consigning the Town Car (together with the rebuilt engine) to the 1996 Auburn Kruse Auction; however, transporting the largely dismantled car to the site proved to be impractical, so it was withdrawn. Instead, arrangements were made for accepting bids by telephone and Livonia, Michigan, resident and Eldorado Brougham collector Dick Baruk had the highest bid.

Prior to bidding on the car, Baruk asked his good friend and Brougham Owner Association member Larry Muckey to carefully inspect the unique automobile to evaluate its condition. Muckey first became aware of the car's existence in the mid-1970s, and even came close to owning it in 1978, but decided the $7,500 asking price was just too high. Muckey found the Town Car to be 99-percent complete and that the few missing parts could be cast, or existing stock Eldorado Brougham parts used or modified as needed.

The Town Car was in surprisingly good condition considering its exposure to the elements for three decades. Even so, much of the interior, including the solid wooden dash, had received significant damage and the plating inside and out was in poor condition. Fortunately, the unique windshield was still like new although the side glass and divider window were both broken. The decayed wooden dash was replaced with a steel dash from a Brougham parts car.

Baruk secured the services of several professionals to get the elegant dream car in top form as well as receiving assistance from GM tech center representative Steve Wolken (since retired), who performed valuable research that included providing original photos of the various

# CHAPTER SIX: THE GM MOTORAMA OF 1956

details of the interior. However, the Town Car was left as a non-runner and without the engine and transmission rebuilt for it. Baruk sold the car in 2005.

In February 2006, the Eldorado Brougham Town Car was sold by RM Auctions in Boca Rotan, Florida, which is fitting because the car was proudly displayed in Miami 50 years earlier during the Motorama. By then, the Eldorado Brougham Town Car finally had its engine and transmission installed and was made drivable for the first time. Leonard and Michele Worden of Windham, New Hampshire now own it.

## Cadillac Castilian, Gala, Maharani, and Palomino: The "Mood Cars"

Four modified production cars labeled Castilian, Gala, Maharani, and Palomino were also shown on the 1956 GM Motorama circuit. All four of these special Cadillacs were dubbed "mood cars" in a 1956 GM press release about that year's GM Motorama.

An Eldorado Seville served as the basis for the Castilian, a Starlight Silver and white car with an interior upholstered in black and white calfskin with silver nylon. Other than its paint scheme, the only outward change made to the show car was the addition of longhorn emblems to the upper door moldings. The Castilian's upper door and quarter trim panels were modified with special metalwork.

*The interior of the Castilian was upholstered in black and white calfskin with silver nylon. Its upper door and quarter trim panels were modified with special metalwork. (Photo Courtesy Lou Commisso Collection)*

The Gala, also know as "the wedding car," was a Sedan de Ville painted pearlescent white with a pearl-white leather, satin, and nylon interior. Carpeting was white mouton. Armrests in the front doors housed small umbrellas with silver and rhinestone-covered handles.

The Western-themed, metallic beige Palomino was created from a Series 62 convertible. Soft, natural palomino hides covered its upper door panels, which were

*All four of the 1956 Cadillac "mood cars" are shown in this photograph. At left is the Palomino, the Gala is on a platform and appears just beyond the Palomino, the Castilian is near the center, and at right is the Maharani. (Photo Courtesy GM Media Archive)*

*Of the four Cadillac "mood cars" built for show at the 1956 GM Motorama, only the Maharani is known to have survived. At the time this photo was taken in 2008, the car was still fitted with its original tires and had been driven less than 1,700 miles.*

divided from the lower portions covered in natural basket-weave leather by a gold-riveted horizontal belt. Seats were upholstered with natural palomino hide (bolsters) and buffalo grain leather. Pale gold hardware and seat finish moldings with gold rivets were additional enhancements.

A Series 60 Special was converted into the metallic maroon Maharani. Its most unusual feature was its roll-top cabinet occupying the front passenger compartment. Underneath the roll-top were a kitchen sink, recessed toaster, hot plate, cutlery tray, folding dining table, cooling unit, coffee and water dispensers as well as a ladies vanity, safe, and safety deposit box. The coffee and water dispensers were supplied by tanks located under the hood and the cooling unit was mounted in the trunk. Presumably, GM's Frigidaire Division made the kitchen appointments. The interior was upholstered in snakeskin with satin print inserts and its floor was carpeted with lambskin.

Of these four "mood cars" only the Maharani is known to still exist. In fact, as of 2008, it was still equipped with its original tires! It was sold at an auction in 2009 to a

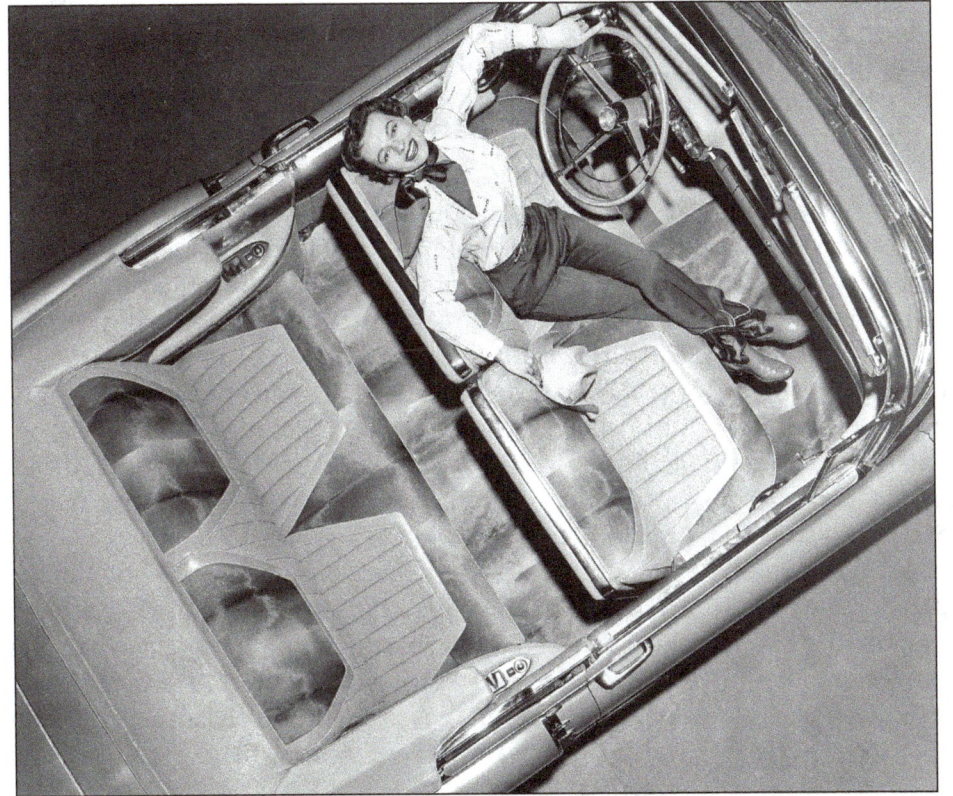

**This rarely seen overhead view of the Palomino provides a good look at the car's special interior. Palomino hides covered its upper door panels; the lower portions were covered in natural basket-weave leather. (Photo Courtesy Lou Commisso Collection)**

# CHAPTER SIX: THE GM MOTORAMA OF 1956

*The most unusual feature of the Cadillac Maharani is the roll-top cabinet occupying the front passenger compartment. Underneath the roll-top were a kitchen sink, recessed toaster, hot plate, cutlery tray, folding dining table, cooling unit, coffee and water dispensers as well as a vanity, safe, and safety deposit box. The show car's upholstery is snakeskin with satin print inserts and its floor is carpeted with lambskin. The interior of the Maharani remains original.*

bidder reportedly in Dubai. At last report it had been sold again with its new owner residing in Italy.

## GM Firebird II: Next Generation

General Motors built on the lessons learned with the Firebird I when the next turbine-powered research car (two of which were built) was designed, the 1956 Firebird II (XP-43). It was "the first American gas turbine passenger car *specifically* designed for family use on the highway," according to a GM-issued press release. The claim was indeed correct. Chrysler Corporation tested a turbine engine in a nearly *stock* 1954 Plymouth Belvedere, a car adapted for a turbine engine rather than designed from the start for turbine power.

The new Firebird II was more than a turbine engine research project, however. It was used to test experimental suspension and braking systems, too.

Another innovation tested was titanium for body construction. One of the two Firebird IIs (SO 2418) was built using this metal. It was the nonfunctional car shown on the Motorama circuit. The other (SO 2683) was of fiberglass. It served as the actual turbine research vehicle.

Both Firebird IIs are part of the collection of the GM Heritage Center. The running car received a refurbishment several years ago. It is shown at special events across the country.

Incidentally, General Motors built another car named XP-500, which was nearly identical in appearance to the Firebird IIs, but its nose was a flattened oval shape without the pair of cone-like projections. In addition, it lacked the shark-like dorsal fin on the rear deck. This fiberglass car was built using the body constructed for close-up scenes in the movie, *Design for Dreaming*, and was used to test a free-piston engine.

### Titanium Challenges

Harley Earl ordered the titanium-bodied car, which served as an experiment in using alternative materials for automobile construction. Titanium presented many obstacles. An article about the Firebird II in the April 1956 issue of *Motor Trend* noted that the metal works "about as easily as spring steel." In addition, it can be filed vigorously with a coarse metal file "for half an hour before the surface is scratched." Stamping it into the desired shape required the metal to be heated to 920 degrees Fahrenheit. Welding it darkened the surface and this proved to be a significant problem because Earl demanded the surface of the metal to be burnished instead of painted. Because welding was not an option, General Motors Research Laboratories developed an epoxy resin that bonded the titanium skin to the body framing.

Another of Earl's conditions was for the body of the Firebird II to also have a brushed-satin finish. To achieve this, hand-finishing blocks with Pyrex glass particles bonded to the blocks were used to get the desired surface appearance. Several coats of satin-finish lacquer clear-coat sealed the surface to keep it from being smudged with fingerprints.

*The Firebird II captured the front page of the February 3, 1956, copy of the* Miami Herald. *It optimistically proclaimed in one story that a, "Fantastic New Era Looms in Gas Turbine Age." The newspaper was also filled with information about the opening of the GM Motorama at the Dinner Key Auditorium. It was a major event for the area.*

In the end, the body of the Firebird II was almost as light as a comparable aluminum-bodied version but it was almost as strong as a steel body.

### Working Innovations

The sloping nose of the Firebird II contained a set of oil-cooling fins located immediately behind the electronic sensors in the cone-like projections, all fitted in deep recesses. Behind this equipment were what looked like turbine blades; these prevented larger objects from getting into the engine air inlet.

The experimental car's small headlights retracted into the body when turned off, leaving only the turn signal/parking lamps exposed. When the headlights were turned on, they extended outward several inches and emitted a strong beam of light. A set of flaps in front opened automatically to allow heat to escape.

The second-generation Firebird, just as the original, received a dorsal fin in back to aid directional stability. It was adorned with the red, white, and blue GM Air Transport Division insignia. Also in back were two 10-gallon fuel pods over which the rear fenders flared outward. Taillights appeared to be absent in daylight as they were housed in a large reflector that created a chromed effect; however, they had the appearance of a glowing jet exhaust pipe at night.

The entire trunk floor rose like a freight elevator to fender height to eliminate the need to lean over for access to the trunk. Inside the trunk were eight pieces of fitted luggage as well as twin 12-volt batteries.

The frame of the running car had to be built rigidly enough to prevent the clear, bubble-like canopy from cracking. Flip-up panels on the canopy opened when the magnetic key was inserted

*The non-functional Firebird II, with its titanium body, served as a show car at the GM Motorama. This photograph was taken at the show in Los Angeles.*

# CHAPTER SIX: THE GM MOTORAMA OF 1956

into a slot on the car's body-side panels to ease entry and exit from the car.

The functional Firebird II was also equipped with air conditioning and a heater. Air conditioning was vital because the bubble canopy created a greenhouse effect and it was particularly necessary when testing at the Mesa, Arizona, Proving Grounds. In addition, a set of three flaps in the center of the canopy could be opened to cool the interior.

An experimental air-oil suspension system designed by the Delco Division was installed in the road-test car. The Delco-Matic units replaced conventional shock absorbers and springs. A cushion of air provided soft springing; a hydraulic leveling system compensated for light or heavy loads to keep the car level. According to General Motors, the Firebird II was the first American car to have leveling in both the front and rear. When the car was moving, the leveling system switched off and provided a smooth ride with air cushioning.

Moraine Products Division designed the experimental all-metal Turbo-X brakes for the Firebird II. The Turbo-X brake system included cast-iron discs that rotated with the car's wheels and a set of metal-lined pads. Applying the hydraulic brakes squeezed the disc between a movable pad on the inboard side and a fixed pad on the outboard side.

### The Engine

Dr. Lawrence Hafstad, vice president of the GM Research Laboratories staff, was placed in charge of engineering the engine and chassis for the Firebird II. He and his team made important advancements toward making the turbine-powered car more like a typical passenger car.

The GT-304 Whirlfire for the Firebird II benefited from a more efficient regenerator that recycled 80 percent of the exhaust that was heat wasted in the GT-302 powering the Firebird I. As a result, fuel economy improved to almost that of the average piston engine of the day. Exhaust gases, which traveled through a set of stainless steel pipes running through the rocker panels (terminating at ports on top of the rear fenders), exited at approximately the same temperature as gases from a conventional automobile. Noise was also reduced to nearly that of a conventional car through the use of a silencer built into the nose of the Firebird II.

The GT-304 was a less powerful engine (only about half as much at 200 gross hp at 28,000 rpm) and it had to carry more than double the weight as its predecessor. However, the Firebird II was not meant to test high-speed aerodynamics as the Firebird I did, so the sacrifice in performance probably was not considered especially important.

*Both Firebird IIs still exist and are a part of the collection of the GM Heritage Center. Shown here is the non-functional titanium-bodied car. Beyond it are the Firebird III and Cadillac Cyclone.*

*Function was behind the look of the 1956 GM Firebird II. Oil cooling fins were located immediately behind the electronic sensors in the conical projections. Behind these were what resembled turbine blades; they served to prevent larger objects from getting into the engine air inlet. The small headlights retracted into the body when turned off, leaving only the turn signal/parking lamps exposed; when turned on, the headlights extended outward several inches, and although diminutive, they emitted a strong beam of light. (Photo Courtesy GM Media Archive)*

*This full-color advertisement promoted the showing of the GM Motorama at the Pan Pacific Auditorium in Los Angeles. Despite the drawing, the Firebird II never appeared in red.*

# CHAPTER SIX: THE GM MOTORAMA OF 1956

*The titanium-bodied Firebird II appeared at the Paris Salon where it drew the attention of many thousands of onlookers. (Photo Courtesy Wayne Ellwood Collection)*

Starting the advanced car was performed by inserting a magnetic key and depressing the starter button. A Delco-Remy motor then brought the gasifier section up to 4,000 rpm, enough to make ignition automatic. The starter then continued to assist up to 15,000 rpm.

### Interior Components

The interior of the nonfunctional Firebird II was equipped more for show than the road test version. It included higher-grade trim, a pair of cathode ray tubes for information readouts, luminescent headliner, red-glowing courtesy lamps on the door panels, reclining seats, and a double-handled aircraft-style steering wheel.

The functional car had a full array of real instruments to provide data on the Whirlfire power plant to the driver.

Both cars had reclining aircraft-style seats with adjustable headrests and wraparound rear seats. The seats and door panels were molded in supple plastic foam and covered with plastic upholstery with the texture and color molded into them.

### Highway of Tomorrow

The Firebird II pioneered the concept of futuristic electronic highways in which cars of the future might be controlled electronically for speed, direction, and spacing interval in order to eliminate driver error. General Motors produced a special movie presentation showing how such highways could function; it was shown on a large screen to visitors to the Motorama. When the short presentation ended, the screen lifted to reveal to the audience the Firebird II as well as the actor and actress seen in the film.

The movie, *Design for Dreaming*, opened with the scene of a family enjoying a vacation drive during a contemporary setting, but soon they encounter a frustratingly congested highway and begin to dream of what might be 20 years later, in the year 1976. In their dream, the family is suddenly traveling in a Firebird II on the radar-controlled highway of tomorrow free of traffic jams.

The idea was presented in a manner to suggest that such convenience could be possible with the flip of a switch. An automatic control system would be activated that allowed electronic impulse-emitting metal strips embedded in the road surface to communicate with electronic pick-up coils placed inside the pair of cone-like projections on the front of the Firebird II. Electronic signals controlled steering, speed, and braking through the car's onboard computer that freed the occupants to talk, play games, watch television, or just watch the scenery.

Occupants could communicate with control towers along the "Auto-Way" to obtain directions, find motel vacancies, make reservations, or get other information. The control tower operator could communicate as well by flashing messages on the two TV screens in the car or through voice communication. As soon as the driver entered the roadway, the control tower operator could check the fuel level and engine operation of the car and synchronize speed and direction while the driver manually positioned the car over the metal strips.

If anything was found to be amiss with the vehicle at any time along the way, the car could be guided automatically to a safe place out of traffic.

The "highway of tomorrow" systems on the Firebird II show car were only simulated. About two years after the 1956 GM Motorama, functional systems were installed on the road-test car and were successfully demonstrated to the press by GM engineers.

The interior of the Firebird II used for show was equipped with simulated "Highway of Tomorrow" systems. Included was a pair of screens used to display information sent from control towers envisioned as part of the advanced highway system. Both Firebird IIs had reclining aircraft-style seats with adjustable headrests.

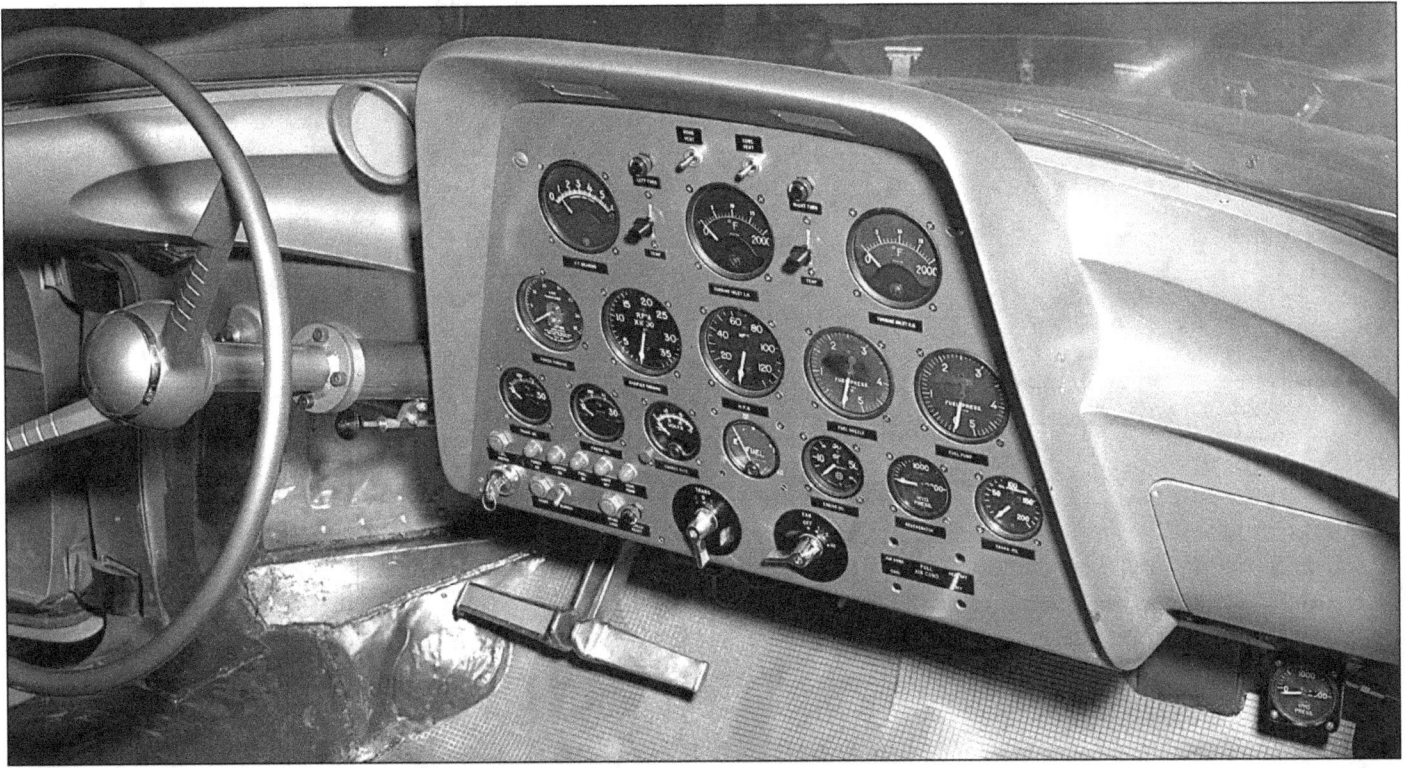

The running Firebird II had a full array of instruments, including tachometer, fuel pressure indicator, hydraulic pressure indicator, etc., to monitor turbine engine performance. (Photo Courtesy GM Media Archive)

MOTORAMA 175

# Other Notable Exhibits of the 1956 GM Motorama

Harley Earl's 1956 Nomad, shown at least once (at the Pan Pacific Auditorium in Los Angeles) during that year's GM Motorama, was equipped with a special interior, probably of leather. (Photo Courtesy GM Media Archive)

A Starfire and a couple of Holiday four-door hardtops were among the Oldsmobiles shown at the 1956 GM Motorama. Note the engine display titled "Oldsmobile Rocket T-350 Engine." (Photo Courtesy GM Media Archive)

Among the automobiles on exhibit at the 1956 GM Motorama was Harley Earl's Nomad painted in an unknown, non-production two-tone paint scheme and upholstered with what was likely leather in a non-production pleated pattern. A monotone white Pontiac Safari was also shown.

In addition to the all-white Safari, another special Pontiac was displayed: a four-door hardtop painted aquamarine blue with an opalescent Mylar fabric roof covering.

A late addition to the tour (at the final venue, in Boston) was a Chevrolet model 10700 commercial truck specially built for show purposes. Its uniquely crafted rear compartment housed multiple cutaway engines, transmissions, and differentials to show "the broad array of truck powertrain options" offered for Chevrolet trucks. An electric motor animated the

A special 1956 Star Chief Custom Catalina four-door hardtop was displayed over a pool of water from which color-lighted jets of water were sprayed while the car revolved on a turntable. It was painted aquamarine blue and had exotic star sapphire–trimmed leather upholstery. The roof was covered in aqua-tinted opalescent Mylar fabric. The four-door hardtop was a new addition to the Pontiac line this year.

A Pontiac Safari in a non-production monotone white paint scheme was a special display at the 1956 GM Motorama. Like its Chevrolet companion, the Nomad, the Safari was in its second year of production. (Photo Courtesy GM Media Archive)

engines and rotated the differentials. It required 25,000 man-hours over nine months to construct. After the show in Boston, the truck appeared at many locations across the country.

GMC also displayed its prototype tractor-trailer combination equipped with an air-ride suspension system in place of leaf springs.

Another Buick show car on display at the 1956 GM Motorama was a dressed-up Roadmaster convertible with a non-production paint scheme. It was tilted sideways and sat behind a railing and a wall with an arched opening cut into it to give a jewel box effect. References gave differing accounts of the color scheme of the car; one said it was pearlescent peach and cream and another said it was two-toned blue. Perhaps two different cars were used on the tour or the display car was repainted.

A mannequin was placed at each end of the convertible. One was attired in an evening gown and $2 million worth of jewelry; the other was wearing the Hope Diamond then valued at $1 million. Two (live) armed guards and additional law enforcement personnel in civilian attire were stationed nearby to discourage theft.

The Electro-Motive Division of General Motors was also represented with a large-scale model of the Aerotrain. Designed under the direction of Chuck Jordan, the actual Aerotrain was intended to provide a luxuriously smooth ride via an air-suspension system. Unfortunately, the sleek train looked much better than it rode,. Its air suspension produced just the opposite effect intended and, ultimately, only three examples were built. All three survive at museums.

*This specially built Chevrolet Task Force truck was used to display the broad array of engine, transmission, and differential offerings for the GM truck division. It was displayed at the final venue of the 1956 GM Motorama before going on a nationwide tour. (Photo Courtesy GM Media Archive)*

*At the 1956 GM Motorama, General Motors displayed a scale model of the new Aerotrain that was equipped with an air-ride suspension. Ultimately, only three of the trains were built; the air-ride suspension did not produce the comfortable ride expected.*

## Chapter Seven

# The Final GM Motoramas

General Motors canceled the Motorama for 1957 in the United States, but resumed with a limited number of shows for the 1959 and 1961 model years. Absent from these shows, however, were the dream cars representing each passenger car division. The turbine-powered 1958 Firebird III was the only dream car put on display at the 1959 and 1961 GM Motorama shows.

GM Canada, though, went forward with the Motorama for 1957 and they continued uninterrupted through 1961. The Canadian Motoramas actually began with the 1955 exhibition. The Motorama for 1957 was the last to have an array of dream cars; several of those were from the 1956 GM Motorama.

### GM Canada Motorama

For the 1958 event, GM Canada apparently did without dream cars and instead displayed a full array of products.

As in the United States, the Firebird III was on exhibit for shows in 1959 in Canada while the 1959 Cadillac Cyclone was exhibited for the 1960 GM Canada Motorama. For the 1961 Motorama, the Firebird I, Firebird II, and Cyclone returned.

### 1959 Motorama

General Motors put the spotlight on their production cars; one from each of their five divisions participated in the 1959 shows held only in New York City and Boston. During the stage show, which was managed by stage

*In 1955, GM Canada began hosting a Motorama just as extravagant as those held in the United States. This advertisement promoted the event held in Regina, Saskatchewan.*

*The Firebird III was included in the 1959 GM Canada Motorama. Note the saucer-shaped platform upon which the Firebird III was parked. (Photo Courtesy CNE Archives, Alexandra Studio, MG-5899-9)*

GREATER
MORE
THRILLING
THAN EVER
STARTS TOMORROW!
GENERAL MOTORS
motorama OF 1955
The sensational 'Firebird', the first gas turbine automobile built and tested in North America.
The Chevrolet Nomad, a six passenger station wagon in the revolutionary styling pioneered by the Chevrolet Corvette.
The Cadillac 'El Camino' a dream design in fibreglass and hand-brushed aluminum.
ADMISSION FREE!
REGINA
EXHIBITION AUDITORIUM
PASQUA STREET
OPEN DAILY 12.00 noon to 10.30 p.m.
FREE PARKING
APRIL 27th to 30th
The Buick Wildcat I, one of the most famous of all General Motors experimental cars.

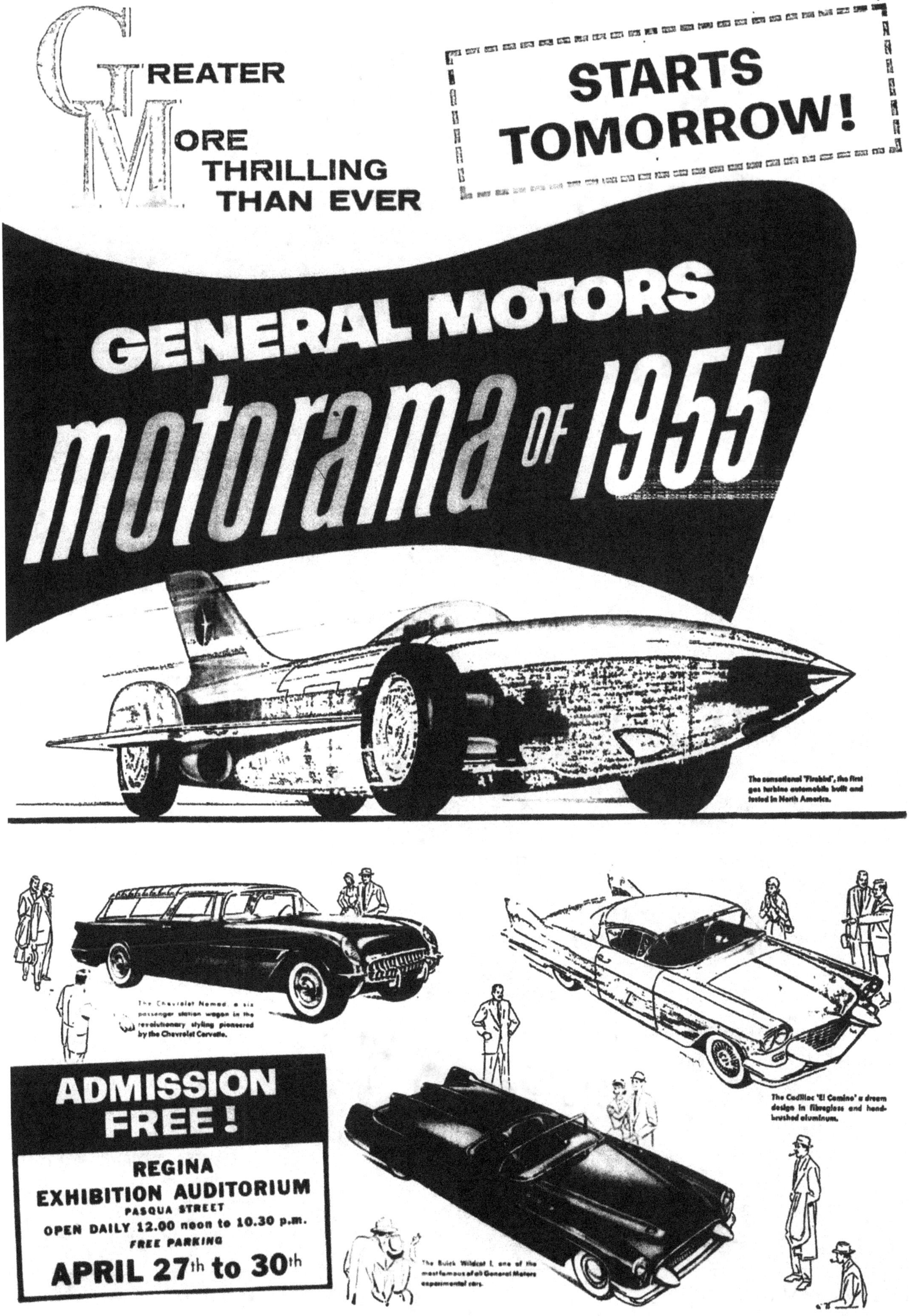

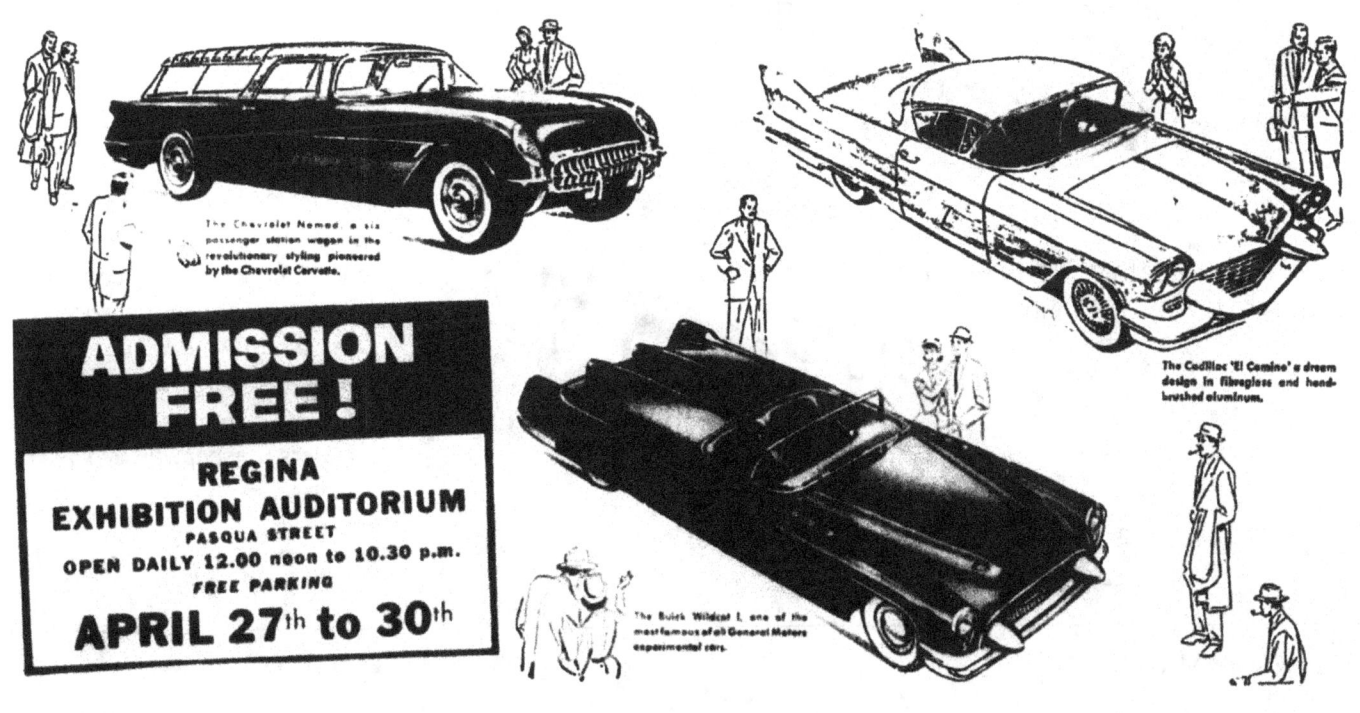

CHAPTER SEVEN: THE FINAL GM MOTORAMAS

*The 1956 Buick Centurion was shown at the 1957 GM Canada Motorama. This photo was taken at the show in Toronto. (Photo Courtesy CNE Archives, Gilbert Milne Collection, MG 6-302-1)*

*For GM Canada's Motorama, the show cars of 1956 were on exhibit with the exception of the prototype Eldorado Brougham. Also included was the large scale-model of the Aerotrain. Among the entertainers present was Eydie Gorme.*

*The GM Canada Motorama for 1958 was apparently without any dream cars. All the emphasis (at least based on the advertising) was placed on the entire line of passenger vehicles of the company including the GM Coach buses.*

*The Chevrolet exhibit at the 1959 GM Motorama included a little of everything, from the Corvette to full-size Chevys to various truck models.*

## CHAPTER SEVEN: THE FINAL GM MOTORAMAS

and screen actor Maurice Evans, five identically painted cars were brought on stage with a 95-ton "grasshopper" mechanism.

As Bruce Berghoff described it, "Following a short fantasy film depicting *Imagination in Vehicles,* the June Taylor Dancers introduced each car line in song and dance. With each introduction, the huge grasshopper arms delivered one production car up and over the audience for a brief spin, and then retracted behind a barrier to await the finale. The stage show ended with five cars spinning. With three cars high, two low, the orchestra blaring, and the dancers kicking, the audience roared with approval."

The five cars were painted a special color developed by DuPont called Pearl-Mist White. The paint, which looked great for a while, was a very fragile pearlescent finish subject to rapid oxidation and yellowing. Consequently, three decades passed before the paint industry sufficiently developed pearlescent paint suitable to offer it as a regular production finish.

Other displays at the 1959 GM Motorama included a Bonneville convertible mounted upside-down allowing visitors to see the car's new "Wide Track" chassis.

Oldsmobile drew attention to its three-car turntable with an aviary housing fifty cockatiels imported from Holland.

*For the final GM Canada Motorama, both the 1954 and 1956 Firebirds were brought back for display. Also shown again was the 1959 Cadillac Cyclone, which had been updated with more conservative tail fins.*

The Firebird III was the only dream car on exhibit at the 1959 GM Motorama held only in New York City and Boston. This photo was taken at the show in New York City. (Photo Courtesy GM Media Archive)

This 1959 Corvette fitted with wire wheels was shown at that year's GM Motorama in Toronto. No other details are available about this show car. (CNE Archives, Alexandra Studio, MG5-5899-10)

CHAPTER SEVEN: THE FINAL GM MOTORAMAS

*The GM Motorama in Canada was similar to those held in the United States. On stage were examples of the passenger cars of each division. These were probably the same cars used in the U.S. shows, which were painted a special pearlescent white color. (CNE Archives, Alexandra Studio, MG5-5899-13)*

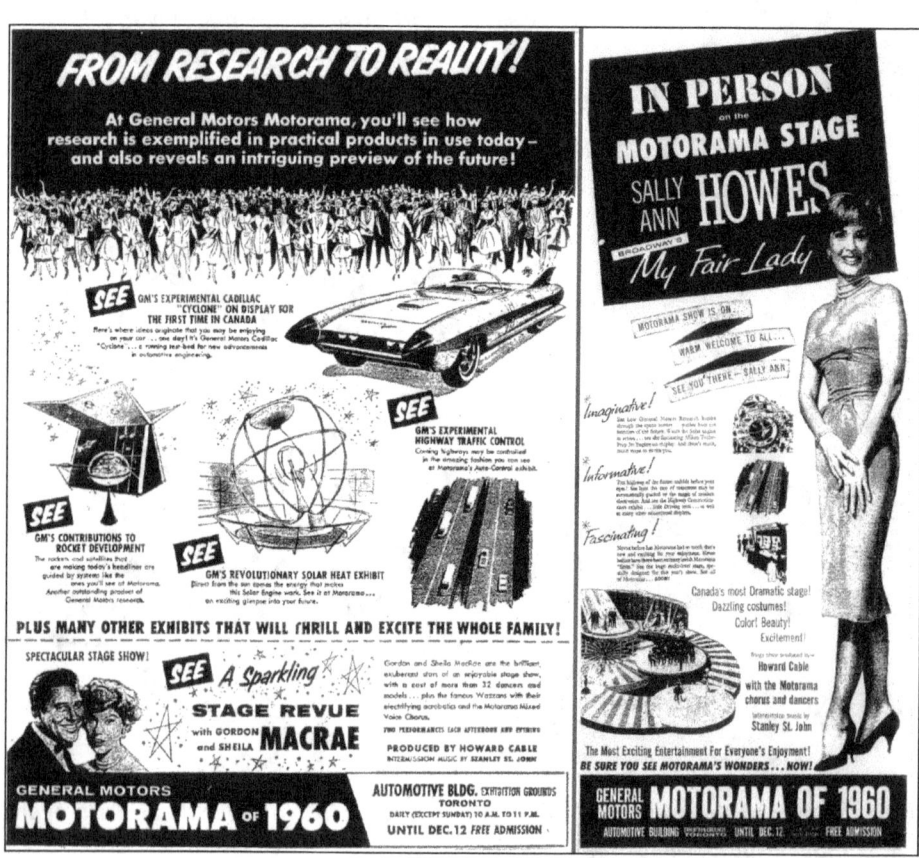

*The 1959 Cadillac Cyclone was not shown at any of the GM Motorama shows in the United States, but it was on exhibit at the 1960 and 1961 GM Canada Motorama.*

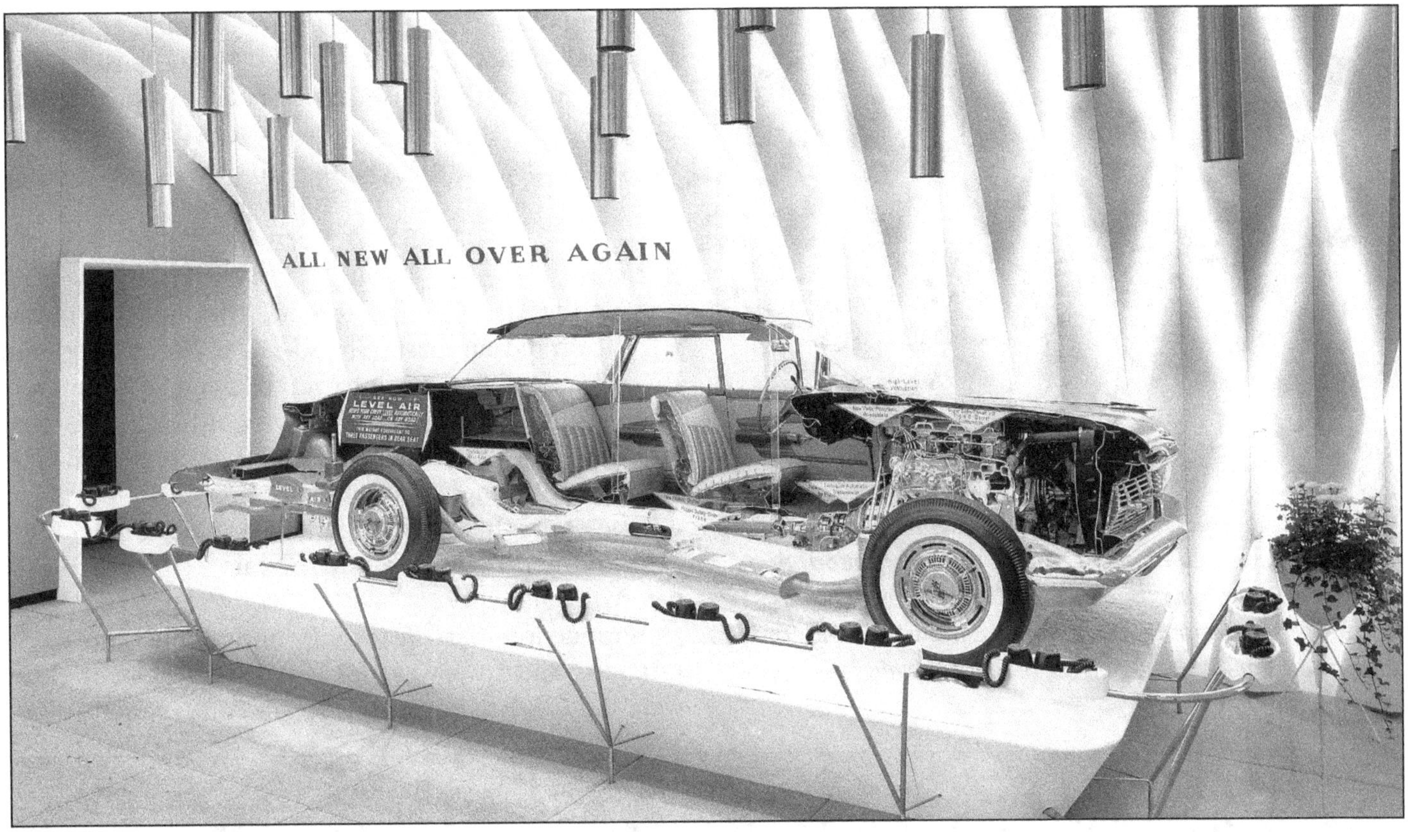

*A cutaway 1959 Chevrolet four-door hardtop must have been an eye-catching exhibit at that year's GM Motorama. The car was equipped with the optional Lever-Air suspension, Turboglide automatic transmission, and a 348 with triple 2-barrel carburetors. The troublesome Level-Air suspension was in its final year of availability as an extra-cost option.*

*This exhibit offered onlookers the opportunity to see the 1959 Buick Electra 225 convertible on display from multiple angles at once thanks to the mirrored panels placed above and behind the car. It was equipped with the optional bucket seats. (Photo Courtesy GM Media Archive)*

# CHAPTER SEVEN: THE FINAL GM MOTORAMAS

*The ultra-luxurious Cadillac Fleetwood (foreground) and Eldorado Brougham (background) were shown at the 1959 GM Motorama. Pininfarina assembled the Eldorado Brougham for 1959 as well as 1960 after which the model was discontinued.*

A cutaway 1959 Chevrolet four-door hardtop was equipped with the optional Lever-Air suspension, Turboglide automatic transmission, and a 348 with three 2-barrel carburetors. The troublesome suspension system was dropped after this year, though.

## 1961 Motorama

For the 1961 GM Motorama, the production cars were again the emphasis. The so-called grasshopper from the 1959 show was put into action again with cars representing the five GM car divisions, although this time without the pearlescent white paint. A high point was when 29 performers from the stage show, *The Magic Man*, danced through skits written and produced by Gil Stevens and Bob Haymes, while the cars were brought out before the audience.

Production cars featuring non-production paint, interiors, and trim were also on the show floor. They were the Chevrolet Impala Special, Pontiac Moda d'Oro

*A car from each of GM's passenger car divisions appeared during the stage presentation at the 1961 GM Motorama. Unlike those of the 1959 GM Motorama, these cars were painted in standard colors. (Photo Courtesy GM Media Archive)*

186  MOTORAMA

convertible, and Buick Flamingo. One other special Buick shown was a convertible painted metalflake coral with a white bench-seat interior. In addition, a couple of special Cadillacs (one an Eldorado) were on display.

The Impala Special convertible was finished in pearlescent white paint and was equipped much like the Impala Super Sport offered for the 1962 model year. However, its bucket seats and console interior were upholstered in a special gold and white scheme; wire wheels were installed.

Distinguishing the Moda d'Oro from an ordinary Bonneville convertible was accomplished with a golden pearl exterior finish, gold-plated instrument panel, and gold cloth and ivory leather interior. Moldings, sill plates, and other trim for the interior were gold-plated. Mouton carpeting covered the floor and lower door panels of the car.

The Buick Flamingo was painted pearlescent orange and featured paisley upholstered seats; the passenger-side bucket seat could be rotated 180 degrees to face the rear-seat passengers.

Another Pontiac show car present was the tilt-body Tempest. It was a new compact model fitted with a transaxle and flexible driveshaft. The first Tempest, a four-door sedan probably painted Shelltone Ivory, was modified with a set of hinges at the rear that allowed the car's body to be tilted upward to flaunt the advanced driveline. All engine and chassis components were finished to show-quality standards; the underside floorpans were fully painted and even the tires were dressed up with wide white sidewalls on both the inner and outer sides.

This car was probably scrapped once it was no longer needed for display. The second 1961 production Tempest, which was also displayed during the final GM Motorama, still exists and is owned by General Motors.

Oldsmobile's flashiest car on display was the new Starfire, set for release later in the model year. This example was in a monotone scheme with an Autumn Mist metallic exterior and a matching interior. The Starfire

*Several production cars with non-production paint and interior schemes were exhibited at the 1961 GM Motorama. Shown here is the Impala Special, a convertible painted pearlescent white and equipped with essentially the Super Sport interior, although the upholstery was unique to this car. Its design is credited to Blaine Jenkins. (Photo Courtesy GM Media Archive)*

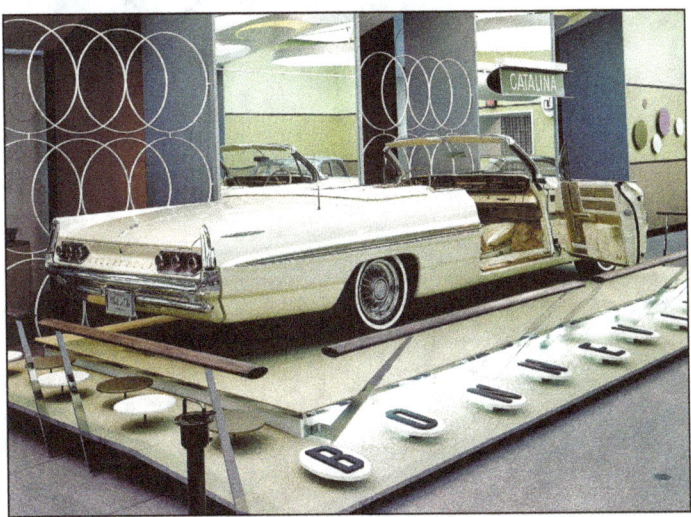

*The 1961 Pontiac Moda d'Oro was a Bonneville convertible modified with a golden pearl exterior finish, gold-plated instrument panel, and interior of gold cloth with ivory leather. (Photo Courtesy GM Media Archive)*

*The Buick Flamingo show car was painted pearlescent orange and was upholstered in a matching paisley cloth with leather. Its passenger-side bucket seat could be rotated 180 degrees to face the rear-seat passengers. (Photo Courtesy GM Media Archive)*

## CHAPTER SEVEN: THE FINAL GM MOTORAMAS

The tilt-body Tempest was a four-door sedan modified with a set of hinges at the rear to allow the car's body to be tilted upward to flaunt the car's flexible driveshaft and transaxle. This compact model was new to the Pontiac line in 1961. (Photo Courtesy GM Media Archive)

A pearlescent white Eldorado Biarritz with narrow-band whitewall tires was another special show car at the 1961 GM Motorama. Its interior was likely modified, but documentation about this car is lacking. (Photo Courtesy GM Media Archive)

For 1961, Oldsmobile released a new Starfire model offered only as a convertible. The car shown at that year's GM Motorama was painted Autumn Mist, one of several colors offered. Standard equipment included bucket seats, console, and tachometer. (Photo Courtesy GM Media Archive)

was a sporty version of the Super Eighty-Eight convertible equipped with bucket seats, console, tachometer, brushed-aluminum side moldings, and a 345-hp version of the 394-ci Rocket V-8.

The Cadillac Park Avenue was a short-deck version of the Sedan de Ville. This model (7 inches shorter than a regular Sedan de Ville) was released for the 1962 model year so the car exhibited was evidently a prototype. (In 1961, a short-deck Series 62 Town Sedan was offered, although it did not wear the Park Avenue script.) The short-deck car was offered because of complaints from some Cadillac owners regarding difficulty in parallel parking and their cars not fitting into their garages.

An Eldorado Biarritz "special" was also on exhibit, with a pearlescent white finish and narrow-band whitewall tires.

### End of an Era

With the final showing of the 1961 GM Motorama in Los Angeles, the traveling road show came to a permanent end. The cost of producing the Motorama had grown to the point where there were now more economical ways to promote GM products. Special one-offs continued to be built and shown at various events around the country, but not on the large-scale of the 1950s GM Motorama. The high-cost of producing the extravaganza was not the only matter bringing an end to it.

The late Chuck Jordan explained the sudden departure of the GM Motorama: "After the 1956 Motorama, things changed. Because of continually increasing costs and new corporate marketing opportunities, the 1957 Motorama was canceled. GM Styling's annual crop of dream cars also came to an end because, as the style leader, General Motors was giving away too many valuable design ideas to our competitors. GM Styling's program of concept cars continued, but now in secret behind locked doors.

"One fact was certain: Our Motorama experience had taught us the importance of creativity and the value of advance design as we charged ahead."

### 1958 GM Firebird III

Turbine engine research moved ahead with the 1958 Firebird III (XP-73, SO 90238). It proved to be the last of its kind, although for 1964 General Motors trotted out the Firebird IV, which was said to be turbine-powered. In fact, it was a non-functional show car without an engine.

Among the original specifications for the Firebird III was that its fiberglass exterior surfaces were to be vacuum-nickel-plated, and because such panels were easily marred, a complete set of extra panels were to be made available. The process for this was known to be lengthy and this may have contributed to the reversal of this decision and to instead paint the car Lunar Sand, a warm gold tone. At some point, the car was repainted the silver-gray color it is today.

According to GM's booklet *Flight of the Firebirds*, Harley Earl "envisioned an entirely different type of car, 'which a person may drive to the launching site of a rocket to the moon,'" when he considered the styling for the next turbine car. For the times, the styling, which included a twin-bubble canopy and multiple tail fins, certainly fit Earl's vision.

Contained within the car's fiberglass skin were a regenerative gas turbine GT-305 and a separate 2-cylinder 10-hp aluminum engine to run the electrical and hydraulic accessories that consisted of steering, braking pumps, brake flaps, air suspension, and air conditioning. The engine represented a significant advance over the GT-304; it was 25 percent lighter, more compact, developed 225 hp at 33,000-rpm gasifier speed, and provided a 25-percent increase in fuel economy. The engine, transmission, and differential were mounted as a unit behind the passenger compartment. Its transaxle included a

*Technicians with General Motors are shown here beginning the process of installing the GT-305 turbine engine in the 1958 Firebird III. This engine was lighter, more compact, and developed more power than the GT-304 used in the Firebird II. (Photo Courtesy GM Media Archive)*

CHAPTER SEVEN: THE FINAL GM MOTORAMAS

# BILL MITCHELL: BORN FOR THE JOB

*Here is Bill Mitchell posing with his personal 1961 Cadillac "Le Mans" show car built from a production Eldorado. The car was displayed at the 1962 Chicago Auto Show. (Photo Courtesy GM Media Archive)*

William L. Mitchell began his long career at General Motors during the final days of 1935. Landing there must have been predestined. Mitchell was the son of a Buick dealer, could draw well, and loved automobiles, especially the fast ones. He eventually succeeded Harley Earl as the head of GM Design.

Mitchell was born July 2, 1912, in Cleveland, but grew up in Greenville, Pennsylvania. As a child he sketched automobiles (and kept his scrapbook of drawings for the remainder of his life), but his parents did not see the value of it. Hoping he would find more to draw than cars they sent him to Carnegie Institute of Technology in Pittsburg. However, in 1931, he began attending night school in New York City at the Art Students League to further his skills as an artist. During the time he attended the school, Mitchell spent his lunch hour in the showrooms along 57th Street where he gazed upon European automobiles such as the Hispano-Suiza, Isotta Fraschini, Mercedes-Benz, and Rolls-Royce.

Four years earlier he had been hired to work part time as an office boy for Barron Collier Agency and became a full-time employee upon graduating high school. At that point he served as a layout man and illustrator. There he created the first MG ads in America and was introduced to sports cars by Collier's sons, who got him interested in such cars as well as road racing. In fact, he joined them in racing and designed the patch logo for the Automobile Racing Club of America (ARCA), which predated the Sports Car Club of America (SCCA).

In his book, *Corvette: A Piece of the Action*, Mitchell wrote, ". . . [I] found out what driving was all about. Those foreign sports cars, they would go like hell over a gravel road. The fun with the car was to almost lose it; I mean to always drive on that narrow edge. No windshield, a cut-down door. It was you and four wheels. You felt every twitch, everything the car was doing . . . And I drove like crazy. One of these cars, and then another, and then another. I wished to God the United States had something like them."

In the summer of 1935, an insurance agent, Walter Carey, attended a Collier competition. One of Mitchell's sketches caught his attention so he introduced himself and asked Mitchell if he had ever thought about designing cars. Carey was a personal friend of Harley Earl. This meeting led to Mitchell creating some sketches for evaluation by Earl. On December 15, Bill Mitchell joined General Motors and within six months was made chief designer of the Cadillac Studio. His first major assignment was the design of the 1938 Cadillac Sixty Special, which according to Mitchell's account, emerged as the "first 'youth image' Cadillac."

Around this time, Mitchell requested a leave of absence from General Motors to pursue his passion of racing. He very much wanted to join Mercedes for a while. "To me, there were no American race cars; Indianapolis and all those funny-looking high roadsters didn't stir me at all . . . Mercedes and Auto Union were having their great duels, and I wanted to be there and be part of it . . . General Motors said no," wrote Mitchell in *Corvette: A Piece of the Action*. So, he "devoured every issue of *Autocar*, drooling over the racing paintings of Gordon Crosby, and reading every other foreign journal I could get my hands on, and suffering the strange looks of everyone around Detroit who really didn't know what I was about. Except Harley Earl. He had a feeling for cars."

Six months after Mitchell's arrival at General Motors, Harley Earl put him in charge of the Cadillac studio. There, Mitchell sketched the design of what ultimately became the 1938 Sixty Special, a trendsetter with integrated trunk, no running boards, and 3 inches lower than other Cadillac models. It was Cadillac's bestseller that year.

Bill Mitchell joined the U.S. Navy during World War II. Upon his return he joined the Harley Earl Corporation, an industrial design firm. He returned to General Motors as assistant director of styling in 1953.

Much more can be written of Mitchell's career, enough to fill a book. Some of the other notable contributions include the Corvette Sting Ray and Buick Riviera. When he took over as Harley Earl's handpicked successor to head GM Design at the end of 1958, Mitchell took the company in a new direction in terms of styling marked by razor-edge lines. He retired from General Motors in 1977.

---

Hydra-Matic transmission mounted directly to the differential case.

Building on the Highway of Tomorrow research done with the Firebird II, this car received a revised version called Autoguide. Other advanced gadgetry of the Firebird III included a functional Cruisecontrol to automatically maintain a constant speed as well as a Unicontrol system for driver control of steering, acceleration, and braking. It was controlled with a swivel stick accessible from either seat. Moving it engaged servos controlled by three analog computers that compensated for too much driver input such as a sudden turn at high speed. Pushing it left or right steered the Firebird III; a forward or backward push caused the car to accelerate or brake, respectively. Rotating the handle 20 degrees in either direction engaged reverse and an 80-degree rotation in either direction engaged "park."

In GM's booklet, *Imagination in Motion: Firebird III*, the research being done with the car was called "human engineering" and was explained this way: "Automotive engineers have long recognized an area of development known as human engineering. . . In this car, the driver has been viewed as a challenge rather than as a limitation to automotive engineering possibilities. Here is an opportunity to use new simplified control devices, to provide improved air-conditioned comfort, and the armchair ride of an entirely new high-pressure air-oil hydraulic suspension system." The Firebird III was the first completely electronically controlled car.

Still another area of research conducted with the Firebird III was an anti-lock braking system. Although such systems are commonplace today, it was quite high-tech for the day. The 11 x 4-inch Turb-Al brake drums were cast into the alloy wheels and faced with iron. Brake shoes had sintered metallic linings. Cast-in cooling passages between the drum and wheel brought cooling air in through the hub and spun out through the slots. At speeds above 30 mph, the airbrake flaps were deployed to aid in braking. In addition, a "grade retarder" using oil-cooled friction discs on the rear axle shafts went into action above this speed.

*Tail fins sprouted from many places on the Firebird III. This, of course, was part of the design specified for the car by Harley Earl. (Photo Courtesy Wayne Ellwood Collection)*

CHAPTER SEVEN: THE FINAL GM MOTORAMAS

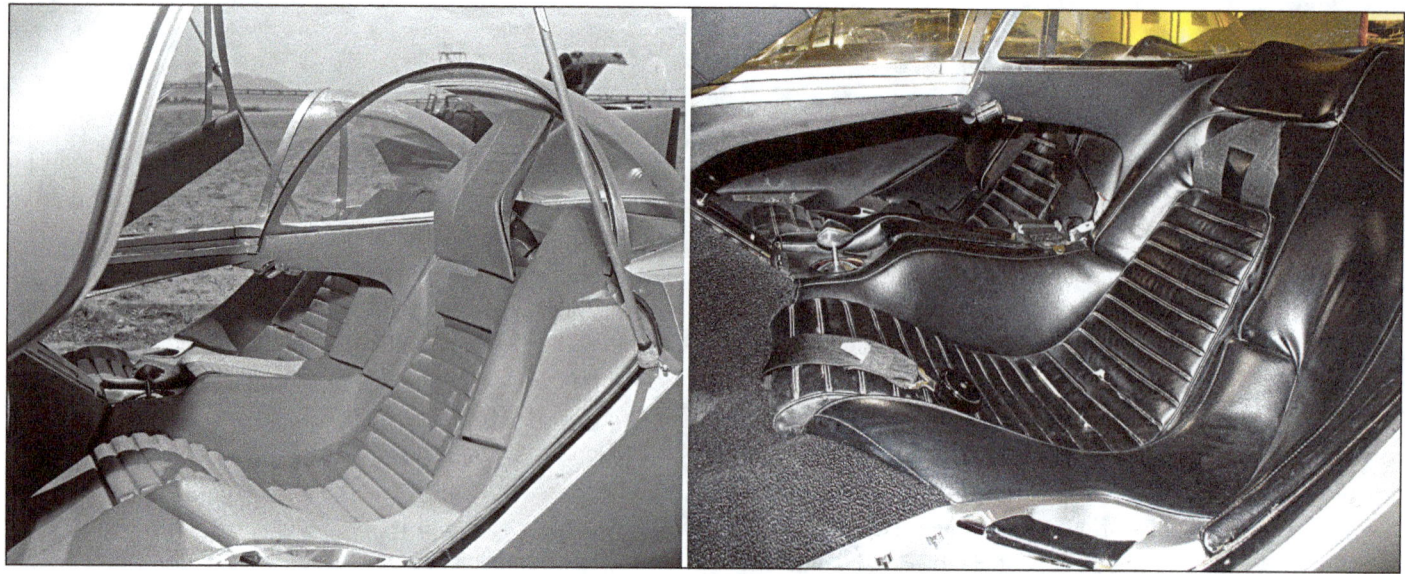

Here is a then (left) and now (right) comparison of the interior of the Firebird III. Originally, the interior of the turbine-powered dream car was red. By the time it appeared at the 1962 World's Fair in Seattle it had been changed to black and remains so today. Note the elaborate extended headrest shown in the photo from 1958. Also visible is the Unicontrol handle on the car's console. Access to the interior was via an ultrasonic key. Just pointing the ultrasonic key at the door caused it to swing upward and forward; the side panel and bubble canopy were joined as one unit to form the door. (Photo Courtesy GM Media Archive/Photo by author)

This optimistic advertisement from General Motors' AC Division suggested that the Firebird III could be the sort of car available in 1969, then a decade away.

The Firebird III's experimental suspension system included solid axles anchored to the sub-frame with four control arms on each, an arrangement that reduced the car's overall height and kept the wheels perpendicular to the road at all times to improve handling. The air-oil springs at the front and rear were interconnected to cause vertical forces acting on a front wheel to be simultaneously applied to the rear wheel to suppress pitching motions for a smoother ride. The car's air-oil unit

The Firebird III was on display for the participants of the 1959 Glidden Tour, which made a stop at the GM Tech Center. The gentleman is pointing to the decal on the Firebird III's hood.

*The Firebird III is a part of the GM Heritage Collection and is still shown at various events across the country. It is fitted with clear canopies. An aluminized set that filtered sunlight was used when the car was undergoing test drives.*

(operating at 3,000 psi) had a variable spring constant that gave a strong spring action when the car was heavily loaded and a relatively weak spring action when lightly loaded. Height control valves maintained a fixed road clearance, regardless of the load carried (within design limits of course).

Electronic systems filled the trunk of the Firebird III; the "black boxes" sat on one side and a pair of 12-volt batteries sat on the other. Access to them was through a deck lid on each side of the central fin.

In August 1958, the Firebird III (along with its predecessors, Firebird I and Firebird II) was sent to GM's Mesa, Arizona, Proving Grounds where the three were photographed together for publicity. It was later tested on public roads and must have been a surprising sight in traffic! It also appeared at the 1959 GM Motorama in Toronto as well as at the Seattle World's Fair in 1962.

A movie was made showing the Firebird III in action with the supervisor of testing, Emmett Conklin, in the driver's seat and GM staff engineer Mauri Rose in the passenger seat. The movie was shown to Motorama audiences during the two-city tour in the fall of 1958

The only Firebird III to be built still exists and underwent a refurbishment a number of years ago. General Motors still displays the car at various events around the country. A vibrantly painted Firebird III chassis was also exhibited. It was recently removed from storage and is part of the collection of the GM Heritage Center.

Turbine research continued at General Motors with a series of trucks including the 1965 Chevrolet Titan III.

### 1959 Cadillac Cyclone

Unlike many dream cars that preceded it, such as the Le Mans, the Cyclone was built as a 100-percent-functional car from the start. There was plenty of gadgetry on board, too. Up front was proximity warning radar to alert drivers via a warning light and an audible signal when an object or automobile was approaching. Initially, when something came into the path of the Cyclone, the warning light flashed and

*The 1959 Cadillac Cyclone made its public debut at the inaugural Daytona 500 in February of that year. Alongside it was Harley Earl's 1959 Oldsmobile F-88. Originally, the Cyclone was painted pearlescent white. (Photo Courtesy GM Media Archive)*

## CHAPTER SEVEN: THE FINAL GM MOTORAMAS

*The Cadillac Cyclone was not painted pearlescent white for long. It was repainted silver-gray and remains this color today. (Photo Courtesy GM Media Archive)*

a digital readout appeared on the "proximity and stopping distance" display window.

As the distance decreased between the Cyclone and the other object, the audible alarm activated; the pitch of the signal increased as the driver got closer to the object. Before an impact could occur the system automatically applied the brakes if no action was taken. That was the theory at least. Reportedly, no one actually tested the last part of the setup.

Normal braking action was accomplished via a power-boosted system using a pressure servo drawing pressure from the air-ride reserve tank. Up front, the wheels and brake drums were designed as an integral unit; rear brakes were conventional cast iron and mounted inboard.

An autopilot system controlling both speed and steering through a sensor bar underneath allowed the car to follow a guide wire buried in the road surface. This idea appeared earlier on the 1956 GM Firebird II as part of the Highway of Tomorrow concept. Thought was given to such highways in the future; the concept was successfully tested at the GM Proving Grounds in Arizona.

Powering the unique show car was a 325-hp Cadillac 390 topped with a low-profile 4-barrel carburetor, its air cleaned of dust through a filter in the hood scoop. The muffler and exhaust system was located within the engine compartment with the combustion gases exiting through ports built into the front fenders ahead of the front wheels. A cross-flow aluminum radiator with twin cooling fans designed by GM's Harrison Radiator Division maintained the proper operating temperature. An experimental Hydra-Matic transaxle with a 2-speed differential transferred the 390's power to the rear wheels.

All engine-driven accessories (air conditioning compressor, air suspension compressor, generator, power steering pump, and water pump) were mounted in front of the engine and were belt-driven via the crankshaft pulley.

Supporting the steel unitized body was a short-lived air suspension system that proved troublesome from the beginning. It experienced a failure just prior to being driven on the pace lap of the Daytona 500, but was repaired just in time. Eventually, a conventional coil-spring suspension replaced the air suspension system.

The doors were another unconventional feature of the Cyclone. They didn't swing open. By activating an electric switch, they popped out 3 inches and then were manually slid back over the quarter panels; ball bearings provided smooth operation. When either door was opened the electrically operated plastic canopy automatically rose if it were in use. When not in use the one-piece canopy was stowed in the rear storage compartment.

A cable release hidden behind the driver's side gas filler (one was placed on each side) unlocked the entire rear section (deck and quarter panels), which swung back as a unit.

Occupants (who had the canopy in place) could communicate with the outside world by using a two-way intercom. A small panel on each door acted as a pass-through for exchanging small objects such as coins.

The two-passenger interior compartment of the Cyclone was upholstered in silver-blue leather. Seating was thickly padded and offered substantial lumbar support. Instrumentation was clustered immediately in front of the driver and on the dash just above the console; dials in front of the driver were a 200-mph speedometer with trip meter, an 8,000-rpm tachometer, and a coolant temperature gauge. Instruments over the console included an Air Force–style chronometer, manifold pressure gauge, fuel level gauge, and an amp gauge.

A two-tone competition-style steering wheel was equipped with buttons to operate the horn and was linked to a variable-ratio Saginaw rotary-valve power steering unit. A red-capped lever on the console served to operate gear selection and a T-handle was used to set the parking brake.

The gas heater and air conditioner were combined into a system similar to that of a home; a dial was used to set the desired temperature. These two units were housed in the cowl sections on either side of the passenger compartment doors.

Originally, the Cyclone was painted pearlescent white with GM's Air Transport Division logo on the fins, but was soon repainted the color it is today but without the logo.

The car's tall tail fins were befitting the Harley Earl era of automotive design, but evidently that feature was not in tune with Bill Mitchell's sense of style. When Mitchell succeeded Earl at GM Styling he immediately went to work on more conservative designs for the 1960s. The Cyclone's tail fins were refashioned to resemble those that appeared on the 1961–1962 Cadillacs. The show car's lower fins or "skegs" went into production on these same models. The Cyclone's taillights were relocated from the concave panel to simulated rocket exhaust ports. Its 14-inch cast-aluminum wheels were also altered.

This show car is part of the GM Heritage Center collection and is occasionally displayed at different venues across the country.

*The two-passenger interior compartment of the Cyclone was upholstered in silver-blue leather. Seating was thickly padded and offered substantial lumbar support. Instrumentation was clustered immediately ahead of the driver as well as on the dash just above the console. Among the myriad of dials were a 200-mph speedometer, 8,000-rpm tachometer, Air Force–style chronometer, manifold pressure gauge, fuel level gauge, and amp gauge.*

*A 325-hp Cadillac 390 topped with a low-profile 4-barrel carburetor powers the Cyclone. Air entering the carburetor is cleaned of dust through a filter in the hood scoop.*

*The 1959 Cadillac Cyclone has been preserved through the decades and is a part of the GM Heritage Collection. It is sometimes shown at various events across this country and was an attraction at the 2013 Amelia Island Concours d'Elegance featuring Cadillac concept cars.*

## Chapter Eight

# MODERN CONCEPT CARS

One of Harley Earl's lasting legacies is the concept car. They are still designed and built in the 21st century (although in secrecy) and will be until the automobile becomes an obsolete mode of transportation. Following are some of the personal favorites of the current head of GM Global Design, Ed Welburn.

The 2012 Cadillac Ciel (French for "sky") was unveiled at that year's Pebble Beach Concours d'Elegance. Many wondered if it represented a preview of a new flagship model from Cadillac, something Cadillac officials promptly denied. Its jaw-dropping styling was apparently influenced by German design trends. Among its features are 22-inch wheels, carbon-ceramic brake rotors, 125-inch wheelbase, holographic instrumentation, touch-sensitive pads on each door handle for individual passengers' climate controls, and even "Snuggies" that can be deployed from each passenger-seat headrest for warmth. (Photo Courtesy GM Media Archive)

## 2003 Cadillac Sixteen

The 2003 Cadillac Sixteen was dramatically styled. The four-door pillarless hardtop, with an all-glass roof, exudes the look of grandeur seen in the original Cadillac V-16 models of the classic era. It also made the most of modern technology in the extensive use of aluminum, Baer six-piston-caliper brakes, Bose sound system, rear-seat DVD information system, power-operated hood, LED headlights and taillights, and fifth-generation OnStar in-vehicle safety and security communication equipment. The aluminum body sits on a 140-inch wheelbase, aluminum-steel chassis, and rolls on 24 x 9-inch aluminum wheels. (Photo Courtesy GM Media Archive)

The name, "Sixteen," was chosen for Cadillac's concept car to emphasize the V-16 of 1,000 hp and 1,000 ft-lbs of torque under its long hood. This experimental 830-ci, 32-valve V-16 features Displacement on Demand technology that allows eight cylinders to shut down during normal driving and automatically and seamlessly reactivate them for more demanding conditions. The engine is coupled to an electronically controlled Hydra-Matic 4L85-E 4-speed automatic transmission. (Photo Courtesy GM Media Archive)

CHAPTER EIGHT: MODERN CONCEPT CARS

## 2007 Chevrolet Volt

The 2007 Chevrolet Volt concept car introduced at that year's North American International Auto Show was built on a new platform dubbed E-flex. It was based on a platform nearly the size of a Chevy Cobalt's and weighed approximately 3,200 pounds. A 161-hp electric motor and a lithium-ion storage pack with 16 kWh of capacity provided power to the front wheels. An Ecotec turbocharged 71-hp 3-cylinder engine sat under the hood to spin a 53-kW generator as one means to charge the battery pack. The other method was via a pair of plugs (one on either side) for charging by a standard 110-volt connection.

When the 2007 Chevy Volt concept car was introduced, General Motors was quick to explain some of its technology was not yet production ready; beginning in December 2010, it was judged ready. The Volt put into production, however, differs greatly from the concept car version to reduce costs and for a much improved drag coefficient (from .43 to .28). It uses the Delta II platform (the same as the Chevrolet Cruze) and is a four-passenger rather than a five-passenger car. So far, sales of the model have not taken off because of a high price tag, although the price is expected to drop significantly over time. (Photo Courtesy GM Media Archive)

## 2008 Buick Riviera

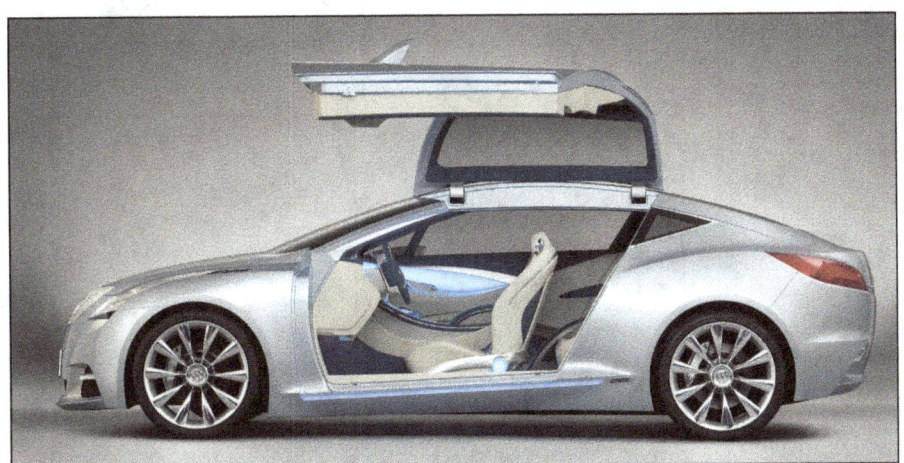

The purpose of the Shell Blue 2008 Buick Riviera concept car was to showcase Buick's new global design direction. It was unveiled in 2007 at China's Auto Shanghai. Ed Welburn, vice president of GM Global Design, said of the concept car that it, "reflects PATAC's [Pan Asia Technical Automotive Center] growing role within the GM Design family and China's significance as the world's largest Buick market." Among its features are carbon-fiber body panels, gull-wing doors, ambient light strips applied across the console and door liner, and the capability to accommodate the new hybrid system that went into production the following year at Shanghai GM. (Photo Courtesy GM Media Archive)

## 2012 Cadillac Ciel

Genuine Italian olive wood trim was used within the interior of the 2012 Ciel concept car. Additional special features include transparent gauges framed within a brushed-aluminum housing; "floating" full-length center console equipped with hidden connectivity portals for each passenger (allowing each to make dinner reservations, check the weather, or even upload photos to social media); heated and cooled seats; a drawer containing sun lotion, sun glasses, and towels; and aromatherapy that can be controlled from the rear armrest. (Photo Courtesy GM Media Archive)

## 2013 Opel Monza

At the 2013 Frankfurt Auto Show, Opel (GM's German subsidiary) introduced the stunning Monza concept car with a 2+2 seating configuration. Access is gained via large gullwing doors. Underneath its stylish skin are an electric motor and a turbocharged 1.0-liter 3-cylinder range extender powered by natural gas. However, Opel says the Monza Concept can be fitted with a wide range of powertrains thanks to its modular chassis. The dashboard contains a first: a cutting-edge, multifunction display powered by 18 LED projectors. The door-to-door instrument panel can be configured via voice commands or steering-wheel-mounted controls. Much like GM's concept cars of the 1950s, Opel says this concept car will inspire future models for the brand. (Photo Courtesy GM Media Archive)

CHAPTER EIGHT: MODERN CONCEPT CARS

## 2013 Cadillac Elmiraj

"A modern update to the classic format of a two-door grand coupe, Elmiraj is a pure expression of streamlined design and engaging rear-wheel-drive performance. This new vehicle architecture expands the brand's commitment to lightweight rear-wheel-drive performance . . ." said General Motors of its new concept car of 2013. The Elmiraj is powered by a 4.5-liter twin-turbocharged V-8 delivering an estimated 500 hp. It was designed on the baseline technology of Cadillac's Twin Turbo V-6 featured in the 420-hp 2014 CTS-V Sport edition. (Photo Courtesy GM Media Archive)

The instrumentation of the 2013 Elmiraj features a transparent analog tachometer and speedometer. Directly behind the analog gauges sits a wide-screen high-resolution display that projects information for the driver as well as the output of a front-mounted camera. A 10-inch touch screen for navigation and connectivity can be concealed inside the instrument panel when not in use. The 2+2 layout of the Elmiraj includes high-performance seats designed to support lively driving. In late August 2014, the Elmiraj was reportedly to be the basis of a new flagship model for Cadilac. The sedan, named CT6, is to be unveiled at the 2015 New York Auto Show. (Photo Courtesy GM Media Archive)

## 2014 Chevrolet Corvette C7

The prototype of the C7 Corvette was presented at multiple venues across the country. Here it is shown at the Amelia Island Concours d'Elegance in March 2013. A day earlier, Ed Welburn, head of GM Global Design, unveiled it to 900 enthusiasts after his presentation about the car in the Grand Ballroom of the Ritz-Carlton Hotel.

## 2015 Chevrolet Corvette Z06

"At the intersection of Le Mans and the Autobahn sits the best of American automotive design and engineering," says Chevrolet of its new 2015 Corvette Z06. Its supercharged 6.2L aluminum V-8 will deliver "at least 625 hp and 635 ft-lbs of torque." A choice of two transmissions is offered: a 7-speed manual or an all-new paddle-shift 8-speed automatic. (Photo Courtesy GM Media Archive)

## 2015 Cadillac ATS Prototype

The 2015 Cadillac ATS prototype was unveiled at the 2014 North American International Auto Show in Detroit. Its 2.0L Turbo engine is an upgraded version of the current ATS sport sedan that delivers nearly 14 percent more torque and helps the ATS coupe achieve an estimated 0-60 time of 5.6 seconds. By the time this book is in print, the new ATS coupe will be available for purchase. (Photo Courtesy GM Media Archive)

# APPENDIX A

# Number Built and Status of the Motorama Show Cars

| Car | Number Built | Status/Comments |
|---|---|---|
| 1951 Le Sabre | 1 | Owned by GM |
| 1951 XP-300 | 1 | Donated by GM to Alfred P. Sloan Museum in Flint, Michigan |
| 1953 Corvette prototypes | 3 | 2 show cars and 1 test car; original car reported destroyed in test |
| 1953 Parisienne | 1 | Updated for 1954 auto shows, but restored to 1953 configuration; presently in Bortz Auto Collection |
| 1953 Starfire | 3 | 2 scrapped; 1 unknown |
| 1953 Wildcat I | 4 | 1 known survivor presently in Bortz Auto Collection |
| 1953 Le Mans | 4 | 2 exist; 1 destroyed in 1985; 1 reported scrapped |
| 1953 Orleans | 1 | For sale in early 1960s; location unknown |
| 1954 Corvair | 5 | 1 reported scrapped; 1 disappeared from Warhoops Used Auto & Truck Salvage in late-1970s |
| 1954 Nomad | 2 or 3 | Evidence indicates up to 3 built; at least 1 rumored to exist; 1 reported scrapped |
| 1954 Corvette w/prototype hardtop | 3 or more | At least 2 were built from 1953 models; possibly 2 or 3 more prototypes built; at least 1 still exists |
| 1954 Bonneville Special | 2 | 2 exist; original car is unrestored and second car is fully restored |
| 1954 Strato-Streak | 2 or 3 | Probably only 2 built; none known to exist |
| 1954 F-88 | 4 + 1 body | See Chapter 4 |
| 1954 Cutlass | 1 | Reportedly sold by GM |
| 1954 Landau | 1 | Restored; presently owned by Bob Coker |
| 1954 Wildcat II | 1, perhaps 2 | 1 for Motorama shows donated by GM to Alfred P. Sloan Museum; 1 reported to have been destroyed in auto accident |
| 1954 La Espada | 2 | 1 rumored to exist |
| 1954 El Camino | 1 | Only 1 confirmed built; reportedly scrapped |
| 1954 Park Avenue | 1 | Unknown but probably scrapped; last reported to have been sent to Cadillac Engineering Department in April 1955 |
| 1954 Firebird I | 1 | Still owned by GM |
| 1955 "50-millionth" GM automobile | 1 | Bel Air Sport Coupe with Anniversary Gold paint and gold-plated trim; still exists |
| 1955 Biscayne | 1 | Fully restored; presently in Bortz Auto Collection |
| 1955 Strato-Star | 1 | Unknown but presumably scrapped |
| 1955 88 Delta | 1 | Wheels advertised for sale in 2017 on the AACA forum |
| 1955 Wildcat III | 1 | Reportedly scrapped |
| 1955 Eldorado Brougham | 1 | Unknown but presumably scrapped |

| | | |
|---|---|---|
| 1955 LaSalle II Sedan | 1 | Under restoration; presently in Bortz Auto Collection |
| 1955 LaSalle II Roadster | 1 | Restored, now drivable; presently in Bortz Auto Collection |
| 1955 L'Universelle | 1 | Unknown but probably scrapped |
| 1956 Corvette Impala | 1 | Reportedly scrapped |
| 1956 Club de Mer | 1 | Rumored to exist |
| 1956 Golden Rocket | 1 | Rumored to exist |
| 1956 Centurion | 1 | Donated by GM to Alfred P. Sloan Museum |
| 1956 Eldorado Brougham | 1 | Unknown but probably scrapped |
| 1956 Eldorado Brougham Town Car | 1 | Fully restored; currently owned by Leonard and Michele Worden |
| 1956 Firebird II | 2 | Both are restored and owned by GM; display chassis also built and presumably scrapped; a third body shell was made for close-ups for the GM-produced movie, *Highway of Tomorrow* |
| 1958 Firebird III | 1 | Owned by GM; shown at 1959 and 1961 GM Motorama; display chassis also built and is part of the GM Haritage Center collection |
| 1961 Tempest show car | 1 | First production Tempest modified with tilt body; probably scrapped |
| Various production show cars with special paint, trim, upholstery | Many | A few are known to still exist |

# APPENDIX B

# Motorama Dates and Locations

## In the United States

**1949 (Transportation Unlimited)**
January 20 to January 27 — Waldorf Astoria, New York, NY
April 9 to April 15 — Convention Hall, Detroit, MI

**1950 (Mid-Century Motorama)**
January 19 to January 27 — Waldorf Astoria, New York, NY

**1953**
January 17 to January 23 — Waldorf Astoria, New York, NY
February 11 to February 17 — Dinner Key Auditorium, Miami, FL
April 11 to April 19 — Shrine Convention Hall, Los Angeles, CA
May 1 to May 7 — Civic Auditorium, San Francisco, CA
May 16 to May 24 — Fair Park, Dallas, TX
June 6 to June 14 — Municipal Auditorium, Kansas City, MO

# APPENDIX B: MOTORAMA DATES AND LOCATIONS

### 1954
| | |
|---|---|
| January 21 to January 26 | Waldorf Astoria, New York, NY |
| February 6 to February 12 | Dinner Key Auditorium, Miami, FL |
| March 6 to March 14 | Pan Pacific Auditorium, Los Angeles, CA |
| March 27 to April 4 | Civic Auditorium, San Francisco, CA |
| April 24 to May 2 | International Amphitheatre, Chicago, IL |

### 1955
| | |
|---|---|
| January 20 to January 25 | Waldorf Astoria, New York, NY |
| February 5 to February 13 | Dinner Key Auditorium, Miami, FL |
| March 5 to March 13 | Pan Pacific Auditorium, Los Angeles, CA |
| March 26 to April 3 | Civic Auditorium, San Francisco, CA |
| April 23 to May 1 | Commonwealth Armory, Boston, MA |

### 1956
| | |
|---|---|
| January 19 to January 24 | Waldorf Astoria, New York, NY |
| February 4 to February 12 | Dinner Key Auditorium, Miami, FL |
| March 3 to March 11 | Pan Pacific Auditorium, Los Angeles, CA |
| March 24 to April 1 | Civic Auditorium, San Francisco, CA |
| April 19 to April 29 | Commonwealth Armory, Boston, MA |

### 1959
| | |
|---|---|
| October 16 to October 22, 1958 | Waldorf Astoria, New York, NY |
| November 8 to November 16, 1958 | Commonwealth Armory, Boston, MA |

### 1961
| | |
|---|---|
| November 3 to November 11, 1960 | Waldorf Astoria, New York, NY |
| January 7 to January 15 | Civic Auditorium, San Francisco, CA |
| January 28 to February 5 | Pan Pacific Auditorium, Los Angeles, CA |

## GM Canada

### 1953*
| | |
|---|---|
| March 20 to March 28 | Eaton's Donald Street Annex, Winnipeg, MB |

### 1954*
| | |
|---|---|
| April 14 to April 24 | Eaton's Donald Street Annex, Winnipeg, MB |

### 1955**
| | |
|---|---|
| November 19 to November 27, 1954 | Show Mart Building, Montreal, QC |
| December 3 to December 11, 1954 | Exhibition Place Automotive Building, Toronto, ON |
| March 17 to March 26 | Hudson's Bay Co. Retail Store, Winnipeg, MB |
| April 1 to April 8 | Kerrisdale Arena, Vancouver, BC |
| April 15 to April 19 | Saskatoon Arena, Saskatoon, SK |
| April 27 to April 30 | Regina Exhibition Auditorium, Regina, SK |
| May 4 to May 7 | Edmonton Exhibition Grounds, Edmonton, AB |
| May 11 to May 14 | Stampede Corral, Calgary, AB |
| May 23 to May 28 | Western Fairgrounds Agricultural Building, London, ON |

### 1956
November 25 to December 3, 1955    Exhibition Place Automotive Building, Toronto, ON
December 9 to December 18, 1955    Show Mart Building, Montreal, QC

### 1957
November 9 to November 18, 1956    Show Mart Building, Montreal, QC
November 25 to December 3, 1956    Exhibition Place Automotive Building, Toronto, ON

### 1958
November 8 to November 17, 1957    Show Mart Building, Montreal, QC
November 27 to December 8, 1957    Exhibition Place Automotive Building, Toronto, ON

### 1959
November 29 to December 10, 1958    Exhibition Place Automotive Building, Toronto, ON
January 9 to January 18    Show Mart Building, Montreal, QC

### 1960
December 4 to December 12, 1959    Exhibition Place Automotive Building, Toronto, ON
January 1960    Show Mart Building, Montreal, QC

### 1961
November 25 to December 10, 1960    Exhibition Place Automotive Building, Toronto, ON
January 6 to January 15    Show Mart Building, Montreal, QC

*These were smaller exhibits and thus not the elaborate shows for which the GM Motorama is known. There were likely additional venues.

**The shows held in Toronto were full-scale Motoramas; those in Montreal may have been, too. The remaining shows for this year were probably limited to relatively small exhibits.

# INDEX

## A

Ahrens, Don E., 35
Amelia Island Concours d'Elegance, 35, 68, 93, 103, 107, 145, 195, 200
America on the Move, 165
Amgwert, John, 46
Antique Automobile Club of America, 46, 68
Auto Shanghai, 199

## B

Balthasar, Tony, 42
Barris, George, 63–64, 66
Barstow, Richard and Edith, 40, 72, 120
Blair, R. F., 106–107
Bloch, Bill, 42
Boyer, Harold R., 61, 63
Brown, Norm, 33, 39, 78–80
Bucci, John, 125
Buick models
    Centurion, 23, 150, 152, 161–164, 180
    LaSalle, 13, 14
    LaSalle II, 120, 123–125, 140–145
    Ranger, 38–39
    Riviera, 21, 30, 33–34, 36–38, 53, 116, 148, 159, 191, 199
    Skylark, 30, 56, 58, 62, 70, 105, 107, 117, 119, 148
    Wildcat (I), 23, 40, 53–59, 66, 104, 106, 119, 124, 132, 133, 164
    Wildcat II, 25, 67, 104, 107–110, 132, 133, 164
    Wildcat III, 120, 128, 131–134, 164
    XP-300, 16–23, 30, 40, 53, 91
    Y-Job, 14–16, 20, 43, 53
*Buick Wildcat: Trial Flight in Fiberglass and Steel*, 53, 58

## C

Cadaret, Bob, 150
Cadillac & LaSalle Club, 38, 56, 60, 64, 66, 68
Cadillac models
    Ciel, 196, 199
    Coronation Coupe, 38–39
    Coupe de Ville, 30, 32–35, 39, 59–61, 71, 116–117, 148–149
    Cyclone, 28, 102, 172, 178, 182, 184, 193–195
    Debutante, 35, 38
    Eldorado, 10, 30, 59–63, 69–71, 81, 110, 112, 119, 123, 134–135, 137, 148–150, 156, 161, 164–168, 180, 186–190
    Elmiraj, 200
    Le Mans, 12, 40, 54, 60–69, 110, 115, 158, 190, 193, 201
    Orleans, 40, 59–60, 62, 87, 110, 134, 137
    Series 61, 36
    Series 62, 30, 36–38, 117, 135, 167–168, 189
    Series 75, 32, 36, 59
    Sixteen, 197
Canadian National Exhibition, 22, 25, 28, 30, 37–39, 49–50, 61, 67, 77–78, 83, 115, 154, 163, 178, 180, 183–184
Chayne, Charles, 16–17, 19, 22, 137, 141
Cherry, Wayne, 126
Chevrolet models
    Bel Air, 30, 32–33, 38, 43, 74, 76–78, 80, 146
    Biscayne, 40, 81, 120, 122–126, 141, 143, 154
    Corvair, 25, 57, 72, 74, 79–83, 86, 122, 124, 140, 145
    Corvette, 20, 25, 40, 42–47, 51, 54, 58, 62, 66–67, 72, 74–84, 86, 90–91, 93–95, 99, 102, 104, 122, 124, 133–134, 141, 147, 150, 152–154, 157–159, 161–162, 181, 183, 190–191, 200–201
    Nomad, 12, 25, 46, 57, 72, 74–79, 81, 83, 137, 146–147, 176
    Royal Canadian, 37–39
    Special Delivery, 38–39
    Volt, 198
Chicago Auto Show, 22, 24, 56, 82–83, 96, 113, 153–154, 190
Chicago Museum of Science and Industry, 24
Conklin, Emmett, 118, 193
Cord, E. L., 33, 57, 102–104
*Corvette American Legend Vol. 2*, 78
Corvette Prototype, 46, 74–75
*Corvette: A Piece of the Action*, 190–191
Cunningham, Briggs, 42
Curtice, Harlow H., 13, 15–16, 28, 56–58, 85, 104, 106–107, 109–110, 120, 140, 146
Custom Car Show, 48

## D

Denver Auto Show, 48
*Design for Dreaming*, 170, 174
Dolza, John, 141
Durant, William, 12

## E

Earl, Harley, 10, 13–18, 20–23, 25–26, 28–29, 40, 42–43, 60–63, 65, 68–69, 76, 83, 96–103, 109, 115, 118, 133, 135–136, 140, 158, 164, 170, 176, 189–191, 193, 195–196
Earl, Jacob W., 13
Eyes on Design, 56

## F

Faloon, Larry, 125, 143
Featurama, 24
Fisher, Lawrence, 12–13, 44, 48, 62, 68–69
*Flight of the Firebirds*, 189
Ford, Henry II, 29
Frances, Phillip Jr., 141
Francis, Mel, 125
Frankfurt Auto Show, 199
Furse, Lee, 21
Futurama, 23–24
Futurliner, 25, 26, 27

## G

General Motors World, 32
Geneva Concours d'Elegance, 56
Gillan, Paul, 48, 83, 86–87, 126, 154
Glidden Tour, 52, 65, 192
Glowacke, Ed, 16–17, 115, 135, 165
GM Canada, 25, 28, 38, 39, 150, 178, 180–182
GM Heritage Center, 10, 23, 56, 60, 63, 65, 67, 69–70, 96, 99, 101, 104, 112, 115, 143, 170, 172, 195
GM models
    Firebird I, 57, 72, 111, 115, 117–119, 170, 172, 178, 193
    Firebird II, 115, 150, 170–175, 178, 189, 191, 193, 194
    Firebird III, 25, 28, 172, 178, 183, 189, 191–193
    Futurliner, 25, 26–27
    LaSalle II, 120, 140, 143
    Le Sabre, 10, 15–23, 30, 38–40, 42, 83, 98, 102, 141, 164
    L'Universelle, 23, 136–139
GM Styling, 14–15, 17, 23, 44, 47, 56, 59–61, 81, 83, 86, 101–102, 104, 108–109, 113, 164, 189, 195
"Going Places," 72
Goodman, James E., 62, 68–69

## H

Hafstad, Dr. Lawrence, 172
Hall of Wonders, 48
*History of Cadillac's Motorama Dream Cars*, 110
Holls, Dave, 62, 104, 115, 125
Humbert, Jack, 95, 104

## I

*Imagination in Motion: Firebird III*, 191
Ingle, John, 47
International Motor Revue, 64
International Motor Show, 49

## J

Jalopy Journal website, 66
Jones, G. R., 25, 78, 147
Jordan, Chuck, 14, 23, 42, 56, 66, 117, 126, 136–137, 163–164, 167, 177, 189

## K

Kaptur, Vince Sr., 25, 42
Keefe, Don, 46, 81, 84–85, 134

Kettering, Charles, 26
"Key to the Future," 150
Kidd, Michael, 150
Knudsen, Semon "Bunkie," 156

## L

LaGassey, Homer, 48, 58, 83, 86–87, 132–134
Lange, Bill, 136
Larson, Matt, 60
Lauve, Henry, 19
Lee, Don, 10, 13, 21
Los Angeles Auto Show, 108, 165
Lucas, Ed, 57, 66, 101, 103–104

## M

MacKichan, Clare "Mac," 42, 78–79, 122
Martino, Marty, 124–126, 143–144
McCuen, Charles, 118–119
McDade, Jim, 79
McLay, Leonard, 22
McLean, Robert, 42, 118
Meadowbrook Concours d'Elegance, 87
Miami show, 56, 82
Michigan Motor Show, 48
Mid-Century Motorama, 24, 30, 35–38
Milwaukee Auto Show, 49, 52
Mitchell, Bill, 14, 42, 84, 98, 101, 103, 158, 161, 190–191, 195
Motorama venues
    Boston, 25, 28, 120, 176–178, 183
    Canada, 10, 12, 25, 28–30, 37–39, 48, 57, 67, 82–83, 89, 93, 115, 128–129, 150, 178, 180–182, 184
    Chicago, 22, 24, 56, 72, 82–83, 87, 93, 96, 113, 120, 124–125, 131, 153–154, 190
    Dallas, 40, 72
    Detroit, 13, 30, 36, 48, 58, 61, 69, 78, 86, 97, 112, 124, 191, 201
    Kansas City, 24, 40, 71–72
    Los Angeles, 24–25, 40, 72, 82, 102, 110, 120, 132, 152, 157, 171, 173, 176, 189
    Miami, 29, 40, 44, 56, 71–72, 79, 82, 88, 92, 104, 120, 147–148, 154, 158, 162, 168, 171
    New York, 15, 25, 28, 30, 34, 40, 47, 56, 72, 86, 93, 104, 106, 113, 120, 165–166, 178, 183, 190, 200
    Regina, 57, 178
    San Francisco, 25, 40, 42, 120, 132, 140
    Toronto, 22, 25, 28, 30, 37–38, 49–50, 61, 67, 78, 83, 180, 183, 193
    Vancouver, 57, 75, 114
    Waldorf-Astoria, 10, 23, 25, 28, 30, 32–36, 40, 42–43, 47, 49, 55–56, 59, 62, 71–72, 74, 76, 79–81, 87, 93, 104, 108, 116–117, 119–120, 125, 129, 135, 147–148, 165–166
"Motorythms and Fashion Firsts," 40

## N

National Auto Show, 15
National Corvette Museum, 43
National Corvette Restorers Society, 46
National Motor Show, 28
Nichols, Ned, 20, 108–109
North American International Auto Show, 69, 198, 201

## O

Oil Progress Exposition, 65
Oldsmobile models
    88 Delta, 120, 129, 130, 131
    Caribbean, 30, 33–34, 38–39
    Cutlass, 57, 90–93, 99, 103, 111, 131
    F-88, 25, 52, 57, 66, 90–104, 109, 193
    Fiesta, 10, 62, 70–71, 76, 119
    Golden Jubilee, 37
    Golden Rocket, 71, 155, 158–161
    Ninety-Eight, 36, 148
    Palm Beach Holiday Ninety-Eight, 36
    Rancher, 38
    Starfire, 40, 51–54, 66, 92, 119, 148, 163, 176, 187–188
    Westward-Ho, 37
Olley, Maurice, 42
Ollier, Pierre, 75
Opel Monza, 199

## P

Pacific International Auto Show, 64
Pan Pacific Auditorium, 25, 72, 82, 102, 108, 152, 157, 173, 176
Parade of Progress, 25–27, 29, 100–101, 113–114, 118
Paris Salon, 21–22, 117, 161, 165–166, 174
Pebble Beach Concours d'Elegance, 49, 56, 59, 85, 196
Perkins, John, 14, 52, 54, 101, 103
Perkins, Ralph, 52
Petersen Automotive Museum, 69
Petersen Motorama, 64
Pillar of Progress, 30, 36
Pontiac models
    Bonneville Special, 25, 83–87, 89, 132
    Catalina, 30, 33, 38–39, 51, 176
    Club de Mer, 125, 154–158, 161
    Fleur de Lis, 37
    Magnificent, 37, 54
    Parisienne, 10, 40, 44–50, 61, 79, 115, 118–119, 134, 140, 170, 172, 174, 193
    Plainsman, 38
    Strato-Streak, 89
    Strato-Star, 126–129
Powerama, 24
Preview of Progress, 39
Progress on Parade, 26
Proving Grounds, 22, 44, 46, 61, 79, 172, 193–194

## R

Renner, Carl, 74, 76, 78, 140, 141, 150
Rose, Mauri, 68, 117–119, 140, 171, 193–194
Ross, Arthur "Art," 51–52, 90, 93, 103, 158
Rover J.E.T., 118–119
Roxas, Fran, 86, 125
Rybicki, Irv, 92, 101

## S

Sanders, Russell, 47
Schemansky, Joe, 42
Sloan, Jr., Alfred P., 12–13, 15, 21–23, 26, 34, 107, 110, 164
Sports Car Club of America, 56, 190
Spotlight on Detroit, 58, 61
St. Louis Auto Show, 52
Stylerama, 29

## T

*The Buddy Holly Story*, 69
The GM Motorama, 10, 12, 23–25, 27–28, 44–45, 47–48, 55–56, 62–63, 71–72, 74, 79, 81–83, 85–88, 94–96, 99, 101, 104, 106, 113, 119–120, 136, 140, 146–147, 150, 153–154, 157–158, 160, 162, 164, 166, 171, 173, 184, 189
The Hot One: Chevrolet 1955–1957, 78
The Solid Gold Cadillac, 36
Transpiration Unlimited, 24
Transportation Unlimited, 23, 30, 32–35
Turlay, Joseph, 17

## V

*Vingt-Quatre Heures du Mans*, 60, 62

## W

Walker, George, 29
Wayne, John, 62, 64, 83, 126, 174, 191
Welburn, Ed, 126, 196, 199–200
Wiles, Ivan, 107, 109, 132
Wilson, Charles, 32, 34, 59–60
Wonderama, 24, 28, 67, 83, 128, 131
World's Fair, 14, 23, 26, 192–193

## Y

York, Richard, 15, 25, 28, 30, 34, 40, 47, 56, 72, 74, 80–81, 86, 93, 104, 106, 113, 120, 165–166, 178, 183, 190, 200

www.ingramcontent.com/pod-product-compliance
Lightning Source LLC
Chambersburg PA
CBHW081443070526
44586CB00019B/2217